T0330119

Competitiveness in Research and Development

Competitiveness in Research and Development

Comparisons and Performance

Ádám Török

*Professor of Economics, University of Veszprém and Head,
Research Group Regional Development Studies and
Micro-Integration, Hungarian Academy of Sciences, Hungary*

with

Balázs Borsi

Research Fellow, GKI Economic Research Co.

András Telcs

*Associate Professor, Department of Computer Science,
Budapest University of Technology and Economics, Hungary*

Edward Elgar
Cheltenham, UK • Northampton, MA, USA

Published by
Edward Elgar Publishing Limited
Glensanda House
Montpellier Parade
Cheltenham
Glos GL50 1UA
UK

Edward Elgar Publishing, Inc.
136 West Street
Suite 202
Northampton
Massachusetts 01060
USA

A catalogue record for this book
is available from the British Library

Library of Congress Cataloguing in Publication Data
Török, Ádám.
   Competitiveness in research and development : comparisons and performance /
Ádám Török; with Balázs Borsi.
      p. cm.
   Includes bibliographical references.
   1. Research—Economic aspects—Hungary. 2. Technological innovations—
Economic aspects—Hungary. 3. Research—Economic aspects—Developing
countries. 4. Technological innovations—Economic aspects—Developing countries.
5. Competition. 6. Comparative economics. I. Borsi, Balázs. II. Title.

HC300.295.R4T67 2005
658.5'7—dc22   2005048434

ISBN 1 84376 921 2

Typeset by Cambrian Typesetters, Camberley, Surrey
Printed and bound in Great Britain by MPG Books Ltd, Bodmin, Cornwall

Contents

Contributors

Ádám Török is Professor of Economics at several Hungarian Universities, including the University of Veszprém and the Budapest University of Technology and Economics, and a Corresponding Member of the Hungarian Academy of Sciences. He has dealt extensively with issues of technology policy and competition policy and has taught at a number of universities in North America and Europe (University of Denver, York University, Université Paris I, Université Nancy II, Catholic University of Leuven). A former head of the Hungarian government's agency on technology policy, he is currently an adviser to the EU Commissioner on Research.

Balázs Borsi is a Research Manager at the GKI Economic Research Co., formerly a Researcher at the Budapest University of Technology and Economics. His main research topics include the knowledge-driven economy and competitiveness. He is co-editor of books and several conference proceedings in the field.

András Telcs is Associate Professor at the Budapest University of Technology and Economics. He received his Ph.D *doctor rerum naturlis* at the Eotvos Lorand University of Sciences, and is a member of the Hungarian Academy of Science. His main field of interests are probability theory, potential analysis, statistics and applications to social sciences. He is the author of books, journal articles and research papers on pure mathematics, and on applied mathematics in the social sciences, which have been published as printed material and online lecture notes.

Introduction

The idea of this book surfaced in the year 2000 after long deliberations on the future of the research and development (R&D)[1] sector in Hungary. The author had worked on R&D policy issues for a number of years, partly as head of the Hungarian government's agency on R&D and innovation. It was striking to see that this sector had gradually been losing its financial support, resources and prestige, and seemed to be one of the losers of the transition process. Although a number of political and also policy efforts have been made to reverse this development, only some of them could improve the conditions of R&D and innovation in Hungary.

Some preliminary analysis of the perspectives of the innovation system in Hungary in particular and in the transition economies in general made it clear that without exception, the changes led to the degradation of the science and technology (S&T) sector with serious losses of human and physical resources in the process.

In spite of the permanent waste of time and human effort, Hungarian (and Czech, and Polish, and Russian . . .) R&D could still produce a number of results well received internationally.

The assessment of the sector's condition and perspectives was in rather sharp contrast with the opinion of the European Commission at the time. This opinion was expressed in the paragraph on S&T of *Agenda 2000*, the first European Union document assessing the ability of candidate countries to join the EU. This paragraph gave an extremely favourable assessment of the Hungarian S&T sector, ranking it among the top 20 in the world (*Agenda 2000*, 1997, 38).

The statement was nice as a compliment, but the necessary footnote was missing and no methodological background or ranking lists were provided in order to corroborate it. The EU's assessment was welcomed with much enthusiasm in the Hungarian S&T community which had not been flooded by good news over the previous ten years or more. However only very few questions were asked as to the relevance of this seemingly very good news. Did it really reflect the truth?

This contradictory picture cries out for analytical evidence and resulted in an ambitious research project on the problem of international comparison of policies and performances in R&D. The project obtained generous support from the Hungarian government's National Program for Research and Development launched in 2001.

This book is a product of that research, the scope of which has undergone quite significant changes between the first questions asked and the last answers provided. The focus of the project gradually shifted from a more or less simple assessment of the international position of Hungarian R&D or the S&T sector towards a much more ambitious goal, namely a comparative investigation of the problem of competitiveness in R&D.

It turned out during research that the international literature on the S&T sector lacked, in principle, any competitiveness-oriented analysis of R&D. The fact that the concept of competitiveness is not enjoying generally accepted support in the economics profession could not be disregarded. Still, the evident weaknesses of the concept could not explain why there had been an almost complete lack of analyses of competitiveness in R&D in the literature.

In fact the only attempt at combining different R&D indicators of individual countries and then ranking them based on this synthesis had a quite limited scope and no theoretical ambition (Niwa and Tomizawa, 1995). Several other efforts, subsequently surveyed in this book, were made to assess comparative positions of countries in innovation performance, but innovation does not equal R&D, and many policy tools used to stimulate innovation may not be linked with R&D to the slightest extent and vice versa.

The problem of partial overlaps between the terms 'R&D' and 'innovation' caused much headache to the authors during their work. The focus of the book is R&D competitiveness, but this topic cannot be discussed without frequently touching upon various problems of innovation. To give the most obvious example, a quite frequently used indicator of R&D output, patent counts, is much more about innovation than R&D even if it reflects the results of R&D quite well in a comparative approach. It is extremely important to note at this point however that science does not mean R&D, just as R&D does not equal innovation. This distinction has to be emphasized due to the fact that these three terms are not always used carefully enough with respect to each other in the press, by politicians or sometimes even in scientific publications.

The basic analytical tool for assessing the structures and performances of national systems of R&D is called NIS (national systems of innovation, or national innovation systems) in the literature. It would have been completely useless to introduce a new term such as for example 'national systems of R&D' just to avoid superfluous or redundant references to innovation in our text. As kind of a practical compromise we have tried to refer to 'R&D and innovation' if our original focus on R&D could not be observed rigorously. Even this heavy-handed solution proved impossible however in cases when we had to stick to established terms (for example NIS or R&D spending), in spite of the fact that we had narrower or broader definitions of such terms in mind.

The first chapter is devoted to some theoretical and methodological issues of competitiveness analysis, with special emphasis on their applicability for R&D. A key problem to be addressed here is how competitiveness can be used and interpreted for products and markets of R&D. This chapter also gives an overview of the main terms, concepts and models of the systems of R&D (or S&T) and innovation. Since the book is an attempt to analyse the R&D competitiveness of countries, the concept of R&D competitiveness is also presented.

The second chapter deals with the measurement of competitiveness. In the 'classical' competitiveness studies the supply- and demand-side measurement is usually not reconciled. High-tech trade and trade in technologies are some-what related to R&D competitiveness at the country level, yet – besides the fact that each country is a different case study – there are also methodological considerations, which are not easy to resolve. Further, it needs to be considered whether comparison should be made on the basis of usual country indicators regardless of country size, or whether per capita (or other 'relative' or 'efficiency') data would give a more appropriate picture.

This question is usually not asked in 'mainstream' competitiveness analysis, since most of such attempts are rooted in classical and neoclassical trade theory in which countries have no spatial dimension and country size does not matter. It is however interesting to see how the per capita approach modifies the international competitiveness picture in R&D and innovation, and the extent to which smaller countries can cope with the lack of economies of scale in this field.

If there is more than one indicator used, another problem emerges and it is related to how different ranking lists using different indicators can be combined into one. The most important ranking methods used so far in the literature are presented briefly.

The most important question as regards the measurement of R&D competitiveness at the country level is 'Which indicators shall we use?' The data based upon which 'absolute' and 'relative' indicator measurements can take place are thoroughly discussed at the end of the second chapter. Despite methodological problems, we have found that in general the number of researchers and GERD (gross domestic expenditure on R&D) as input indicators and the number of publications and patents as output indicators are sufficient enough to describe the R&D competitiveness positions of countries. Nonetheless a word of caution must also be included here. The impact of R&D on a society is difficult to measure, and even if it is done with success, the result of any cross-country comparability will remain questionable because of the different socio-economic contexts of the different countries. To this end, a very important constituent of the national systems of innovation, education, is not discussed in this book. The business and social impacts of R&D (including innovation effects such as spillovers) also had to be kept out of the set of indicators that can be used for cross-country analysis.

The third chapter presents the quantitative measurement of R&D competitiveness. It is the work of Balázs Borsi and András Telcs, who have also contributed to finalizing the manuscript. The chapter is experimental in its approach. Based on all the previous methodological deliberations on the theoretical and policy background, and also the useability of the various important R&D indicators, it uses a quantitative analysis. The investigation involves the selected indicators, carefully chosen methods and interpretations in a rather understated style. It presents different ways to construct composite ranking lists of countries including different indicators. In a sense it shows the progress of our research, going from the first, intuitive attempt at creating an international ranking list towards methodologically more demanding ones. Among these, we have used principal component analysis, a genetic algorythm and Data Envelopment Analysis (DEA). We have produced several results based on the different methods and, quite interestingly, kind of a 'meta-result': the different ranking lists overlap to a significant extent and together they seem to colour the general picture in a coherent way. Nonetheless the verification of the selection of the indicators, methods and approach used should come from the communities linked to R&D in one way or another when the results are being confronted and compared to other findings. Repetition of the measurement and investigation of longer time series would be desirable as well. Finally, the macro-level study cries for detailed case studies as to how R&D activity becomes embedded in the economy and society.

The quantitative picture calls for urgent policy action in Europe and also in the transition countries. As far as international competition in R&D is concerned, the European Union is losing ground vis-à-vis North America and the Far East. At the same time, the competitiveness positions of the countries of Central and Eastern Europe are increasingly challenged by the newly industrialized countries (NICs) of Asia and Latin America.

Policy conclusions are presented along with institutional aspects of R&D competitiveness in the two subsequent chapters. The fourth chapter is devoted to the analysis of such participants of international R&D competition which represent more or less atypical cases of national innovation systems (NIS), and where policy answers have to be found to the challenge of increasing competitiveness in R&D. Special attention is given here to two groups of countries. The case of transition economies is explained in more detail because some of these countries are already members of the OECD and also of the European Union, but their NISs still have a number of characteristics not found elsewhere in the developed world. Third World countries are included owing to the fact that some of them have shown spectacular improvements of R&D competitiveness and are approaching the best in the world, while others are at best marginal players in international R&D. It is beyond doubt that Third World countries are a very heterogeneous group regarding R&D (which they are not with respect to problems of economic development, export competitiveness or policy choices), but it is still an open question whether their NISs show any particular aspects related to the Third World.

Both the case of transition economies and that of so-called developing economies have interesting theoretical implications with respect to a quite new and very stimulating approach to the role of R&D and innovation in economic development – the one offered by evolutionary economics (for an in-depth survey of its fundamental literature see Nelson, 1995). The main focus of the book is narrower and slightly more technical than the usually quite comprehensive approach used by evolutionary economics.

We shall however try to interpret our special country cases of national innovation system development from an evolutionary economics point of view as well. Some issues to be tackled here, but also in further comparative NIS research, include the patterns and directions of the evolution of innovation systems undergoing transition, the problem of innovation as an endogenous factor of growth on both the firm level and the national economy level, and the patterns of institutional development. The problem of path dependency often encountered in evolutionary economics literature may have a special meaning in such transition economies where systemic evolution through transition is accompanied by a shrinking of the NIS and a decomposition of its institutional framework.

The fifth chapter presents the conclusions, with special emphasis on a global picture of competitiveness in R&D. The focus of the research turns to the developed world here, with a brief assessment of the R&D aspects of the EU's Lisbon Strategy.

The author of the book would like to thank his co-authors Balázs Borsi and András Telcs for their contribution to this book and also for the fruitful but sometimes long discussions. Judit Ványai coordinated the research project and also offered great support for the final version of the manuscript. It would be practically impossible to give an exhaustive list of the members of our team, all of whom worked on various important aspects of the research, but the most important participants were András Bakács, Andrea Balla, Zita Bedőházi, Lilli Berkó, László Csernenszky, Zsuzsa Deli, Beáta Horánszky, Judit Karsai, Beatrix Lányi, Iván Major, Éva Pintér, Zoltán Román, András Schubert, Szabolcs Sebrek, Gábor Túry, Attila Varga and Erzsébet Viszt. Two anonymous referees also made important suggestions in order to make the text more coherent and clear. The authors thank all the colleagues listed above for their precious contibution to the work, and consider them blameless for any deficiencies of the result.

This text could not have been produced without the generous financial support of the Hungarian National Programme for Research and Development, the Hungarian–Spanish Exchange Programme of Researchers and the Joint Research Group on Regional Development Studies and Micro-integration of the Hungarian Academy of Sciences and the Dániel Berzsenyi College. The administrative background of the work was provided by the University of Veszprém. I am also grateful to my colleagues at the Department of Economics at the University of Veszprém and at the Budapest University of Technology and Economics for their readiness to help if my research tasks made necessary some exemption from my teaching duties. Last but not least, my family deserve my greatest gratitude for their lasting tolerance and support, without which this book could not have been written.

1. Approaches to competitiveness

1.1 THE COMPETITIVENESS CONCEPT

A Survey of Theories

The intensification of global competition and the increasing openness of national economies seem to have led to an interesting consequence apparently neglected by economic theory so far. Statistical indicators based on the concept of competitiveness have been used more and more as a tool for measuring and benchmarking the performance of national economies. A widely known example is the ranking lists published in the IMD series of Competitiveness Reports.

This new conceptual development has a major shortcoming however: the content of competitiveness has not been clarified in the literature. Many authors have used the term, but a single meaning has not been generally accepted. It is used as a measure of performance on markets in some cases, and others consider it as an indicator of macroeconomic performance. It also happens that competitiveness is regarded as an indicator of the technological level or the state of modernization of an economy.

A telling example is the UNCTAD's *World Investment Report 1995* (WIR) (UNCTAD, 1995) and also to some extent its successor published seven years later (UNCTAD, 2002). The title of the 1995 report includes the notion of competitiveness, but it is not defined throughout the report at all. Furthermore the authors do not explain what they understand by this term. It could potentially be concluded from this fact that there is a general consensus on what 'competitiveness' means.

The 1995 WIR offers however a somewhat confused picture. The first two chapters of WIR 1995 speak of understanding competitiveness as a non-measurable term. It is used in these chapters as a dummy-like attribute of an economy or a firm: either they are competitive or they are not. In later parts of the WIR though (for example UNCTAD, 1995, 238), the increase of competitiveness is brought in the picture, which means a tacit recognition of measurability. However only measurements of productivity and performance on markets are offered, the latter being described by market shares.

Some surveys of literature go even so far as to speak of 'personal' definitions of competitiveness by most authors (Palkovits, 2002, 48). A seemingly good and quite open definition of competitiveness on the national economic level can be formulated as the ability of a national economy to increase the yield of its own factors of production by way of producing, distributing goods or offering services in conformity with the requirements of international markets (see Cohen, 1994; Chikán, 1998). This general formulation appears however as a combination of conditions. As a consequence, measurability does not appear in this definition which makes it inappropriate for international comparison in its present form.

Another general formulation of competitiveness came from Ernest Braun and Wolfgang Polt: 'Competitiveness is a many-faceted concept and can only be meaningful in conjunction with long-term national goals. Competitiveness achieved through price competition alone might lower the national standard of living and therefore is not advantageous.[2] ... true competitiveness must be defined as the ability to balance foreign trade without abandoning vital national interests and goals' (Braun and Polt, 1988, 203).

This definition leaves open a few important questions. For example the effort towards determining 'vital national interests and goals' leaves much space for political arguments yet much less for economic analysis, but it can be helpful in establishing a linkage between competitiveness analysis and the wider focus of the evolutionary approach to economic development. The 'ability to balance foreign trade' can often remain an ability, without achieving balanced trade in reality. Controversially, such an improvement can also potentially take place owing to a deterioration of terms of trade, which can be a result of playing the price competition game in exports.

Few attempts at classifying available definitions of competitiveness are known. It is truly exceptional when not only the economic, but also the social and regional approaches to competitiveness are included in a scheme of classification.

Such a scheme has been offered by Horváth (2001) who speaks of competitiveness in the 'practical', 'environment-related' and 'development-oriented' sense. The first approach means an ability to adopt best managerial or technological practices used elsewhere with success. The second interpretation of competitiveness means an optimal combination and use of elements available for the firm in its business environment – in fact the effectiveness of the firm's adaptation to this environment. This includes the firm's ability to develop its structure and competences reflecting the changing technological requirements of its particular industry (see Utterback and Suarez, 1993). The third approach focuses on the ability to attract investment and the accumulation of resources. None of these three approaches concentrates on market performance (our preferred interpretation of competitiveness), but each of them has elements that will appear later in this chapter when concepts of competitiveness are reviewed.

The conceptual vagueness surrounding the term might not be too evident when competitiveness is referred to in the political or business press almost every day. It causes real problems when publications with titles such as 'Competitiveness Report' or 'The Road to Competitiveness' appear on the market. Many of these limit themselves to one-sided or simplified interpretations of competitiveness, or evoke only some of its factors. If however we want to extend this concept to the world of international R&D where it has not been used thus far, we need a clear and solid conceptual background to it.

The case of emerging economies, and more specifically of the new member states of the European Union, poses new challenges to competitiveness research. The ten new member states were declared 'to have reached an adequate level of competitiveness' in the 2002 Country Reports of the European Commission. The methodological background of this statement, repeated for each of the ten new member countries, remains to be clarified.

We can assume from other EC documentation that this interpretation of competitiveness was understood as 'an ability to resist pressure from markets', again a formula problematic from a theoretical point of view. It could potentially mean the percentage share of firms able to survive in the new competitive environment, but this indicator would be biased owing to the great number of firms competing only on local (sheltered) markets.

Competitiveness Analysis in the Literature

The conceptual vagueness surrounding the use of the term 'competitiveness' can be demonstrated with a brief survey of literature. This survey proves that many experts of international economics avoid using the term, while it is often applied outside the realm of theoretical economics.

Three widely used textbooks of international economics from the 1970s, 1980s and 1990s (Marcy, 1976; Caves and Jones, 1985; Krugman and Obstfeld, 1991) share the complete neglect of the term 'competitiveness'. The later edition of Krugman and Obstfeld's textbook (Krugman and Obstfeld, 2000, 275–6) reserves some space for the term, but only in trying to dissuade readers from using it in macroeconomic and international economic analysis:

> *Paul Krugman* sent an obvious message to his readership with the title of one of his former articles (*'Competitiveness: a dangerous obsession'* – Krugman, 1994). It is somewhat contradictory though that the same author applies this term rejected by himself when he speaks of the competitiveness problems of the American economy in the first half of the 1990s. (Krugman, 1996, 117–19)

As Krugman and Obstfeld put it (see Krugman and Obstfeld, 2000, 275–6) international trade is not a zero-sum game like war. Referring to the classical and neoclassical theories of international trade, they consider international trade a positive-sum game where cooperation between the parties would yield pay-offs to each of them. This is a very convincing argument, but some foot-notes could be added to it.

Let us take a practical approach. International business based only on co-operation between governments and only on competition between firms is quite hard to imagine. If governments encourage their firms to compete aggressively with their foreign counterparts they might lose part of their cooperative image in international trade. If firms try to become more cooperative with their competitors they might risk ending up in cartels with dire legal consequences. It is therefore quite unlikely that governments purely cooperative on the international level can undisturbedly coexist within the same national economy with firms only competing in international trade.

The fact that the term 'competitiveness' does not appear in many textbooks on international economics does not seem to influence (or intimidate) a string of authors on strategic management. A survey of the most influential authors of the field (Moore, 2001) mentions competitive advantages 19 times, defines them three times, and refers to the term 'competitive positions' another five times. Authors quoted with respect to competitiveness include Ansoff, Porter, Henderson, Ohmae, Rumelt, Salter, Weinhold, Hofer, Schendel, Kazanjian, Pearce, Robinson, Thompson, Strickland, Johnson and Scholes.

Our brief survey of literature seems to confirm Krugman's approach to a certain extent. Economics and international economics seem to ignore competitiveness while management sciences seem to take it quite seriously. Could we infer from this observation that competitiveness can be regarded only as a term applicable in business analysis, but not at all on the level of national economies?

The Theoretical Framework of Competitiveness

Our starting point is a term which originally, at the beginning of the nineteenth century, was still used in both macroeconomic and business analysis (Mucchielli-Sollogoub, 1980). This term is 'comparative advantages', approached in a quantitative way with 'comparative costs'. The basic idea of comparative advantage is that, in the case of two producers and two products, the international division of labour can be mutually beneficial even if one of the two producers is more efficient in producing either product (that is this one has the absolute advantage in both products). This basic idea makes it possible to assume that international trade can make any producer competitive if compared with anyone else if both have to choose from the same set of products.

The literature looking into the motives of international trade has devoted most of its attention to the development of the concept of comparative advantage. The classical and neoclassical theories of comparative advantage (Smith, Ricardo, Mill, Heckscher and Ohlin) are built on the model of comparative costs. The measurement of comparative costs proved quite difficult in practice as the debates on the Leontief paradox proved it. The empirical counterpart of the theories of comparative advantage increasingly became the measurement of export performance (see Balassa, 1965 and 1977) based not on supply-side data, but rather on export and import data with the latter reflecting the demand side.

The neoclassical approach lacked any specific technology-related content which was in apparent contradiction with the fact that innovation has become a key factor of export growth. The neoclassical concept of comparative advantage was substantially modernized in the 1960s in the form of the neo-technological theories of international trade (Linder, 1961; Posner, 1961; Wells, 1969; Hirsch, 1974 and 1975; Vernon, 1979). Not much later, a number of studies demonstrated that firms or countries tend to show relatively good trade performances if they are relatively successful in developing and designing new products, or improving old ones or their technologies of production (for a survey of such analyses see Freeman, 1988).

The neo-technological theories were in fact not about the factors of comparative advantage because they did not look at comparative costs as the factors of export specialization. Their contribution to theory was important rather because they broke with the exclusively supply-side based explanations of export performance and trade structure, and they emphasized the importance of adjustment to the demand side. These were the first theories of international trade in which the apparently favourable comparative cost structure of exports was not understood as a guarantee of export success or, to use the term the genesis of which we are just discussing, an appropriate level of export competitiveness.

These were the first influential theories of international trade based on the assumption of imperfect competition. The correction of market failures became, in this theoretical framework, a government task. Competitiveness had to be understood in the model of imperfect international markets as a concept including government policies promoting competition and potentially competitiveness as well.

The appearance of theoretical models of imperfect competition and of entry barriers gave a substantial boost to theoretical debates on the measurement of competitiveness. Competitiveness measurement has no sense in monopolistic markets, but this measurement also becomes problematic if the market has a substantial degree of contestability or is characterized by monopolistic competition.

Calculations made from trade data available about imperfect markets may show low levels of export performance if the smooth functioning of markets is inhibited by various entry barriers. In other words, market performance expected from the volumes and relative costs of inputs will not become a reality owing to market imperfections. The application of the models of imperfect competition to international trade entails that market performance and competitiveness have to be grasped and measured on both the supply and the demand side.

Expected competitive performances calculated from supply-side (for example input) and demand-side (for example trade) data can differ substantially for a number of reasons:

1. The microstructures of demand and supply can prove strongly different. This may be the situation in monopolistic competition.
2. The visible size of entry barriers and the intensity of competition are in an apparent contradiction with each other. This is the case of contestable markets.

These two models of imperfect competition can even coexist in practice:

*   in a situation of monopolistic competition, both supply-side and demand-side substitutions are limited. This fact could explain why seemingly unfavourable cost structures in output do not prevent export performance from being good and competitiveness measured on the demand side being high. If the model of monopolistic competition describes the structure of the given market well, supply-side competitiveness can be good even with high costs of inputs, and demand-side competitiveness would be shown by high market shares.[3] These two different aspects of competitiveness would be brought in harmony with each other either when costs of production or market shares go down for the market player whose competitiveness is evaluated.
*   According to the model of contestable markets (see Baumol et al., 1982; Maskin and Tirole, 1988) monopolists or oligopolists should strive for high levels of competitiveness because low entry barriers permanently expose them to the danger of 'hit-and-run entry'. Competitiveness measured on the demand side might seem favourable on a contestable market but the really decisive factor of competitiveness could only be the level and the structure of costs of production. High market shares on a market with low entry barriers can speak of a *de facto* high level of competitiveness only if this is justified by relatively low costs of production.

The models of monopolistic competition and contestable markets can coexist if substitution is limited and entry barriers are low at the same time.

These could be cases in which levels of competitiveness measured on the supply and the demand side would differ substantially.

The measurement of competitiveness should be started, at least in an ideal case, with the assessment of the type of competition. This would however raise the problem of relevant markets (see Scherer and Ross, 1990). This problem appears in any case of anti-competitive behaviour when determining the scope of the harm done to competition makes it necessary to narrow down the market to a point where substitutability disappears. Determining the relevant market does not mean, on the other hand, that the type of competition can easily be identified.

The case of contestable markets may show why it can sometimes be hard to establish the type of competition in a quantitative way. Contestable markets show high levels of concentration. If however the height of entry barriers (customs duties, taxes related to imports, the difference between the nominal and the real exchange rate of the national currency, the size of transport costs and so on) is measured, this measurement can also result in apparently good competitive conditions.

One possible scheme distinguishes three types of entry barriers: (1) Physical barriers such as distance or geographical obstacles to trade; (2) Administrative barriers including quantitative restrictions, customs duties or exchange rates, and (3) Strategic barriers related to market structure and industrial organisation (see Kühn et al., 1992). The least visible barriers are the strategic ones, and their measurement is especially difficult because, as mentioned above, it should go much further than just measuring concentration.

The models of imperfect competition have fundamentally stirred up the concept of comparative advantage. This occurred in spite of the fact that the majority of the international economics community seems to subscribe to Ricardo's approach to comparative advantage – albeit only in a reformulated and very much generalized version. This reformulated version can be summed up as: 'the international division of labour is a cooperative and positive-sum game'.

Still, assuming the existence of comparative advantage is conditional not only on the productive behaviour of the players (as Smith, Ricardo, or much later Heckscher and Ohlin supposed it), but also on their competitive behaviour. This difference led to a number of cases where assumed (or expected) and measured comparative advantages (as for instance in the case of the Leontief paradox) did not overlap at all.

A good practical compromise to solve this problem was Bela Balassa's concept and indicator of 'revealed comparative advantage' (RCA) (see Balassa, 1965, 1977; Fertő and Hubbard, 2002). It is, in the first place, a tool for mapping international trade specialization (Laursen, 2000. 36), and it cannot be regarded as a measure of competitiveness. But a map of international specialization certainly reflects competitiveness to some extent if it is accepted that specialization is based upon the perception of competitiveness by market players.

The compromise underlying the use of the RCA index was made on the assumption that the measurement of comparative advantage is a theoretical illusion. Does this mean however that measuring competitiveness is equally impossible?

Not at all. In the first place, competitiveness is a concept much broader than comparative advantage. Comparative advantage is related only to the supply side, and it does not involve a number of factors influencing competitiveness, such as for example demand, the type of competition, technological and supplier relationships.

The idea of 'revealed comparative advantage' speaks of a certain level of understanding of the problem, but the authors elaborating this concept remained in the classical–neoclassical framework of explaining the pay-offs from trade liberalization. Michael Porter's work beginning in the 1980s (see Porter, 1990) helped to expand the concept of comparative advantage towards the much broader idea of competitive advantage (on the possible links between absolute advantage, comparative advantage and competitive advantage, see Neary, 2003).

Discovering the 'Diamond'

The analyses of competitive advantage are based upon a methodology clearly distinct from the methodology of mainstream economics. This less analytical and more visual methodology is used in strategic management and marketing, and its basis is much more on company-level and sectoral data than national accounts statistics ('its emphasis is on the ways in which factor productivity and firm competition interact', Neary, 2003, 458).

The most often cited analytical tool of competitive advantage analysis is the 'Porter diamond' (Porter, 1990, 72) which is a rectangular scheme of four groups of factors of competitiveness. Its revised form for the purposes of innovation analysis is presented in Furman et al. (2002).

This model distinguishes between supply-side factors in the classical–neoclassical sense based on relative cost, and demand-side factors also including entry barriers. Porter brings new elements into competitiveness analysis with the third and the fourth group of factors: supplier industries on the one hand and market structure and corporate strategies responding to market developments on the other. These four groups of factors of competitiveness on the company level enlarge the scope of competitiveness analysis to a considerable extent, but it remains to be seen how the model could be applicable for country-level competitiveness analysis.

The four groups of competitiveness factors described by Porter's model can be clearly interpreted on the macroeconomic level, although such interpretations are not known from the international literature yet. The probable reason is the fast-increasing role of transnational firms in international trade from the late 1980s which seemed to have made the analysis of country-level competitiveness largely irrelevant.

This argument is however refuted by several authors (see Laursen, 2000 and different issues of UNCTAD WIR, WEF and IMD reports) but there seems to exist a down-to-earth counter-argument as well. Namely, if competitiveness on the national level becomes an empty or irrelevant term, then international or foreign trade measured on the country level is also nothing more than a statistical illusion. If however this statement is accepted then all international trade statistics showing country-level exports and imports should be condemned as useless and irrelevant.

The competitiveness of foreign-owned firms shapes the pattern of competitiveness of the host economy since such firms use mostly local factors of production. International investment and trade data are interpreted by UNCTAD (2002) – although without a detailed explanation of the theoretical background of this approach – in such a way that the trade performance and the competitiveness of a subsidiary of a transnational or multinational firm count as elements of the trade performance and competitiveness of the host, and not of the mother economy.

The diamond model does not introduce a new model of competitiveness but it offers a scheme of the explanatory factors of competitiveness trends on enterprise and sectoral level. Chapter 1 of Porter's book explicitly describes the Smith–Ricardo paradigm as a theoretical framework inappropriate for modern competitiveness analysis. After this judgement however, the book leaves the world of theory and tries to identify the factors of export success in a purely practical approach. Some of these factors are found by Porter not only outside the exporting firm, but also outside the exporting country.

Competitiveness on the supply and the demand side should be given separate attention for various reasons. One reason is linked to theory. No such theoretical approach is known so far which would have been able to integrate the supply- and the demand-side factors of export specialization. A further reason is policy specific. The development of competitiveness depends on different policies such as industrial or technology policy on the supply side and trade or competition policy on the demand side.

For such reasons, the problem of defining and measuring competitiveness will be analysed first in a supply-side approach and second in a demand-side approach.

1.2 FIELDS OF COMPETITIVENESS

Competitiveness on the Supply Side

The key concept of classical and neoclassical trade theories is comparative advantage. The exploitation of potential comparative advantage makes it possible to create appropriate levels of competitiveness, a term which was still unused by and probably unknown to earlier authors dealing with comparative advantage. Pre-war economic theory neglected the demand-side factors of comparative advantage and the problem of market structures to a large extent, since its tacit point of departure was that goods produced find their own markets:

> This idea was referred to in former literature as the 'Say law', but Schumpeter showed that the French author did not publish this idea in the form often attributed to him. (Schumpeter, 1954, 616–17)

The abstract approach of the Heckscher–Ohlin theory also assumes that markets accept the goods produced if relative product costs are in conformity with relative factor costs. These patterns of relative cost emerge if structures of factor endowment and factor price reflect each other in a given national economy. The Leontief paradox and a number of subsequent analyses have been able to prove that a country's trade structure may evolve in a way substantially different from what could be concluded from its factor proportions (see Leontief, 1954 and 1956; Swerling, 1954; Balogh, 1955; Hoffmeyer, 1958; Kindleberger, 1962; Mucchielli and Sollogoub, 1980).

International economics literature has apparently left unobserved an interesting parallel with the so-called SCP (*structure–conduct–performance*) model of market structures and market behaviour (on the model see Caves, 1964; Scherer and Ross, 1990). The two cases are similar in the sense that both speak of the lack of conformity between market structures and the factors of competitive performance. The theoretical approaches arising from the Leontief paradox identify such divergences between factors of production and export structures, whereas the SCP model explains differences between market structures, competitive behaviour and competitive performance.

Measured structures of factor endowment would point to real (but never absolutely exactly identifiable) comparative advantage in Heckscher–Ohlin inspired models of international trade. The quantitative picture of export structures diverging from the ones expected on the basis of factor endowment shows visible (or revealed) comparative advantage as in calculations made with the RCA indicator by Balassa, the indicator of net exports, or other indicators described in detail in Bowden (1983).

Such differences between real and measured (revealed) comparative advantage appear if for example an economy rich in physical capital does not specialize in capital-intensive industries such as steel or petrochemicals, but rather in labour-intensive industries as textiles, footwear or furniture.

The divergence between theoretically assumed (real) and quantitatively measured (revealed) comparative advantage is also the basis of the difference between comparative advantage and competitiveness. This difference is mainly due to the imperfect functioning of markets in international trade.

Strategic trade policies in a string of East Asian countries have repeatedly tried not only to adjust structures of production and exports to the patterns of real comparative advantage, but also to shape them on the basis of its expected trends of change (see Inoue et al., 1993). Cases referred to in the source cited speak of such industrial and trade policies first in Japan, and subsequently in Hong Kong, South Korea, Singapore and Taiwan, which focused on industries offering comparative advantages not on the basis of current but rather of prospected comparative advantage.

Literature on comparative advantage and competitiveness devoted much effort in the 1970s and 1980s to linking economic development to export performance. Balassa identified close linkages between the stages of economic development and comparative advantage. His conclusion was that comparative advantages shift in the function of the national accumulation of capital towards manufactured goods with a higher technology content (Balassa, 1977).

In Porter's first model of the development of competitive advantage, each stage of national economic development is based upon different factors of competitiveness such as (1) factors of production, (2) investment, (3) innovation, and (4) accumulated wealth (Porter, 1990). The revised version of Porter's model has only the first three factors of the previous variant. The omission of the fourth one is based on the recognition that accumulated wealth can serve as a factor of competitiveness only for a limited amount of time (Porter, 2003). In addition to that, accumulated wealth is often the basis for exports of capital, which is a case where competitiveness is enhanced abroad rather than in the domestic economy.

The supply-side indicators of competitiveness are based on the assumption that unit factor costs below the cost levels of competitors would make it possible to increase profits or market shares as compared to the competition. This is however a strongly *ceteris paribus* type assumption which can hold only if at least three other conditions are fulfilled. Measurements of unit factor costs often neglect the three conditions below, which limits the field of practical application of supply-side techniques of competitiveness measurement. These conditions are as follows:

1. Exporters need not bear any costs of changing their levels of capacity utilization.
2. Any decrease of export prices increases demand and makes it possible to increase exports. This is a simplified reformulation of the Marshall–Lerner–Robinson condition according to which the sum of the price elasiticities of exports and imports has to be higher than 1 for a devaluation to generate a surplus of exports over imports (Krugman and Obstfeld, 1991, 466).
3. Changes of relative factor prices of exporter A in time period t are answered by competitors with such a delay that their reaction does not modify market shares in time period $t+1$. Prices and market shares of exporter A change in this time period $t+1$ only as a result of the changes in its factor prices during t.

These three conditions are however quite difficult to be fulfilled in practice. Some comments:

1. The most evident costs of changing the level of capacity utilization include inflexible labour costs (if the level of employment remains the same in spite of a decrease of capacity utilization), severance payments (in the case of employment cuts), and training costs (if employment increases). Such costs are usually relatively high in countries with regulated labour markets such as most member countries of the European Union, and much lower in countries with less regulated labour markets such as for example the United States. The European Commission recognized in the late 1990s that the inflexibility of labour markets may harm competitiveness, but it did not take politically risky steps to lower job security. Its strategy for increasing labour market flexibility has taken a different direction, namely the stimulation of lifelong learning. This strategy was enacted at the European Council meeting in Stockholm in March 2001 (European Commission, 2002, 47).
2. There exist a number of manufactured goods, mainly luxury and prestige items, where price cuts could deteriorate competitiveness. Such products are namely characterized by high negative, or even positive price elasticities of demand.[4]
3. Factor prices and market shares usually do not change in a continuous way. Therefore the size of the time lag in question can be determined only when very short t periods are analysed.

Literature on the methodology of competitiveness measurement often relegates such theoretical problems to footnotes when the main indicators are to be explained. It is less a measurement problem but rather a methodological problem that most of the currently used indicators of competitiveness are based on several *ceteris paribus*-type assumptions stemming from quite outdated elements of classical and neoclassical trade theories.

The fundamental problem with the currently most frequently used methods of competitiveness measurement is similar in kind, as we are going to see shortly. The supply-side measurement of competitiveness quite often supposes a given level of demand. On the other hand, the demand-side measurement supposes a given level of supply. It is difficult to prove in either of the two cases that these conditions exist in reality. Furthermore the traditional indicators of supply- and demand-side competitiveness (these indicators will be surveyed in detail in Chapter 2) are of limited use for competitiveness analyses of technology or skill-intensive products, because they are quite insensitive to qualitative differences between inputs, and differences in the technological levels of outputs.

An often used and simple indicator of the technological competitiveness of manufacturing exports could be the export share of high-tech products. It can be considered as an indicator of competitiveness only with serious reservations. We will deal with it in a separate sub-chapter where the relationship between export structure and technological competitiveness will be analysed.

In spite of the problems referred to above, the supply-side measurement of competitiveness poses less dramatic methodological problems in cases where countries with similar levels of development are compared. For example labour cost-based indicators such as unit labour cost (ULC, surveyed also in Chapter 2) are more reliable indicators of competitiveness in developing countries whose exports consist primarily of labour-intensive goods. Such indicators may also be relevant in more developed economies for smaller statistical aggregates such as firms or regions. For example their use can be recommended to assess the competitiveness of an industrial location which competes with its rivals on the basis of its level of labour costs.

Demand-side Competitiveness

The demand side of comparative advantage and competitiveness gained attention in the 1960s. It turned out at the time (Linder, 1961) that the growth of world trade is carried less by Heckscher–Ohlin type specialization based on complementary factor endowments than by trade between industrial countries with apparently similar factor endowments.

This trade was called 'intra-industrial' because it took place mainly between similar industries in the partner countries (for example cars were exported and other types of cars were imported, or assembled cars were traded for car components). The differentiation of supply can be of great help in adjusting to demand, and price competitiveness may play a secondary role only. In practice, this is the end of the 'one product, one price' principle of neoclassical economics, since one product can exist in a number of versions some of which may even carry a similar price tag.

The non-price factors of competitiveness and their measurement techniques are surveyed in Stout and Swann (1993). That survey established a surprising relationship between the competitiveness in manufacturing exports and the competitiveness in R&D or innovation, and we shall base our analysis of competitiveness in R&D on similar kinds of relationship. They proposed synthetic indicators for assessing non-price competitiveness on the demand side, and these indicators are very much technology related. One of these proposed is GERD (gross domestic expenditure on R&D) as a percentage of GDP, and another is the number of patents per country in an international comparison.

The British authors consider the comparison of the qualitative parameters of exported goods a good technique for measuring non-price competitiveness, but no example of implementing such a technique is known from international literature:

> This fact does not mean that no such measurement has been carried out at all: a former article (Salgó and Török, 1980) made an attempt to assess the non-price competitiveness of exports on the basis of data taken from product tests. The article came to telling results in assessing the competitive structure of Hungarian imports of engineering products for households. The same method was reapplied in a project in the mid-nineties also in Hungary. (Penyigey, 1996)

The model of monopolistic competition dominates such markets where non-price competitiveness is decisive. In this model, supply consists of segments within which most goods are only limited substitutes of each other. Competitiveness might be greatly influenced here with minimal changes in product parameters if these changes have a strong impact on substitution.

In monopolistic competition the competitiveness of products depends largely on their exact position on the list of supply, and also on which size, purchasing power and taste-based parameters of demand they have to face. New Economic Geography adds to this picture that the exact positioning of products on the market also depends on the respective geographical locations of supply and demand (Fujita et al., 1999).

A further factor making it necessary to base demand-side competitiveness analysis on qualitative parameters is that increasing product differentiation does not suppose any physical change in the products themselves. Advertising is a good example to this. It increases the degree of product differentiation only in consumer perception. It also increases competitiveness as a kind of sunk cost that functions as an exit barrier for incumbents on the market (Sutton, 1991).

The demand-side measurement of competitiveness should reflect the impact of a number of competitive factors which have been identified by industrial organization theory such as for example economies of scale, market structure, behavioural variables and, in a more general approach, the potential of developing and exerting market power. Techniques are however still mostly missing which would make it possible to identify the impact of such factors on competitive performance.

The scope of the methods currently available range from the quite simple to the more sophisticated.

Theoretical Problems of Harmonizing Supply-side and Demand-side Competitiveness

We have seen that the theoretical meaning of competitiveness is different on the supply side from that on the demand side, and their indicators have few elements in common. We could call the aspect of competitiveness measured on the supply side the 'cost-side factor of competitiveness', and competitiveness as appearing on the demand side the 'reflection of competitiveness on the market'. It depends largely on the factors of this reflection how competitiveness approximated with the methods listed above is perceived by market players. Some of these factors are discussed below.

Competitiveness measured on the supply side appears in the form of cost advantages, and competitiveness measured on the demand side takes shape in performance on the market. There is however no generally valid and appropriately tested causal relationship between cost advantage and sales success. If therefore a strict theoretical stance is taken, then the only possible conclusion is that the results of competitiveness tests do not offer watertight proofs of the existence of a certain level of competitiveness. Low relative costs speak of a competitiveness potential only (the exporter can sell well above his or her low costs). Good relative export performance shows that the market has accepted the product favourably, but the costs of this good performance are missing from the picture.

The theoretical problem of linking supply-side and demand-side competitiveness to each other has led to a process of searching for alternative solutions. The first of these does not mean a radical break with conventional methods of assessing competitiveness, but it can help in increasing the accuracy of applying such methods. The second one however is an attempt at generalizing the scope of competitiveness analysis in order to skip the problem of harmonizing the supply-side and the demand-side measurement.

The Fields of Competitiveness

International comparisons of competitiveness might yield surprising or even wrong results if the country sample for comparison is not well designed. It might be, in general, quite misleading to compare countries with great differences in economic development, country size, factors of competitiveness or structures.

Giving a correct comparative picture of Polish competitiveness, for example, requires much more a comparison with Mexico, Spain, Ireland, Hungary or Turkey, than with the United States, Germany, Japan or China.

The factor of country size deserves our special attention at this point. The successes of some small European nations (Switzerland, Finland, Sweden, Ireland, Denmark, Austria) in international R&D or innovation competition are sometimes interpreted as a proof for the equality of chances in this competition. A balanced view is expressed on this subject by Vivien Walsh who states that 'small countries have much more limited resources (money and people) for R&D than large countries, but the variety of possible disciplines, projects and industrial sectors is not necessarily smaller. Thus small countries either spread their resources more thinly over the available areas, or else select certain areas as priorities for R&D investment' (Walsh, 1988, 42). It will be discussed later that, in the early years of the new millennium, the highest GERD rates in the world belong to relatively small countries with genuinely strategic R&D policies: Sweden and Finland.

The choice of the right country sample is especially important in our case, where the international comparison of R&D competitiveness is envisaged: R&D as a sector exists only in no more than 100 countries, and differences in competitive factors and performances range on a wide scale even among these countries.

Choosing a more or less optimal sample should be based on more than just intuition. For a start, we use a logical but not too far-reaching analogy with prospective (future) research where it is quite common to apply three scenarios (Lesourne, 1979). The central scenario (the 'normal' or 'mainstream' one) is based on the continuation of fundamental trends with only minor changes in them. The 'positive' or favourable scenario shows the results of good policies making use of positive externalities, while the 'negative' scenario describes rather unfavourable developments.

The negative scenario plays a certain role in selling the prospective analysis and, in some cases, getting political support for the strategy aimed at avoiding these negative developments. The deterrence factor underlying some negative scenarios can help politicians take unpopular decisions in order to minimize damage later. This means the strategic function of negative scenarios can be in offering implicit support to strategies needed to realize the positive ones.

Our logic in putting together a sample for comparative competitiveness analysis is similar. The dimension of creating three groups is, in this case, not linked to differences in strategic perspectives but to the relative strategic positions of the countries to be compared. Three groups of countries can be created, and we call these groups 'fields of competition'. These groups are identified on the basis of factors known from SWOT (strengths–weaknesses–opportunities–threats) analysis. The country whose competitive positions should be assessed is country A.

The first and perhaps the key group (or field) is where country A is exposed to direct competition. We can call this the field of neighbours. The countries competing in this field are direct competitors of country A in most products. Regarding this field, it is of primary importance to assess the current strengths and weaknesses of country A in order to be able to stand competitive pressure from countries having similar strategic assets and facing similar strategic challenges.

If for example we take again the economy of Poland, countries directly competing with it include Hungary, the Czech Republic, Slovakia, Greece and Portugal, offering more or less similar products and being in the same part of the world. Regarding other continents, South Korea, Turkey, Mexico, Brazil or increasingly China have comparable structures and levels of competitiveness in manufacturing exports which would also make them part of this competitive field for Poland.

The second field includes countries which are well ahead of country A, but catching up with them is still an opportunity for country A within a reasonable time scale. To put it differently, there is still some degree of comparability of the competitiveness of country A and members of this field which we can call the field of targets. These countries can be reasonably targeted from the point of view of competitiveness strategy, since catching up with them is a more or less realistic possibility. For Poland again, Italy, Spain, Ireland or Austria might constitute members of this field if the strategic perspectives of Polish manufacturing exports are considered.

The third field has countries whose catching up efforts are a strategic threat for country A, which can still boast of certain competitive advantages as compared to this group. These countries are the pursuers of or the runners-up to country A, which is in turn a target for them. Regarding Poland, countries wishing to catch up with it as far as competitiveness in manufacturing exports is concerned include Romania, Bulgaria or Ukraine within Europe, and India, Pakistan or Morocco outside it.

A really complete pattern of competitiveness fields for country A would include not three, but rather five groups of countries, but the logic of our approach implies that the 'best' and the 'worst' countries have to be omitted. The reason is the following. There are, for most cases of country A, certain such countries which are either too strong or too weak to be understood as its direct competitors for the largest part of its exports. Sticking to the Polish example, most of its manufacturing products do not compete directly with goods made in Switzerland, the Netherlands, Japan or the United States. To look in the opposite direction, Angola, Bangladesh, Myanmar or even Albania have few products (if any) that can compete with those made in Poland.

The focal point of our approach is the microstructure of exports. This means country A can export goods belonging to the same commodity groups that are also well represented in the export lists of the 'best' and the 'worst' countries omitted from the direct comparison of competitiveness.

The problem is however that few products offered by country A have substantial degrees of substitutability with goods having considerable percentage shares in the exports of the 'best' and the 'worst' countries. In other words, only a small part of Polish exports can be regarded as exact substitutes of exports from Switzerland, and similarly only a minimal part of exports from Angola might be direct substitutes of goods delivered from Poland. This is the reason why direct comparisons of competitiveness between Poland on the one hand and Switzerland or Angola on the other could have a quite esoteric character, and should thus be omitted.

1.3 INNOVATION, R&D AND COMPETITIVENESS IN R&D

R&D and Innovation Systems: Elements and Policies

The terms 'R&D' and 'innovation' have been understood and interpreted in many ways. Both these terms and their measurement have undergone a number of changes during the history of science and innovation. Furthermore these changes were largely influenced by the gradual integration of R&D and innovation analysis in the broader context of the analysis of the development of economic, social and institutional systems offered by the various strands of evolutionary economics (see Nelson, 1995).

The OECD made the first consistent attempt towards elaborating the international standard for terms such as 'R&D' and 'innovation' (Godin, 2003). This standard now is in general use, based on a tacit agreement accepted by the majority of the profession, but this agreement has to a certain extent a convention-like character. The word 'convention' has been borrowed from mathematics: it describes one of several available options of understanding and applying a term. None of these options is necessarily more accurate and useful than any other, but the profession will have chosen the one accepted as a conventional term for reasons of simplicity or practical usefulness.

It seems appropriate to briefly review the OECD's interpretations of the most important terms used in R&D and innovation analysis. This is to make sure that possible misinterpretation is avoided.

The interpretational standards of the OECD for R&D and innovation are set out in the Frascati Manual (OECD, 2002). As one of its key activities, the OECD started to collect data on R&D in the 1950s. A group of experts held a meeting on R&D statistics in the Italian town of Frascati in June 1963, and the output of that meeting was named *Proposed Standard Practice for Surveys on Research and Experimental Development*. This is still the official name of the Frascati Manual.

The first version of the manual was originally meant to serve as a collection of methodological guidelines for surveys of applied R&D and experimental development, and its scope was enlarged later towards basic research. The manual is regularly updated and its latest version is always available on the Internet. We have used the electronic version from 2002.

The manual limits itself to R&D, and seeks consistency with those international norms, for example the ones introduced by UNESCO, which have been created for S&T (science and technology) analysis.[5] Furthermore the manual is meant to serve the needs of OECD countries, most of which can boast of quite advanced economic and scientific systems.

As we shall see later from the analysis, many non-OECD countries have lower levels of economic development and significantly different R&D systems as compared with the OECD countries. This fact also means that the applicability of the manual to the non-OECD countries might be somewhat limited. It has to be noted however that the relative share of the OECD countries in both the world's scientific input and its output is more than 90 per cent (in a more precise manner, Keller argues that the G-7 countries accounted for 84 per cent of world GERD whereas their share of world GDP was only 64 per cent; Keller, 2004, 752). Furthermore only the OECD countries produce more or less comprehensive and comparable statistics on R&D. It is hardly an exaggeration if we suppose that the OECD standards of R&D analysis can be used for the whole world with a fairly high degree of approximation and reliability.

It is hardly necessary to review the whole Frascati Manual in this chapter. There are however a few definitions and concepts which are key to solid analysis of international R&D. They include the main types of R&D, the difference between R&D and innovation, the concept of national innovation systems (NIS, also referred to as NSI, national systems of innovation, in the literature), and the indicators of R&D activity.

Types of R&D

R&D consists of basic research, applied research and experimental development, and can be accurately defined as their combination.

Basic research is 'experimental or theoretical work undertaken primarily to acquire new knowledge of the underlying foundation of phenomena and observable facts, without any particular application or use in view' (OECD, 2002, 30). This is what can be called a 'negative definition', describing what basic research is not. This definition says research can have a basic character only if no particular application is envisaged. Of course it is difficult to say what kind of output had been targeted when a particular research project was launched; however if the purpose was scientific publication then the so-called basic character of the research can hardly be denied, at least in natural sciences. Still, there were interesting cases when theoretical results proved to be very profitable and entailed not only intellectually rewarding applications some time later:

> *Number theory was such a case*: most if not all of its results were long considered without any practical use but, in the early 1980s, a completely new window of opportunity opened up for mathematicians expert in the field. It turned out that number theory can be very well applied for the development of *cryptography*, with many promising applications in information science and technology. (Devlin, 1990, 21–2)

'Basic' research inevitably has a strongly theoretical character, since it can also be regarded as research laying the foundations for practical applications. This is why we would suggest reconsidering this label. 'Basic' also means 'low-level' or 'for beginners' (as in the expression 'the basics of . . .'), whereas 'fundamental' has a slightly different meaning. It includes support for and even a precondition of further research,[6] and is therefore broader in scope than the term 'basic' which involves not only some kind of beginning of a research process but also the simplicity of the achievements. Recently, the 'basic' character of basic research was also questioned by Nelson (2004, 462).

Literature has devoted much effort to grasping the border line between basic and applied research (see David et al., 2000; Salter and Martin, 2001). 'Basic research' overlaps considerably with 'academic research', 'research' and 'science', but the meaning of these terms is not the same. They also emphasize the fact that public research funding does not only go into what is called basic[7] research, because it is also used to support collaboration between academia and industry (Salter and Martin, 2001). Therefore the way of financing research cannot become a dividing line between basic and applied research. The specific feature of the latter is application: applied research 'is also original investigation undertaken in order to acquire new knowledge' (OECD, 2002, 30). Still, it is 'directed primarily towards a specific practical aim or objective' (OECD, 2002, 30).

Applied research is, in a theoretical approach, based on the idea of 'backward linkage' in the Hirschmanian sense.[8] Patterns of development in the sector relying upon results from R&D determine the pattern of applied research, while basic research works rather according to the 'forward linkage' model. In this case, the line taken in R&D determines, often with a considerable delay, how research output will influence trends in industry.[9]

Basic research can be divided into two sub-groups, namely 'curiosity-oriented' and 'strategic' (Salter and Martin, 2001, 510). No such distinction would make sense for applied research, where pure curiosity can extremely rarely stimulate serious research effort. It basically always has a strategic character, and this strategic orientation is closely linked to the strategy of the partner in industry or, in general, on the demand side. The pattern and the line of the given research project depends, at least to some extent, on the researcher in the case of basic research. In applied research however, not only the final word is said, but also the entire strategic line is determined by the partner in non-research business.

What unites basic and applied research is the desire to create new knowledge, even if the initiative comes from different sources. Experimental development is aimed at combining existing pieces of knowledge (based both on research and on practical experience) in a way that is most efficient from the viewpoint of business or society. The output of experimental development can be much more than new devices, products or services. It can include new materials, processes and systems, and also the substantial improvement of already existing pieces of technology or output in the industry.

Experimental development is part of R&D owing to its relatively high exposure to risk, and the fact that it precedes serial production. Exactly as basic or applied research, its important feature is that it has no repetitive character. Each action of experimental development is aimed at a different output and this makes it different from industrial routine.

Linkages between the Types of R&D

The three types of R&D are not necessarily linked to each other in a chain-like model. The causal chain leading from basic and applied research to experimental development and then to serial production is represented in the simple and somewhat didactic 'linear' model of R&D, but the time-consuming and not too efficient process described by this model is quite rare in real life. In any event, the different types of R&D have to complement each other in the best possible way in order to generate the optimal spillovers helping national and international economic development.

R&D takes place much more often according to the 'circular' model in which each stage of the process exerts a permanent influence on each other and none of them is a closed entity. This holds both for processes and organizations, and the circular model does not require the existence of separate R&D organizations. Basic research can, according to this model, continue at the same time as applied research or even experimental development, and experimental development can be followed by a new stage of basic research. This model is able to describe parallel processes of R&D and innovation when one organization simultaneously carries out several R&D projects with partly overlapping contents.

The circular model gives a realistic description only of well organized and transparent national R&D and innovation systems. This is usual in industrialized countries, while elsewhere in the world (mainly in Third World countries and some former Soviet republics) certain elements of structural and financial disorganization or chaos may be also present. Such R&D systems are described by the 'random' model.

The random model may seem to be centralized, but serious problems of coordination between the players make central strategy making and control a mere illusion. This model has a number of special characteristics which do not support coordination between the elements of the systems of R&D and innovation. Most R&D organizations function in isolation from each other and their roles are not always clear. Successful basic R&D is usually not followed by high-quality applied research, and experimental development often takes place outside the country. There might be two reasons for this: either R&D output is sold cheap in order urgently to obtain financing, or intellectual property belonging to domestic organizations is simply sold by individuals on their own account (to be precise: it is stolen from the original owner of intellectual property).

Poor governments and technologically undemanding firms are unable to provide sufficient financing of R&D in the random model. This is why R&D organizations may have to undertake many different inefficient tasks just for survival. The bulk of financing still comes in a quite haphazard way from governments, due to some political pressure from interest groups linked to science or academia. But the irrational character of the system and the weakness of government exclude efficient evaluation and monitoring, and financing becomes independent from the outcome and results of R&D. The R&D and innovation system is maintained simply because some politicians hope the country might still need it in better times.

Regarding the development of organizational models of R&D and taking an evolutionary approach to it, the random model can be considered rather as a detour. In other words, it is a special case applicable only to countries where R&D is carried out in a not friendly economic and political environment, and its role in systemic evolution is neglectable.

The development of economic and sociological analysis of R&D made it necessary to elaborate models with degrees of complexity higher than that of the circular model which is basically limited to the participants of the R&D process itself. The success of the R&D effort depends on the interplay of all of its stakeholders (on the meaning of the term see Williamson, 1985; Milgrom and Roberts, 1992, 41–2). This interplay is probably best described by the 'triple helix' model.

The triple helix model of the organization of R&D takes account of the fact that 'the boundaries between public and private, science and technology, university and industry are in flux' (Leydesdorff, 2000, 243). This is not the chaotic world described by the random model, but its complexity and lack of hierarchy makes a simple description very difficult. The triple helix of relationships between universities, government and industry is understood as a model of evolving networks of communication (Leydesdorff, 2000, 243). The model is based on the competitive dynamics of markets, innovation and control (Leydesdorff, 2000, 244), and its complexity finally leads to a low level of predictability.

The triple helix model is in general terms also called a model of institutional networking. It was thought that this model also renders the analysis of national systems of R&D and innovations unnecessary. Indeed one of its main assumptions is that all kinds of boundaries between organizations interested in R&D are in flux, while international markets for goods and services including the output of R&D have opened up very fast. It has been demonstrated however that international comparisons of national R&D systems can comfortably coexist with the triple helix model (de Castro et al., 2000). This is one of the key arguments (see also Laursen, 2000, 6) which seem to support our view that national systems of R&D and innovation can be analysed in a model of international competitiveness and competition.

Non-R&D Activities

The Frascati Manual is consequent in excluding a number of R&D-related activities from R&D itself. It is important to note these activities since in some countries governments try to overestimate (or inflate) R&D spending in order to give the impression of a government effort towards competitiveness improvement and of a future-oriented technology policy. The existence of rigid institutional frameworks can facilitate such statistical distortions of the R&D picture.

For example, the Hungarian government made a promise in 1999 (just as both its predecessor and its successor) to increase the GERD : GDP ratio (gross domestic expenditure on R&D as a percent of GDP), this time from 0.8 to 1 per cent in a few years. This would have meant an increase of R&D spending by US$ 100 million in an economy with an approximately US$ 50 billion of GDP. Funds were scarce, the willingness of business to give additional financing for R&D was far from evident, and the existing national innovation system[10] was not very well organized. Thus it was questionable whether more money could be raised for this purpose and also whether extra R&D funds could be spent in an efficient way.

Nonetheless, creative accounting did the trick. State universities in Hungary (about 80 per cent of universities in the country, with more than 90 per cent of graduate students) obtain the bulk of government financing for two purposes: education and research. Both amounts have a fixed and a so-called normative element, the latter based on some nominal indicators of input (for example the number of students enrolled) or output (for example scientific production). The government just shifted the proportion between the fixed parts of education financing and research financing to the benefit of the latter. Since then universities seemed to have spent less on education and more on research, which neither deteriorated the quality of life of students nor improved that of university professors doing research. The only outcome was a visible increase in the GERD indicator.

The example illustrates why the OECD wants to give a narrow institutional definition to R&D. While education and training coexist with R&D in a number of institutions (mainly universities), they have different roles in improving the knowledge base of the society and the economy. Education and training do not produce new knowledge in the way R&D does, but they can be instrumental in improving the quality of intellectual input to R&D in the future.

Besides education and training, three other types of activities related to science and technology, but not creating new knowledge, are also excluded from R&D. These are called: (1) 'other related scientific and technological activities' (for example scientific and technical information services, patent and licence work, or testing and standardization); (2) 'other industrial activities' (basically other innovation activities such as technology acquisition or industrial design); and (3) 'administration and other supporting activities'. The latter can greatly contribute to the success of R&D itself through good management of funds and correct accounting, but this contribution has a character strongly different from R&D itself. Furthermore all the activities excluded from R&D can be part of the innovation process defined in much broader terms than R&D.

R&D and Innovation

The boundaries of R&D also need clear definitions with respect to the term 'innovation', so frequently confused with R&D. The concept of innovation goes back to Schumpeter (1912), whose novel approach besides introducing the term itself consisted in defining it in a much broader sense than just technology. Innovation is understood as a complex process at the beginning of which there is usually a good idea (to paraphrase Thornton Wilder: 'perhaps an invention'), and there should appear a successful and competitive product, service or technology at its end.

Innovation includes scientific, technological, organizational, financial and commercial actions (OECD, 2002, 18). All of these activities are undertaken in order to implement technologically new or improved products, services or processes. R&D is only an element in innovation, and not even the one which helps the innovator to generate new ideas. Since these new ideas are needed along the entire innovation process including its final stage of bringing the new products or services to the market, marketing for instance can also be an innovative element without any specific R&D content.

The problem of distinction between R&D and innovation is often raised at the policy level. The simultaneous use of both terms can lead to some confusion. R&D policy is sometimes identified with science policy but, in any event, its scope is limited to the creation of new knowledge without any special emphasis on application. The monitoring function of R&D policy is therefore quite independent from performance on the market, and is mainly based on data reflecting the recognition or acceptance of a given result ('R&D output') by one segment of the research community. Such data are for example publication indicators or citation indexes.

Innovation policy has a much broader meaning and scope than R&D policy, and it is more closely related to the modernization (or 'evolutionary') process of the national economy. Innovation policy might include incentives to R&D as one of its key elements. In addition to that, its scope can comprise fields covered by regional policy or industrial policy. Innovation policy is, in practice, quite difficult to define and delineate due to its many possible overlaps with other policy fields. This may be the reason why usual R&D related policy analysis has a narrower focus, that is R&D policy itself. Innovation policy as such is relatively rarely elaborated, at least as far as it can be judged from the titles of policy documents. This is probably linked to the fact that the R&D community can be more easily identified and delineated than the innovation community, the members of which are not necessarily linked to the sometimes quite isolated world of science and scientists. Government institutions dealing with these two practically distinct fields of policy may also differ.

A typical example of the differences in the institutional backgrounds of policies on R&D and innovation can be found in the European Commission. The Research Directorate is responsible for 'pure' R&D policy with the Framework Programmes as its main policy tool, whereas innovation policy, with its tools outside the scope of the FPs, belongs to the Directorate dealing with enterprises, industry and information technology. Certain parallelisms exist between the two Directorates, and the fulfilment of the Lisbon Strategy goals belongs to the second one. R&D policy is a key element in achieving the Lisbon objectives (see Rodrigues, 2003), and it could thus become kind of subordinated to the innovation policy arm of the Commission.

It seems an interesting contradiction that R&D policy is more often formulated and referred to than innovation policy, but national systems comprising the main actors of the R&D scene are rather referred to as national innovation systems (NISs). Taking a closer look at some conceptual issues of the NISs might help bring the idea of competitiveness in R&D and innovation closer together.

R&D Policy and the Role of Competition

R&D policy in its clear form may run the risk of isolation from economic realities in a kind of 'ivory tower' if it promotes only scientific activities regardless their output. It is an open question (to which our text tries to find an answer) whether the world of science and research really lacks any element of competition. We think it does not, but it has to be seen how competition in this market differs from the traditional approach to competition in markets of goods and services.

One of the classics of the economics of competition policy, Robert Bork emphasized the fact that there coexist a number of concepts of competition in literature used, in general, without references to the others. This creates kind of a confusion since the great number of authors using the term mean various things by it. Bork lists four concepts of competition often used in literature to which he adds his own fifth, 'shorthand' interpretation. The five interpretations are as follows (Bork, 1993, 58–61):

"*Rivalry*": this is basically an interpretation inspired by game theory. Its core element is that one player can improve his/her position on the market only at the expense of a similar combined deterioration of the positions of the competitors. In this approach, competition is seen as a zero-sum game. The problem with this interpretation is that it completely lacks the cooperative element of competition which is very often present even in the absence of a cartel.

The "*liberal*", competition or trade policy related approach: there is competition if no constraints or trade barriers are imposed upon the competitors. It would be more appropriate to speak here of the "competition potential" of a market where such constraints do not exist.

The "*neo-classical*" concept of competition: we could also call this the "textbook of microeconomics" interpretation. According to Bork, this third concept of competition is the one in which no seller or buyer can influence prices with his/her decisions to sell or buy. This is a very narrow and idealised understanding of competition since the majority of markets do not function this way even if they are not monopolised. Would this fact mean competition as such is missing from markets with not completely weak sellers or buyers? Very likely not, and this is why this approach to competition seems to be unsuited for any kind of analysis of competition or competitiveness.

The "*political or social science approach*": in contrast with the previous one, this is a quite broad concept of competition. This approach means that competition can be effective only if a multitude of sectors, markets and firms co-exist within a not too large geographical area. The message here is that the existence of a competitive environment is a prerequisite for competition still before payoffs from competitive strategies, trade barriers and regulations or market structures are considered. Yes, but the existence of a wide variety of possible competitors is really only a precondition for, but not a proof of competition.

The "*shorthand approach*": Bork himself does not say this concept is any better than the others. He simply emphasises that it is at least transparent and easy to understand, and its use can prevent any potential conflict between the various interpretations. This concept says that perfect competition exists only if no government measure can further improve consumer welfare. This is kind of an acid test: not the condition itself is assessed, but the lack of any possibility of improving it indicates that it is probably close to optimal. An asset of the shorthand approach is that it is not defined in a way contradicting with any of the other four concepts. Its practical value is stressed along with the *de facto* impossibility of finding a theoretically appropriate definition of competition.

This string of concepts of competition was surveyed in order to stimulate our thinking on the relationship between R&D and competition. Competition in R&D certainly has a rivalry dimension, since both resources and channels of output (especially publication possibilities) are limited. On the contrary, price competition normally does not exist between R&D products: the availability of a product of R&D is not limited, in many cases, by the price of the individual product.[11] For example articles in scientific journals are sold in packages. The prices of such packages are the tariffs of normal or electronic subscription (although some editors also offer the electronic versions of single articles for sale).

Regarding the liberal approach to competition in R&D, there are very few limitations on or barriers to entry in this field, although certain firm and project sizes are necessary for launching pharmaceutical or electrical equipment research. Barriers of entry do not exist at all in the trade policy sense in the field of R&D but, using the triple scheme of entry barriers[12] introduced by Kühn et al. (1992), some entry barriers of a strategic character can be identified on these markets as well. Such entry barriers may include publication bottlenecks (waiting lists can reach two years or more at the most prestigious professional journals, see Coupé, 2004) and patenting costs (see Griliches, 1990):

Most of these entry barriers are of no considerable size, but researchers or R&D organisations from not too well-off countries might see them as serious stumbling blocks whenever they want to enter international competition for R&D funds, would like to compete for tenure track positions or other payoffs from good former competitive performance in R&D. On the other hand, no research result is known from literature on the specifics and sizes of entry barriers in R&D competition. Mainstream trade policy and Industrial Organisation literature uses the "tax equivalent" or the "customs duties equivalent" as the measurement unit of barriers to entry, but such benchmarks are missing from the scene of R&D competition.

The neoclassical concept of competition can be used for R&D, albeit with some modification. The original form of the concept has to be changed because prices do not act here as the tools of market coordination. The neoclassical concept of competition in the Borkian sense can also be used in the case of non-price competition. According to the extended version of the neoclassical concept of competition then, there is competition in a market if no player is in a situation to influence the conditions of entering this market. This is certainly true, because it can be hardly imagined that any single researcher or R&D organization could be able to influence the conditions of publication or patent registration, except for very narrow and specialized market niches.

A footnote belongs to this general statement: it can't be completely excluded that editorial boards of journals can have editorial policies which act as entry barriers for some potential authors. Such editorial policies could have, on the other hand, a real strategic entry barrier-like character only if they could cover entire fields of science in a monopolistic way thus leaving no other publication option open for researchers working in that precise field of science. This could be a realistic assumption in very narrow and completely isolated fields of science only.

The political or social science based approach to competition can also be made operational for competition in R&D. It is a strongly internationalized sector with only a few fields of locally oriented research carrying no interest for a wider international scientific community. Language barriers are disappearing from international science owing to the expansion of English as a kind of modern Latin. Value or political barriers can completely inhibit the participation of countries in international R&D cooperation and competition only in some isolated cases (for example North Korea, while researchers in Cuba for example already have a limited access to the Internet). In any event, the multitude of players as a key factor of a competitive environment certainly exists in international R&D.

Market failures are quite rare in the R&D sector. This is why the fifth, shorthand concept of competition seems to have a somewhat limited relevance for the R&D sector: the low likelihood of market failures inhibiting R&D competition creates a situation in which government intervention is normally not needed. Barriers to the flows of R&D resources and output are low or non-existent, governments are not expected to touch them, and therefore it can be rightly assumed that the shorthand condition of competition usually exists in R&D.

National Systems of Innovation

The NIS concept is described by the Oslo Manual as an institutional approach which 'studies innovating firms in the context of external institutions, government policies, competitors, customers, value systems and social and cultural practices that affect their operation' (OECD Oslo Manual, 2002, 17). This approach is somewhat reminiscent of the 'contractual asessment' of corporate governance described for example by Williamson (1985, 301–11), and akin to the 'stakeholders approach' (see Milgrom and Roberts, 1992, 41–2) incorporated into Industrial Organization theory.

The common element of these approaches consists in an inclusion of all potentially interested parties in behavioural analysis, and the concept of NIS stresses the complexity of the net of influences of many elements of the society and the economy on the innovation process. It is highly likely that the development of the NIS concept benefited from the broad framework for innovation analysis provided by evolutionary economics. This framework was instrumental in establishing effective linkages between R&D and innovation analysis on the one hand and the analysis of the development of the capabilities, structures and institutions of national economies on the other (see Nelson, 1995 and 2004).

An important contribution of the NIS concept to theoretical thinking on innovation is that the effort of innovative organizations themselves is not at all decisive in determining the final outcome of the process, and a favourable environment is essential for successful innovations. This approach becomes very important when R&D and innovation are analysed in economies in which individual research capacities may be much more developed than the political and economic context of these activities. Such cases are quite frequent in transition economies.

Carlsson et al. (2002) present the evolution of the idea of innovation systems. They point out that NIS is a relatively recent concept introduced only in the late 1980s. This observation seems to be in accordance with our assumption regarding the important role of evolutionary economics in the creation of the NIS concept since the first publications on evolutionary economics appeared in the early 1980s (for example Nelson and Winter, 1982).

In the approach of Carlsson et al. (2002), the NIS is a framework broader than an input–output system consisting of industries and firms, and many other actors active in science and technology, as well as technology policy, are also included. They also emphasize that the NIS concept considers all actors as components of a national system. Their low-key criticism of the model is not directed against its national character, but rather stresses the fact that, at least so far, it could only become the starting point of static analyses instead of more explicative dynamic ones.

The debate on the NIS concept going on in the literature since the 1980s is about much more than just terminology. The problem of the existence or non-existence of NISs is a key issue for our research, since it is strongly related to the definition of the players in international R&D competition. If the existence of NISs is accepted at least as a tool of analysis then it can also be assumed that international competition in R&D takes place between individual researchers, firms and countries. International R&D statistics make only the competitive performances of countries comparable in this respect, and the R&D competition between countries can also be interpreted as competition between NISs.

The real picture is far from simple: part of R&D financing comes from governments which are obviously national in character. The most widely used indicator of R&D financing, the GERD, is expressed as a percentage of GDP. Financing is received by elements of the R&D community which is (and has to be) very open and internationalized (to the extent of course which is allowed by intellectual property-related interests of firms). Besides international R&D networks, it is increasingly frequent that research teams are multinational even if they work in the same university or research centre on American, British, French, Polish or Japanese soil. Many firms using R&D output are also multinational, first of all in the so-called high-tech industries.

In apparent contradiction with this, the statistics of R&D output and performance are published exclusively as country statistics. This is true not only for data on patents or publications, but also for a number of indirect output indicators such as the exports of high-tech products. It seems thus inevitable that the NIS be used as a conceptual framework for assessing international R&D competition. Besides practical arguments such as the ones listed above, a number of theoretical considerations also support this approach.

Lundvall et al. (1999) stress that the concept of the NIS has earned wide international recognition since its introduction in the 1980s. It has been absorbed as part of the analytical perspective of the OECD, the European Commission and UNCTAD, while the initial reluctance of the World Bank and the IMF seems to be fading away. Two countries are also explicitly mentioned by the authors as ones which use the concept of NIS in policymaking. The United States Academy of Science applies it as a framework of science and technology policy analysis. Going even further, the Swedish government established a central agency in the spirit of the NIS called Systems of Innovation Authority.

Lundvall and his co-authors are aware of the fact that globalization makes the use of any economic concept related to the nation-state controversial to some extent. They show with references from empirical literature that, in spite of globalization, the national level has retained a quite high degree of relevance for some innovation-related activities. They quote Pavitt and Patel (1991) who have shown that the national origin of multinational firms has quite strongly contributed to determining the location of innovative activities.

The existence of local innovative networks and their positive impact on economic development is also an argument in support of the viability of the NIS concept.[13] The so-called Aalborg version of this concept has a strong element of Schumpeterian inspiration with making innovation-oriented inter-firm competition a core element of NIS. It brings good arguments (with examples from Scandinavian countries) for the useability of the NIS concept for small and open economies.

This means our NIS-based analysis of competition in R&D can also include the countries of Central and Eastern Europe. Most of them (with the exception of Poland) have very open economies and still partly quite inward-looking national innovation systems (see Papanek 1999). The Aalborg model is however somewhat biased in a geographical sense: Lundvall et al. (1999) cite examples according to which the NIS concept seems to be less applicable to Southern than to Northern countries.

One of the authors of the NIS concept, Freeman (2002), notes that recent literature on national economic systems has been characterized by an attempt to come to terms with social capability for technical change. His study gives a broad historical overview of such paths or national trajectories of economic growth (for example Britain in the nineteenth century, the United States in the twentieth century and certain 'catching-up' economies from the 1970s on) which bear a number of characteristics of NISs.

Freeman's important findings include his interpretation of the relationship between Friedrich List's model of infant industry protection-based economic growth in the framework of the nation-state and the idea of the NIS, and the application of Viotti's (1997) distinction between active and passive systems of learning to the NIS concept. This study makes the linkage between different stages of NISs and the stages of economic development really explicit.

The problem of competitiveness in R&D is closely linked to the comparison of structures and performances of NISs. The problem could in fact be reformulated as the problem of the contribution of different NISs to R&D competitiveness in their respective countries. It may be remembered that one of the starting points of our current analysis was the impact of economic transition on comparative R&D performance. The NISs of advanced economies are quite well known from NSB (2002) regarding the United States, and publications such as Wilson and Soutiaris (2002) on Germany, Lemola (2002) on Finland, Mustar and Larédo (2002) on France, Narula (2002) on Norway, Jiménez Contreras (2003) on Spain, Hayashi (2003) on Japan, and Balconi et al. (2004) on Italy.

Cases from countries outside North America and Western Europe are less widely known, although Mani (2002) gave an excellent survey of innovation systems in several former and present catching-up economies such as Japan, Korea, Brazil, Israel, South Africa, Singapore and Malaysia. Articles by Hadjimanolis and Dickson (2001) on Cyprus, Trajtenberg on Israel (2001),

Lee and Lim (2001) on Korea, Intarakumnerd et al. (2002) on Thailand, Costa and de Queiroz (2002) on Brazil, Katrak (2002) on India and Mathews (2002) on Taiwan surveyed individual country cases, while Sutz (2000) and Katz (2001) gave broader overviews of NISs in Latin America.

Literature on the role of R&D in developing countries is quite sporadic. Still, reflecting upon the problem of emerging NISs seems to be necessary for understanding the relationship between the level of economic development and R&D competitiveness in a perspective broader than the usual OECD-oriented view, and also incorporating some elements of thinking borrowed from evolutionary economics.

It would however be a simplification to speak of the NISs of non-OECD countries in general terms. In fact most textbooks and other pieces of literature tend to describe NISs as structures specific to developed industrial countries. The NISs of the leading countries in international R&D are relatively easy to describe with simple institutional models. Other country cases of NISs are however less of a textbook kind.

Recent enlargements of the OECD brought a number of countries to the organization, which cannot be called industrial in the traditional sense of the term (in conventional usage, 'industrial' does not simply mean an economy with a strong industry, but rather an advanced economy). Out of the new OECD countries the Czech Republic, Hungary, Poland, Slovakia and Slovenia are transition economies which, besides the general problems of their economic development, can be regarded as special cases of NIS patterns between traditional industrial (or developed) countries and the Third World.

The NISs of the advanced OECD economies have been extensively described in the literature, but our analysis of R&D competitiveness cannot be limited only to them. The NISs of the new OECD countries of Europe deserve our special attention as well as the NISs of some developing countries, which have recently become important players in the international competitiveness game. The further two new members of the OECD, Mexico and Korea, have quite powerful export-oriented industrial capacities but, in statistical publications for instance, are still considered as developing countries or parts of the Third World (even if the latter term is becoming increasingly empty and obsolete).

Several transition economies have relatively low levels of economic development together with quite well-performing innovation systems (for example Slovenia and, on a lower level of economic development, Estonia), and could thus be regarded as peculiar combinations of industrial and developing countries. The problem of competitiveness of the economy in general and the innovation system or the R&D sector in particular appears in the case of these countries in a special light, because in these countries the gap between these two aspects of competitiveness seems to be large.[14] Furthermore a trend surprising from the viewpoint of evolutionary economics seems to be unfolding in most of these countries: a fast increase in economic development and export competitiveness is accompanied by a shrinking of NISs in both the financial and the institutional sense. This trend will be assessed in more detail in the chapter on the NISs of transition and Third World countries.

Competitiveness in R&D

The idea of competition in research has a surprisingly long history, although neither the purpose, nor the participants of early forms of such competition were identical to the ones experienced through the twentieth and the early twenty-first century. Arthur Koestler described the origins of conflict (and perhaps competition) between Church and Science in the sixteenth century in his book on the quest for truth in astronomy (Koestler, 1959). This was probably the first case in which monopolies in science were questioned. Or, to express it in modern economics language: it became known that the market of science has a contestable character.

Competitiveness in R&D has, as has been mentioned, two main aspects: (1) the role of R&D in the competitiveness of an economy with its implications for economic development in a broader sense, and (2) the international competitiveness of the R&D sector itself. The second approach is narrower and it is really where an appropriate definition can be sought. As Griliches (1990, 1689) emphasized, R&D-related data such as patent counts have been repeatedly used for comparative 'competitiveness' analyses of various countries.

Competitiveness in R&D can also be understood as the distance of an economy's R&D, innovation and technology sector from the technology frontier. In this sense, the R&D competitiveness of an economy is partly overlapping with its technological capability, and may reflect it quite well. The two terms and concepts are however not identical at all.

Competitiveness in R&D is, regarding both of its aspects referred to above, conditional upon the participation of an economy in the international trade of goods and services, including international flows of knowledge related to R&D and technology (for an in-depth survey of literature on the international diffusion of technology see Keller, 2004). In marked contrast to that, the technological capabilities of an economy may be high even if it is not a participant of, or a good performer in international competition in R&D. There are for example nuclear powers in the Third World (most of them in Asia) with undeniably high technological capabilities but which are not excelling in either the input- or the output-based indicators of R&D competitiveness. North Korea is not a participant in international competition in R&D, and Pakistan is not a good performer in it, in spite of the fact that both countries seem to have been able to develop modern nuclear capacities.

The R&D sectors, or the systems of innovation of different national economies, are exposed to competitive pressure as most other sectors of these economies are. They compete for resources on both the international and the national level, and the competitive strategies of R&D organizations also have strong output-related objectives. Output does not appear on the market as directly in the case of R&D as in that of manufacturing, since publications and some other outputs of R&D are usually not sold.

Still, competitiveness is not an entirely abstract idea here either. Trade in R&D products also has its aspect of trade performance, and R&D output is evaluated by markets in this sector as well. The input- and output-based approach seems to be a good analytical framework for introducing a working definition of competitiveness for the R&D sector. This approach is sometimes also called the 'upstream–downstream' approach, a term taken from business economics, and also supposing a direct link between what is fed into the process and what is realized from it.

As to the input side, an above-average use of inputs can be helpful in creating high levels of competitiveness in R&D and a special version of the Heckscher-Ohlin concept of factor intensity can be applied. We will be focusing on two tools of measurement of inputs, roughly corresponding to what can be called the R&D counterpart of capital and labour intensity. On the output side, several quantitative measures of 'R&D products' will be reviewed and compared to the inputs.

As our survey of international comparisons of R&D performance will show, most attempts at such measurements applied a broader scope, and analysed innovation. Conclusions from comparative analyses of innovation are helpful for our deliberations, but they reflect the use of a different benchmark: industrial application and commercial success. In general R&D does and must serve innovation, but there are also partly different targets in R&D.

These different targets include the advancement of science as a quite general and perhaps philosophical objective, and also the personal advancement of researchers and research teams. Both these kinds of advancement are partly independent from the potential success or failure of the innovation process which R&D may support. This is why R&D performance should be treated as not completely overlapping with innovative performance in spite of the strong interdependence between R&D and innovation.[15]

The problem of R&D competitiveness has three levels of relevance. Competition in R&D takes place between countries (which is our main focus of analysis) in a partly abstract sense, because success in this kind of competition does not promise too much in terms of immediate pay-offs. However the long-term or strategic pay-offs can be identified in a more accurate way. A country's better performance in R&D competition will help its universities to higher-quality students and more generous financing, its research centres (including universities) to more favourable research contracts and, likely but not necessarily, its manufacturing and services sectors to higher levels of international competitiveness.

Still remaining on the macro level, a similar kind of competition can be identified between large fields of science. Namely it makes a great difference whether for example physics can demonstrate faster progress than biology in such a way that one part of available research funds will be reorientated from financing research in biology to financing research in physics. Such major shifts between major fields of science have been observed several times in recent decades.

For example the funding of academic R&D in the United States showed largely diverging trends among major fields of science: the real value of funding of both medical research and engineering increased almost fourfold between 1973 and 1999 (with a major acceleration of spending on medical research from 1984 on), the increase of funding for research in biology showed a more modest but still 2.5-fold increase during the same time period, and all the other major fields of sciences such as physics, environmental sciences, computer sciences, psychology and mathematics had to accept significantly lower increases of funding (NSB, 2002, 5–15).

Social sciences[16] have behaved as a field apart: their funding decreased by about 20 per cent in real terms between 1973 and 1984, and thereafter they obtained a 2.5-fold increase in funding until 1999. This decrease might have been due to the fact that direct welfare implications of research are more difficult to measure in social sciences than in natural sciences. An interesting attempt to carry out such measurement is, for Canada, the article by Landry et al. (2001).

The third level of relevance of competitiveness in R&D is related to the users of inputs and the producers of output such as firms, universities, research centres, research teams and individual researchers. Competitiveness can be measured on this level as well, but only based on questionnaire-based surveys and in narrower fields of competition (for example regions or fields of science). This approach is now gaining ground in literature (for example Acs, Anselin and Varga, 2002), but it is not used in cross-country comparisons.

2. Indicators for measuring competitiveness

2.1 SUPPLY OR DEMAND SIDE MEASUREMENT?

Unit Labour Cost: the Main Indicator of Supply-side Competitiveness

Literature frequently uses ULC (unit labour cost) as an indicator of supply-side competitiveness. Its use is limited however to manufactured goods and sporadically also to services, for the following reason. Endowments with natural resources and also weather or climatic conditions are key factors of the levels of capacity utilization in agricultural and mining production and this is why the ULC indicator cannot be reliably applied for measuring competitiveness in these sectors.

The idea underlying the ULC indicator is the following. If two technically identical goods are compared, the one which is more competitive is the one produced with a lower unit labour cost. This assumption is strong in such a simplified form, and it surely becomes quite contestable if it is brought a bit closer to business practice. Namely it is rather obvious that competition never takes place between goods where their distinction or differentiation is possible uniquely on the basis of labour costs. If this is the case then other differences between these goods will also have an impact on competitiveness.

The ULC indicator has wage and wage-related costs (for example social security and unemployment contributions) in its numerator, and value added created in the given industry or sector in its denominator. The ULC indicator is rarely used in a strictly product-level approach:

$$ULC_i = (W_i + C_i)/VA_i.$$

This indicator is used for competitiveness measurement in international comparative analyses between industries, sectors or other statistical aggregates. It can also be applied in time-series analysis in order to show the speed and the scope of change of unit labour costs in different industries within the same national economy. This kind of application of the indicator calls however for some caution. It would be a mistake to use it for competitiveness comparisons in a cross-sectoral approach, owing to sectoral differences in the levels of labour and capital intensity.

The ULC has been a quite widely used indicator, but its relevance for competitiveness analysis seems to be decreasing. The reason is the low relative share of labour costs within the total cost of production of a growing number of products traded internationally (see the sectoral analyses in Scherer, 1996). To make things worse, the ULC indicator does not show the extent to which the level of technology, or even the presence of modern technology, influences competitiveness levels.

We have serious methodological doubts regarding the applicability of ULC for international comparisons. Namely such application is conditional on the validity of the assumption formulated in the Heckscher-Ohlin theorem that each industry has a same level of factor intensity in every country (that is the ranking list of industries expressing their relative factor intensities is identical in each national economy). Early critics of the HO theorem – among them also Leontief (1954 and 1956) – had already pointed out that this assumption is far from valid since skirts imported to the United States from India are not really comparable with American-made skirts, and there is only limited substitution and competition between these products.

This remark has much relevance for the methodology of competitiveness analysis. Differences in levels of economic development are usually reflected in different microstructures of exports and imports. This may even involve identical brand or product names covering different product parameters and quality.

Global car manufacturers for example produce their mass models in 'cheap' versions for some Third World markets or China, 'favourably priced' and sometimes underpowered versions for East European countries, and 'full' versions for their West European or North American markets. Such differences in the microstructures of exports imply that comparisons of competitiveness between countries having strongly different levels of development may be misleading, because identical names of product groups may include elements not competing with each other.

The ULC indicator is similar in content to the so-called Lary indicator of factor intensity (Lary, 1968). This indicator (value added per capita in each industry) is based on the assumption that sectoral levels of per capita value added show the degree of labour intensity if they are below the average level of manufacturing, and the degree of physical capital intensity if they are above it.

The ULC indicator can be considered as related to the Lary indicator if costs of labour and capital are complementary to each other within total costs of production. Once this assumption is correct, it follows that the ULC indicator is an inverse indicator of relative physical capital intensity. In such cases low levels of the ULC speak of high levels of relative physical capital intensity, and vice versa.

The Unit Value of Exports

The numerator of the UVI (unit value index) indicator of demand-side competitiveness contains the change of the average unit value of manufacturing exports of country a. The denominator expresses the changes of the unit values of exports of the country's main competitors weighted with their relative shares in world imports:

$$UVI_a = \Delta(X_a/Q_a)/\Sigma\Delta(X_i/Q_i)*s_{iw},$$

where X_a is the value of exports of country a, Q_a is the volume of exports of country a, and
   X_i is the value of exports of competitor country i,
   Q_i is the volume (for example the weight) of exports of competitor country i, and
   s_{iw} is the relative share of country i within world imports.

The UVI indicator shows whether the country in question was able to increase the unit value of its exports faster than its competitors or not. This indicates an important aspect of export performance, namely the extent to which the specific demand facing the exports of the given country was resistant to price increases in those exports as compared to direct competition. The indicator is often applied with corrective factors filtering out the short-term impacts of exchange rate fluctuations.

A really serious methodological problem in applying this indicator is related to export subsidies. Subsidies in the unit value of exports are almost never visible, and there is a similar problem with any such competitiveness indicator which is based on price or value data. Practically all demand-side indicators suffer from the same deficiency.

The UVI expresses just the opposite of price competitiveness, the primordial element of supply-side measurements of competitiveness. A good indicator of competitiveness is not produced here if the export price is lower due to lower labour costs. The indicator improves if one supposed unit of exports earns a higher revenue to the exporter. Successful product differentiation or a better adjustment to demand are rewarded with higher prices without decreasing market shares in this approach. Constant market shares are a key element in this competitiveness measurement.

This seemingly well-applicable indicator is seriously flawed in a methodological sense. The main problem is that the basis of comparison lacks solidity in its case. The UVI is based upon the idea that product differentiation within the same statistical product category helps the more competitive exporter to reach higher unit prices. Thus however products which are not really identical products are compared and we are back at the fundamental problem of competition analysis in the model of monopolistic competition.

Calculating unit values makes it necessary to use physical units of products. International trade statistics use such physical units of measurement as pieces or tons, all of which are highly unsuitable for an integrated analysis of high value added and differentiated product groups such as drugs, electronics goods or complex engineering products.

The methodological pitfall of the application of the UVI can be avoided by comparing the unit values of exports and imports of the same commodity groups for each country analysed. This is a practical and in most cases proba-bly feasible compromise, but some constraints have to be kept in mind:

1. Countries with substantial amounts of transit trade (re-exports) are not good test cases for this indicator if the relative weight of products strongly represented in transit trade is high both in exports and in imports. This problem can become a serious bias in competitiveness analyses for coun-tries that have export/GDP proportions above 100 per cent due to high levels of transit trade (like for instance Singapore, or the Netherlands to a smaller extent). Enterprise- or product-level distortions may be caused when an export capacity produces only low levels of value added because it is very much dependent on imports.

2. The problem of transfer prices (see Plasschaert, 1995) can cause substan-tial distortions in the application of the UVI. This may occur for example if multinational firms use intra-firm transfer prices for nothing else than transit trade for the purposes of tax optimalization or the transfer of prof-its. The use of transfer prices implies that the statistical value of imports is artificially diminished and the statistical value of exports is inflated in order to create the illusion of high value added production.

3. The microstructure of exports and imports can differ substantially in spite of the apparent equality of exports and imports on the level of commod-ity groups. 'Intra-industry trade' was first described by Linder (1961) and its indicator was constructed by Grubel and Lloyd (1975). One of its implications on the structure of exports and imports seems to be that a less-developed country usually imports more expensive products than it exports of the same kind. Quality differences usually lead to differences in unit prices or in prices per unit of weight, but it is not necessarily true that unit values of goods exported by technologically more advanced countries are below average. The reason is that 'heavy' is not the synonym of low quality any more. In the car industry for example, lighter Korean

models are proportionally less expensive than some German cars which carry a wide range of security- and comfort-related equipment.

A similar reason is if statistics are unable to separate exports and imports consisting of products not substituting each other, but within the same statistical commodity group. This problem is the most evident if a country has only regular annual exports or imports from one commodity group and occasional or fluctuating trade flows in the other direction.

> The use of the UVI can lead to substantial distortions, for example in analysing the international trade of the United States in aeroplanes. More than 95 per cent of this trade is exports in a quite stable microstructure while US imports are much lower and fluctuate fast which makes the UVI unstable as well.

The application of the UVI in international trade research has decreased during recent years (Pitti, 2002), although it still remains an important indicator of trade performance. It has, on the other hand, a major shortcoming with regard to its application to measuring trade performance and competitiveness. Namely it may show worsening trade or competitive performance if a product consists of new, lighter-weight materials – a good example why the application of UVI-type indicators based on one-dimensional quantitative approximations of quality may lead to confusing results. This is the main reason why UVI-type, quantitative *cum* qualitative indicators have been discarded from our further analysis of competitiveness.

Indicators of Trade Structure and Performance

Recent surveys of indicators of trade performance (see Laursen, 2000) have skipped the simpler indicators of trade structure and performance, perhaps on the ground that these are not frequently applied in modern quantitative research. This is probably true, but just Laursen's analysis shows the extent to which several modern and more sophisticated indicators are direct descendants of simpler ones.

The starting point at the application of simple structural indicators of trade performance is that export surplus shows relative specialization and thus apparent comparative advantage, a likely reason of which is competitiveness above the national average. The opposite is true for those elements of the trade structure where import surplus can be observed.[17]

The main focus of our analysis is not trade statistics, and we pay special attention only to those indicators which have a special relevance to measuring R&D performance or competitiveness. This is why most of the structural indicators of trade will be only briefly explained.

The simplest indicator of export (and import) specialization is the proportion of exports to imports, also known as the indicator of import coverage or the import coverage ratio:

$$C = X_i/M_i,$$

where Xi denotes the exports of commodity i, and M_i the imports of the same commodity.

The relative size of export surplus is shown by $C > 1$. This indicator is sometimes corrected for the bias caused by the trade balance, but this correction is not too frequent since surpluses of exports or imports on the commodity level might have reasons independent from the sign of the overall trade balance.

The import coverage ratio can be used for measuring comparative advantage or competitiveness only under serious constraints. When it is applied to a closed economy it tells much less about its overall level of competitiveness than when applied to a country with a high level of trade openness. As a consequence, this indicator has different explanatory powers for countries with different levels of openness, which limits its field of application to a great extent.

Similarly the import coverage ratio is insensitive to the geographical structure of foreign trade. The mere fact that a country has an export bias towards less-developed economies (that is such countries have a quite high relative share in its exports) while its import structure is in line with the pattern of world trade might produce such import coverage ratios which would show that economy's apparent level of competitiveness to be higher than expected.

The methodological problems surrounding the application of the import coverage ratio may also appear in the case of similar indicators using simple export and import data. We shall see later that analogous methods (such as the TBP – technological balance of payments – indicator) are sometimes used for assessing technological competitiveness, but their wider application is equally hampered by the insensitivity of this type of indicators to trade patterns and structures.

An indicator similar in its logic to the import coverage ratio is the revealed comparative advantage (RCA) extensively discussed in Laursen (2000). It was introduced by Bela Balassa (1965), but also applied not much later by Brown and Kojima (see Bowden, 1983). We here give only a brief discussion of the traditional version of the RCA with special emphasis on its theoretical background. Its more recent applications are discussed in Laursen (2000), including its extension to international flows of high technology (RTA – revealed technological advantage).

The RCA is calculated as follows. Exports of commodity j by country a are denoted as X_{aj}, and total exports of country a as $X_a = \sum_j X_{aj}$. The world exports of commodity j, that is the sum of its exports by all countries, are denoted as X_{wj}, and total world exports (of all commodities) as X_w. RCA for country a and commodity j equals then:

$$RCA_{aj} = (X_{aj}/X_a)/(X_{wj}/X_w)$$

The RCA is based on the assumption that the share of product j in the exports of country a should be equal with the relative share of the world exports of product j within the total exports of the world. If however $RCA_{aj} > 1$, then a revealed comparative advantage, or an indirect proof of above average competitiveness exists, because country a exports more from product j than expected on the basis of the structure of world trade.

This one-country situation can be completed to correspond better to the neoclassical framework. We can imagine a world economy consisting of two countries, a and b. If $RCA_{aj} > 1$ as described above, then $RCA_{bj} = 1/RCA_{aj}$. This means the RCA of country b in product j is complementary to RCA_{aj}, and it speaks of relatively poor competitiveness or revealed comparative disadvantage.

The RCA is an indicator of export performance which does, if regarded in a two-country framework, reflect a neoclassical inspiration. The underlying idea is that revealed comparative advantage or disadvantage is subject to equalization among countries if more than one product is considered. RCA fits into the general equilibrium concept of the Heckscher–Ohlin–Samuelson theory of comparative advantage and international trade specialization. It seems to offer a simple and effective technique for measuring competitiveness on the demand side.

Still, a number of reservations can be expressed. We think devoting some space to them is all the more appropriate in that Laursen's important book on the use of specialization indicators for the analysis of technology-related comparative advantages skipped the problem of potential weak points of the RCA.

Bowden's remarks are key to delineating the field of application of the RCA (Bowden, 1983). In the first place, he argues that this indicator lacks any sophisticated theoretical background,[18] and he points to the RCA's 'ad hoc character'. Another important critical remark of his is that the RCA measures the way comparative advantages appear in exports, and not the way they reflect the structure of production.

This problem has an important policy implication: the old dichotomy of export-oriented versus import-substituting policies seems to have disappeared from the focus of policy debate. Recent literature concentrates rather on how export-oriented economic policy can make use of the competitiveness potential of the economy, and how this potential can serve export success (see

Bruton, 1998). Bowden's latter remark touches upon the same problem: theory has been speaking, ever since Smith and Ricardo, of comparative advantage in production or exports as exactly the same thing.

We would rather be inclined to think that comparative advantage is, strictly speaking, an issue related to production, whereas real-life competitiveness appears when this theoretically competitive production is exported. The same distinction applies to competitiveness in R&D: there are comparative advantages when products of R&D (publications or patents) or innovations are generated with a favourable cost structure, and these become competitive when publications are accepted by journals with high-impact factors or patents are registered in countries with high-cost and competitive systems of IP protection.

The third counter-argument vis-à-vis RCA is that it is based only on trade data without specifications of prices. This is why it cannot be determined from for example $RCA_{aj} > RCA_{bj}$, whether country a is apparently more competitive than country b in the exports of product j for reasons of price competitiveness or any other reason.

RCA is, in spite of all the counter-arguments, a solid and robust indicator of competitiveness if it is understood as a level of export performance. It still has a considerable weakness of a practical character. This is linked to the availability of appropriate data. Multi-country comparisons of export competitiveness require reliable and homogeneous databases including low levels of aggregation at the commodity level. Such data are preferred which can be double-checked for a country from sources of other countries, and these are exports and imports data.

Their homogeneity can be ensured by international organizations. The OECD Trade by Commodities, the UN International Trade Statistics, the IMF Direction of Trade or Eurostat offer either a wide country coverage without commodity-level data, or commodity-level data for a limited number of countries. A relatively wide country coverage of international trade data with an appropriate level of commodity specification is offered by the OECD.

The OECD publishes national trade data for all of its member countries, but it does not cover the entirety of world trade. This is why really reliable RCA indicators cannot be computed from the international trade statistics (for example Trade by Commodities by the OECD). A still simpler indicator would be needed to ensure a satisfactorily wide coverage of international trade which is based only on national trade data at both high levels of aggregation and the commodity level. This simple indicator, also applicable in R&D competitiveness analysis, is the indicator of market shares.

All the counter-arguments against RCA are also applicable against the indicator of market shares, but a number of practical considerations speak for using it. The first of these, namely the availability of data, has been mentioned.

Another set of arguments for the use of this indicator is that other tools of measurement generated from it have been widely used in Industrial Organization (IO) literature (see Tirole, 1988; Shy, 1995) for the analysis of market power. It seems, by the way, that not much cross-fertilization has taken place so far between the methodology of market power analysis in IO and competitiveness analysis in international economics.

It is interesting to note at this point that UNCTAD has taken a tacit stand for applying market shares in measuring competitiveness in international trade (UNCTAD, 2002, 143). It mentions relative shares within world exports as a traditional indicator of competitiveness. The competitiveness development of countries with fast increasing exports can be really reliably shown only when their relative shares within world exports are measured in a long-term approach, for example between 1985 and 2000.

The indicator of market shares is based on an implicit assumption, namely that the share of imports within domestic demand remains constant during the period of analysis. This is needed because the homogeneity of data cannot be assured if national data on domestic supply are used as well. This indicator therefore gives a reliable picture of the changes in competitive positions among direct competitors only in imports. It is generally used in such cross-section analyses where relative positions of countries exporting to a given market are compared. It shows only a kind of snapshot of the competitiveness picture, but it is not applicable for explaining the factors of this picture.

Any change in the indicator of market shares shows, in fact, the impact of two things: one is what we can really call 'competitiveness', that is the gain of market shares due to better performance on the market which can be due to both price- and quality-related factors. The second element of change is, strictly speaking, not competitiveness related. This is the microstructural change in imports, and it means that the exports of the country in question have been concentrating on those commodities which have shown an above-average growth of demand (see Oblath and Pénzes, 2003).

The lack of any solid theoretical background of the indicator of market shares is evident, although Lord Nicholas Kaldor developed an interesting paradox analysing the possible contradiction between increasing market shares and increasing export prices (Kaldor, 1978). Still, it is certainly a good practical tool to identify comparative trends of competitiveness, if they are to be gauged in a demand-side approach.

Statistical Problems in Linking Supply-side and Demand-side Competitiveness

Measuring competitiveness in international trade is complicated by a potentially serious statistical problem. Data used for supply-side measurement is based on sectoral statistics internationally known as the ISIC (International Standard of Industrial Classification) system, while demand-side (or market) measurement uses trade statistics presenting commodity-level data in the SITC (Standard of International Trade Statistics) nomenclature. The ISIC uses an industrial classification system of sectors and subsectors such as for example footwear manufacturing; the SITC has data on commodities such as footwear itself.

The two systems do not overlap in a number of cases. For instance if an engineering firm exports engineering products, there is a high likelihood that production data from the ISIC source correspond to the trade data from the SITC dataset. It can however also export metal products or components, which do not belong to the SITC commodity class comprising engineering products.

A more serious problem arises with respect to imports. The engineering industry exports engineering products, but its imports come, to an important extent, from other sectors abroad. Therefore import competition facing the engineering industry cannot be described with import data of the sector itself. Productive imports as the inputs of a given sector are only partly sold to firms belonging to the sector whose output is generated by them.

All these difficulties mean, in practice, that supply-side measurements of competitiveness cover sectors, whereas demand-side measurements deal with products. This problem is less dramatic in the R&D sector where it can be strongly assumed that 'sectors' coincide with 'products' under the same name. If our above example from the engineering industry is replaced for instance with 'engineering research', then it is likely that its output will also include publications and patents in this field. The input problem however remains basically the same.

The lack of compatibility between supply- and demand-side data makes it impossible to apply the two approaches simultaneously. Furthermore the indicators can only be used if they are computed exclusively from either the ISIC or the SITC database. The ULC or the RCA are such indicators.

It is however not advisable to calculate indicators that take data from both statistical systems. Such a case would be calculating market shares for the entire domestic market instead of imports, because this would make it necessary to directly compare ISIC data for domestic production with SITC data for imports.

The General Approach

The methodological problems of the measurement of competitiveness have given rise to such attempts which get around the dilemma of supply-side versus demand-side competitiveness. These approaches interpret competitiveness as a general condition of the economy.

To use an example from athletics: the supply-side approach measures some parameters of the runner's physical condition and concludes how that runner would fare in the contest. The demand-side approach measures the runner's performance and comes to the conclusion that this performance should reflect his physical parameters. In turn, the generalized approaches take all measurable parameters of the person in question and establish from them a general pattern of performance. It is then from this pattern that his potential performance in the running contest could be approximated, but the key issue is his general condition.

The generalized approach is mostly used for establishing whether an economy could be regarded as competitive at all.[19] A competitive economy is, according to such concepts of competitiveness, one which has good indicators of development and growth, its macroeconomic balances are acceptable, the economic actors are aware of good condition of the economy, and the degree of its openness is also high enough to reach a trade performance corresponding to the statement that the economy is competitive.

The interpretation of this concept of competitiveness might have pitfalls. There are a number of developed economies where there should be a high degree of competitiveness, but this does not obviously appear in export performance. In small and open economies such as Switzerland, the Netherlands, Luxembourg or Singapore, more than 60 per cent of GDP comes from services. In their case, export performance is not such a reliable indicator of macroeconomic success as it used to be.[20]

The generalized approach looks useful if a comparative analysis of competitiveness in R&D is envisaged. As we shall see, the measurement of input and output (or the equivalent of trade performance) is not too evident in R&D or innovation. It is however also an open question whether the condition of an economy in general, that of its R&D sector or of its innovation system is the best starting point for assessing R&D competitiveness.

The mainstream theory of NISs (national innovation systems) does not devote much attention to the problem of economic development measured in statistical terms as a factor of the condition of the NIS, although evolutionary economics offers very useful insights into the complexity of relationships between the innovative and R&D potential of an economy on the one hand and the condition of its institutions on the other. Theoretical deliberations on NISs seem to cover, in the first place, the industrial economies in which there is a quite strong coherence between the level of development of an economy and the overall condition (and also development) of its NIS.

This coherence seems to be the most evident for the best-performing economies of the world, such as the United States, Germany, Japan the Benelux or the Scandinavian countries. A string of other highly developed economies such as France, the United Kingdom, Italy, Austria or Canada still belong to the best performers in both respects, but some parameters of their

NISs are more or less below the top level. Going downwards on the list of the levels of economic development of the OECD countries, an increasing number of cases reveal gaps between macroeconomic performance and NIS condition.

Leaving the OECD group in the search for more complex country cases, there are several national economies with a really wide gap between the level of development of the economy in general and the condition of the R&D or innovation system in particular, which is a great challenge to NIS analysis but, in a broader approach, to evolutionary economics as well. A large number of such country cases among the transition economies and in the developing world can be identified. It has to be seen however how these cases outside of the scope of the traditional NIS-based institutional approach would fit into our R&D competitiveness analysis. This problem leads again to the question of the relationship between the overall competitiveness condition of an economy and the competitive position of any of its sectors, for example the NIS or R&D.

Not all sectors of the economy can be subject to competitiveness analysis with the commonly accepted methods as we have described them. Several kinds of services are such cases, and an interesting example is banking. Competitiveness analysis in the banking sector also uses comparisons of market shares, and the analysis of product differentiation plays an important role as well. Still, a number of analyses of competitiveness in banking focus on client surveys and can be therefore regarded as exercises in marketing. (see Erdei, 2002)

The two widest known and regularly published analyses of the general competitiveness level or competitive condition of important countries are the annual *World Competitiveness Yearbook* of the IMD business school at Lausanne, and the also annual *Global Competitiveness Report* of the World Economic Forum (WEF).

The IMD competitiveness reports consist of two parts. The first part is in line with the generalized approaches to competitiveness. It assesses the economic condition of the countries based on statistical indicators and verbal policy information. The second part uses information obtained in question-naires filled by hundreds of experts in each country. These questionnaires ask for personal assessments of competitiveness in a string of sectors of the economy with R&D being one of them.

The 2002 survey introduced a slightly new method of competitiveness assessment (see http://www02.imd.ch/wcy/esummary). Four groups of factors were established: economic performance, government efficiency, business efficiency, infrastructure. Each group of factors was used to create a ranking list of countries, and the synthetic ranking list was produced out of these four lists. This method is an example of the globalized approach where the macro-economic and policy conditions of competitiveness are examined rather than competitiveness itself.

The 2003 *World Competitiveness Yearbook* was the first in the series trying to give definitions of competitiveness. Two different definitions were given, reflecting the dichotomy between the ways economics and management science approach competitiveness. The yearbook calls them the scientific and the business definitions.

The first considers the competitiveness of nations a field of economic analysis. This analysis is aimed at identifying policies towards an economic environment enhancing the value generation of the enterprises and the prosperity of the population.

The business definition is narrower in scope: it considers country-level competitiveness as the contribution of national economies to a business environment leading to competitiveness improvement on the company level. This definition regards enterprise-level competitiveness as an exogenous variable, as well as a concept not needing any further elaboration since it is widely used in and known from strategic management.

A further methodological innovation was introduced in the IMD competitiveness yearbooks in 2003. It reflects the problem of country size in international comparisons of competitiveness.

The solution to this problem chosen by the IMD is different from the one we propose (as we shall see later, we have opted for using both the absolute and the per capita versions of the main indicators of R&D competitiveness). The 2003 *World Competitiveness Yearbook* (IMD, 2003) introduced the distinction between small and large countries. Large countries are the ones with more than 20 million population, and separate lists of competitiveness are set up for them, as also for the small ones.

Along with this new element, the yearbook also tries to introduce a new level of competitiveness analysis between the country level and the firm level. This is the region, represented in the sample by such sizeable administrative units within large countries as Catalonia in Spain or Lombardy in Italy. Such regions may even compete with smaller countries, and their own governments could also come up with their own solutions for competitiveness improvement.

It remains to be clarified how this intermediate level of international competitiveness analysis could be inserted into the current schemes on either the country or the firm level. These are based on the assumption that countries compete with countries and firms with firms. It is an open question whether regions could be visualized as each other's competitors. For example direct competition between Catalonia and Ile-de-France, or Lombardy and Bavaria, would be very difficult to imagine or measure statistically.

The global competitiveness report by the WEF (WEF, 1999) is available in three versions. The synthetic list of competitiveness (the 'scoreboard') is published by the press each year. Experts participating in the surveys receive the summary report. The entire study is available only to subscribers.

The concept of competitiveness used in this report has become increasingly sophisticated over the years. It makes a distinction between current and growth competitiveness since 2000. Current competitiveness is basically what can be measured on the company level. Its concept has been repeatedly changed since 2000 with a marked shift to the company level. It was renamed 'micro-economic competitiveness index' in 2002, and 'business competitiveness index' in 2003. The main function of this index consists in explaining how per capita levels of GDP vary across countries as a result of microeconomic differences between countries. These microeconomic differences reflect how efficiently countries use their resources and how their productivity potential is translated into effective productivity growth (Czakó, 2004, 124).

Growth competitiveness means a kind of growth potential: an economy might be capable of better growth performance than is made possible by its current market performance.

Both aspects of competitiveness analysis in the WEF report are based on comparisons between potential and performance. The potential for competitiveness improvement is what we call the input-based approach in measuring R&D competitiveness, and the extent to which this potential is exploited is reflected by outputs.

A further example of the globalized approach to competitiveness is the *Competitiveness Report* of the European Union (European Commission, 2002). This is a policy paper rather than a real competitiveness analysis. It gives priority to the quality of human capital as a factor of productivity growth, and economic policy is also presented as a tool of improving productivity and competitiveness. The report does not really give a picture of EU competitiveness as such. In fact this report is also a proof that competitiveness is a somewhat vague 'buzzword' in early twenty-first century economics, and has not yet obtained a meaning generally accepted in the literature.

2.2 TRADE PERFORMANCE AND THE HIGH-TECH SECTORS

The issue of competitiveness in manufacturing has quite strong linkages to competitiveness in R&D.[21] It seems obvious that the best-performing countries in international trade are helped by their strong and performing R&D sectors. Keld Laursen's book (Laursen, 2000) has produced convincing evidence on the multifaceted relationship between competitiveness or trade performance in manufacturing and the presence of high-tech sectors in the economy or technological specialization.

It is worthwhile to survey his findings even if strong technological specialization is not a perfect synonym of competitive and performing R&D. There are a number of emerging economies with significant volumes of foreign direct investment (FDI) where the high-tech oriented specialization of exports is mainly based on R&D abroad (for example Hungary, Poland, Slovakia, Estonia, Malaysia, Mexico; see UNCTAD, 2002 and 2003).

Laursen's calculations have yielded important results for a number of countries which are also in the focus of our research. He calls them 'catching-up' countries, but refers by this to those OECD countries which showed above-average growth rates in the 1970s and 1980s, for example Japan, Austria, Finland, Greece, Ireland, Italy, Portugal and Turkey (Laursen, 2000, 144). Current 'catching-up' countries include those members of the OECD which joined after 1995 (the Czech Republic, Hungary, Poland, Slovakia and Slovenia from Europe, and Mexico and South Korea from overseas), and the country cases investigated by Laursen may serve as a good benchmark for our analysis.

It is true for most advanced economies that technological specialization is mainly based on the high-performance domestic R&D sector which is then the backbone of the highly competitive export structure in manufacturing. Laursen compared export specialization measured by RCA and so-called technological specialization measured by patents registered in the United States. He found that from 1971 to 1991 trade specialization patterns of most OECD countries proved more stable over time than patterns of technological specialization (Laursen, 2000, 87). This stability of trade structures was quite conditional upon the path of economic and technological development for the patterns of both export and technological specialization.

The United States and Japan showed the highest degree of stability in both respects, and some 'catching-up' economies within the OECD (for example Finland, Greece, Italy, Portugal and Spain) proved the most turbulent. The analysis of the long-term changes of specialization patterns also showed that there were no significant differences between low-tech and high-tech sectors with regard to their involvement in outward foreign direct investment (Laursen, 2000, 88).

This finding helps our analysis to a significant extent, since it confirms for a number of OECD countries the relative instability of such export structures which were based on a high percentage share of high-tech products without a significant domestic R&D background. Generalizing this finding (albeit without any direct proof of it for emerging economies), it can be said that at certain development levels there seems to be an inverse relationship between the level of economic development and the strength of the linkage between competitiveness in manufacturing and competitiveness in R&D. We will try to test this hypothesis from our side of the analysis, that is R&D competitiveness.

The special case of the 'catching up' economies demonstrates a parallelism between their rapid export growth and the fast improvement of their technological capabilities, measured again by their relative shares in United States patents (Laursen, 2000, 144). It is, on the other hand, also telling that their patterns of export specialization have shifted in the wrong direction (towards sectors offering low levels of technological opportunity), except for Japan (Laursen, 2000, 144).

Firstly, this confirms again his previously cited finding that 'turbulence' in both export and technological specialization was characteristic of the majority of 'catching up' economies within the OECD. Secondly, it also demonstrates that the linkage between their export expansion and technological development was far from organic (Japan is an exception in this respect as well): their increased R&D and innovation activity was not at all reflected in the development of their export specialization.

Laursen's findings show that the linkage between export competitiveness and some indicators of innovative performance has been quite weak for the former 'catching up' economies of the OECD. This observation means, in other words, that the export sectors and the R&D sectors of most of these economies have developed quite separately, and export competitiveness has probably not been largely supported by the competitiveness of domestic R&D.

Besides this, the separation of the R&D sector from the rest of the economy has been the case for much longer than just the years of economic transition in most of the current 'catching-up' economies of the OECD, basically the new member countries of the European Union. Therefore the analysis of R&D competitiveness of the 'catching up' or the emerging economies can likely help answer only the second question of the two which were asked as the starting points of our research: (1) how does competitiveness in R&D help general competitiveness improvement in the economy? (2) what is the position of the country's R&D sector in international competition in R&D?

Laursen's results provide important elements for the answer to the first question. It is also important that he has established a strong relationship, for the pre-1991 OECD countries in general, between fast-growing sectors and high-tech sectors (Laursen, 2000, 168–9) finding that most of these coincided. His important and convincing analysis did not however directly tackle the problem of competitiveness in exports, nor in R&D.

The two issues could seemingly be linked with each other using a widely popular indicator, the relative share of high-tech products in manufacturing exports. Establishing such a linkage, potentially evident at a first glance, would be misleading, and could be done only on a well established *ceteris paribus* basis. Some comparative data should be considered first.

Hungary belongs to the least-developed economies in Table 2.1, but its high-tech export indicator offers an unexpectedly favourable picture. The problem is this figure is based mostly on R&D carried out outside the country. Hungary seems to be a country which benefits from the international diffusion of technology carried by FDI to a large extent. The theoretical background of

Table 2.1   Relative shares of high-tech products in the manufacturing
             exports of selected OECD countries (1999)

Rank	Country	%
1	Rep. of Ireland	49.2
2	United States	38.3
3	Switzerland	34.5
4	Korea	34.2
5	United Kingdom	33.8
6	Japan	31.3
7	Netherlands	30.3
8	Sweden	27.9
9	Mexico	26.9
10	Hungary	26.3
11	Finland	24.1
12	France	23.9
13	Denmark	20.2
14	Germany	18.5
15	Austria	14.4
16	Canada	13.0
17	Belgium-Luxemburg	12.9
18	Australia	12.6
19	Norway	11.3
20	Italy	10.6
21	Spain	10.1
22	Portugal	9.0
23	Czech Republic	8.8
24	Greece	6.9
25	Turkey	6.8
26	Poland	6.4
27	Slovakia	5.9
28	New Zealand	3.1
29	Iceland	2.6

Source: Export shares (OECD, 2001, 207).

the role of FDI in technological spillovers has not been fully explored yet and empirical evidence on this is not completely convincing either (see Keller, 2004, 760–1, 769), although the role of such spillovers seems to be much stronger in high-tech industries (Keller, 2004, 771) which have been by far the most important targets of FDI in Hungarian manufacturing.

UNCTAD sources make it plain that in the year 2000 (and very likely also in 1999), out of the largest 50 foreign-owned Hungarian firms 12 were car and components manufacturers, 9 produced electronics goods, and 3 were in the pharmaceutical industry (UNCTAD, 2002, 171, Table VI.11). All these industries are considered high-tech by OECD statistics. Also in the year 2000, the first four manufacturing exporters from Hungary (Audi, Philips, IBM and General Electric) with more than 20 per cent of the country's total exports were in high-tech industries but carrying out a significant part of their R&D abroad.[22]

Even the commodity structure of exports is not necessarily a good indicator of the technology level of production in the exporting country itself. IBM Storage Products Hungary closed its plant in the country in October 2002. Statistics on redundant labour seeking new employment made it clear only at that time that most of this seemingly high-tech production was, in fact, nothing else than semi-skilled assembly work made competitive by relatively low labour costs. The plant was not closed owing to its 'footloose' character, and production was not moved to countries with lower labour cost levels. IBM decided to give up its own hard-disk product line and sold such capacities to Hitachi. The Japanese company did not want to maintain this kind of production in Europe and this is why the former IBM plant was closed in Hungary.

Other country examples from the table also go against expectations based on some knowledge of the NISs of the economies listed. Along with Hungary, Korea and Mexico have also surprisingly high ranking positions. Whereas Mexico evidently benefits from the presence of American-owned assembly lines in the country, Korea is not a country with a less-developed R&D sector any more.[23]

High-income countries placed surprisingly low in the list include Canada, Australia, New Zealand and Norway. These four economies have one thing in common: each of them is an important exporter of manufactured goods having a high content of domestically produced raw materials (for example paper and pulp in Canada and Norway). The high value of such exports increases their data of manufacturing exports and thereby apparently decreases the relative importance of high-tech goods.

This is just one argument for the very cautious use of the high-tech export share indicator. Other words of caution are much more related to the problem of the relationship between competitiveness in exports and in R&D:

1. The relative share of high-tech goods in exports may give a distorted picture of competitiveness because it does not show the origin of modern technologies used for export-oriented production.
2. It can also be misleading because it gives no information on why high-tech production was located in the given country.

3.   It does not indicate the technology intensity of production and exports either.

   In spite of all these counter-arguments, the relative share of high-tech goods in exports is used in some international comparisons of technological competitiveness, and we shall make some references to it as well. It can be regarded as an indicator complementary to other measurements of supply-side competitiveness, more or less acceptable between countries of similar levels of development and attracting similar volumes and kinds of foreign direct investment. It is important however that it be used only in combination with other, more robust competitiveness indicators.

2.3   THE TECHNOLOGY BALANCE OF PAYMENTS (TBP)

Analogous problems arise with another technology-related indicator of supply-side competitiveness, namely 'technology balance' or 'technology balance of payments' (TBP).[24] The TBP indicator was constructed to measure international transfers of technology. The original idea was to assess how much 'technology' was imported and exported by a country in a given year. The reliability of this indicator depends largely on what is understood by 'technology' during the measurement, and also on whether qualitative differences between equal nominal amounts of technology trade could be quantified or not.

   The TBP consists of four sub-indicators which helps it give a quite full quantitative coverage of the international transfers of technology a country may be involved in. Each of the four sub-indicators expresses payments for the technology-related items listed in its description:

1.   Trade in techniques: this is the core sub-indicator constituting TBP, and the one most related to R&D generated in the country earning export income with the sales of technology-related intellectual property. It includes the sales and purchases of patents, non-patented inventions, patent-related licence agreements and contracts on know-how transfer. In sum, these flows of techniques are those which embody international transfers of knowledge.
2.   Transactions involving industrial property: this is much less related to R&D. Trademarks, industrial samples and the transfers of industrial methods belong here.
3.   Services with a technical content: engineering studies and technology-related consulting work such as training of experts, maintenance expertise

work or quality management services are the items included. Here again, the R&D or innovation content of the services in question is not too evident.

4. Industrial R&D: this denomination is a bit misleading, since it means R&D financing between countries. For example R&D carried out at a foreign subsidiary of a multinational corporation, but financed from the headquarters of the company, or R&D in country C financed by two independent firms from countries A and B.

It seems quite clear from the list of TBP items that TBP is the sum of flows of payments very different from each other in character, and being related to R&D and innovation in distinct ways. Two problems arise regarding the practical value of TBP as a direct or indirect measure of R&D competitiveness. First, it should be asked whether a country which is a net exporter of technology-related intellectual property and services is really competitive in them.

This is a question analogous to the one asked earlier in this chapter: how can export–import ratios in commodity trade reflect the comparative advantages or the level of competitiveness of an economy if its degree of openness and the geographical structure of its trade are not known?

The second problem is related to the directions of international transfers of technology. If a country has a high TBP indicator this may show that it is a net exporter in most items constituting the TBP, but not necessarily in those with a high content of technology or innovations.

For example a country may be strong in exporting engineering consulting services not based on its own innovations, but weak in sales of patents and know-how. The total could be positive TBP regardless of the real innovative potential of the economy. Similarly if a country's firms order much commissioned R&D work from abroad due to the lower cost levels of the foreign R&D units, the TBP can decrease also in the case of a really innovative economy with competitive R&D.

It would be a misunderstanding to think that the TBP is a trade balance-type indicator describing the trade of high-tech products. The content of the TBP is a comparison of the amounts of 'technology' imported and exported by a country in a given year, but this indicator leaves open whether products or services under the same heading in statistics really do have the same technological value or not. Therefore the TBP as an indicator of R&D or innovation output is quite unreliable in linking R&D competitiveness to apparent competitiveness in one segment of international trade.

This is why the TBP can reflect real levels of technology development and technology-based competitiveness only in an approximative way. Reflecting its controversial character and analytical value, it is treated in different ways by various international statistics on R&D and innovation.

The TBP is not included in *Science and Technology Indicators* (NSB, 2004), one of the most frequently cited statistical surveys of American and international R&D development. That statistical analysis uses only its fourth component called 'industrial R&D'. *The Main Science and Technology Indicators* (published by the OECD twice in a year) includes, however, TBP in its totality.

A strong demonstration of the inadequate character of the TBP indicator can be found in Salvatore (2002). His analysis of the case of the United States has shown that a deterioration of the technology balance went hand in hand with a substantial improvement of multi-factor productivity. This latter trend is an important sign of the expansion of the so-called 'New Economy',[25] while the worsening trend of the TBP of the United States is partly explained by substantial imports of patents used for further innovations based on them.

In any event it is doubtful whether an apparent improvement (increase) of the TBP is a good sign for a country's economic and technological performance or not. In a short-term approach, it may show some kind of improvement of technological or innovation competitiveness, but a negative value of TBP can speak of a country's strong effort to improve its technological potential and also competitiveness in the long run.

The latest available TBP data are only for OECD countries. The most important net exporters of technology based on TBP in percentage of the GDP were, according to Table 2.2: Switzerland, Belgium, Denmark, the United States, the United Kingdom, Canada and Japan in 1999. Most of these countries can boast of high levels of R&D competitiveness as we shall see it from our subsequent analysis.

The Republic of Ireland, Korea, Hungary and Portugal were the most significant net importers of technology on a TBP basis (OECD, 2001, 114). Negative TBPs can equally mean a surge in imports of technology or a sudden decrease in technological exports. Even within the OECD, at least two countries from the above group of four with low TBP indicators, the Republic of Ireland and Korea, are quite well placed in our R&D competitiveness measurement, to be presented later.

The relative unreliability of the TBP as an indirect indicator of R&D competitiveness is also demonstrated by the low values of Germany and Norway, both of which have high GERD levels and respectable R&D potentials. The extremely low TBP level of the Irish economy speaks of a special case, a country massively importing foreign direct investment (FDI) and also technological services and knowledge as part of it. Ireland is in fact one of the world's leading importers of FDI:

> The impact of incoming FDI on a country's economy is measured by the 'transnationality index' (TNI), an average of four percentage shares: 1. FDI inflows in gross fixed capital formation during the last three years of measurement; 2. FDI inward stocks as

Table 2.2   TBP as a percentage of the GDP (OECD countries, 1999)

Rank	Country	%
1	Switzerland	0.63
2	Belgium-Luxemburg	0.35
3	Denmark	0.35
4	United States	0.25
5	United Kingdom	0.21
6	Canada	0.12
7	Japan	0.11
8	Finland	0.04
9	Czech Republic	0.01
10	New Zealand	−0.01
11	Australia	−0.03
12	France	−0.04
13	Italy	−0.07
14	Mexico	−0.08
15	Austria	−0.10
16	Spain	−0.14
17	Germany	−0.18
18	Norway	−0.21
19	Poland	−0.35
20	Portugal	−0.44
21	Hungary	−0.59
22	Korea	−0.71
23	Republic of Ireland	−8.87

Source: Technology balance of payments. OECD Science and Technology Indicators Scoreboard (2001), 197.

compared to GDP in the last year of measurement; 3. The value added of foreign affiliates within GDP in the last year of measurement; and 4. The employment of foreign affiliates within total employment in the last year of measurement. Ireland's TNI was 47.4 in 2000, second only to Belgium (75.6) within the OECD. The highest levels in the Third World belonged to Hong Kong (109.8) and Nigeria (62.8). (UNCTAD, 2003, 6)

A high level of TBP can potentially show a country's poor absorption capacity of new technologies. Similarly the TBP may be low because the country in question tries to export technologies to countries with low levels of technology absorption. To exaggerate a little bit, a negative TBP can equally speak of a strong modernization effort in the country itself or, if it is potentially a significant exporter of technologies, a lack of such effort in the partner countries.

There is one aspect from which the TBP can possibly be used as an indirect indicator of R&D competitiveness, namely if imports of technological knowledge are simple substitutes of domestic R&D and innovation. This can be the case in developing or transition countries whose firms might be biased against domestic R&D and do not want to rely upon it at all. Such country cases may be identified if data on GERD and the expenditure side of TBP are compared.

This comparison is done in Table 2.3 with the ratio of the foreign expenditure (technology imports) element of TBP and GERD. A higher value of this ratio shows that the country in question replaces domestic R&D with imports of technology to a great extent. The degree of substitution decreases if this ratio gets lower.

Table 2.3   The cost of technology imports from the TBP (A), GERD (B), both as a percentage of GDP in 1999 and their ratio (A/B = TBP expenditure per GERD)

Ranking (by A)	Country	A TBP expenditure per GDP	B GERD per GDP	A/B
1	Ireland	9.44	1.21	7.813
2	Belgium-Luxembourg	1.71	1.96	0.873
3	Austria	1.23	1.80	0.684
4	Hungary	1.04	0.80	1.300
5	Norway	0.81	1.70	0.477
6	Germany	0.77	2.53 (2001)	0.305
7	Korea	0.75	2.65 (2000)	0.283
8	Portugal	0.72	0.76	0.948
9	Denmark	0.61	2.00	0.305
10	Czech Republic	0.52	1.31 (2001)	0.397
11	Switzerland	0.51	2.64 (2000)	0.193
12	Poland	0.43	0.67 (2001)	0.645
13	Italy	0.36	1.04	0.346
14	France	0.22	2.17	0.101
15	United Kingdom	0.22	1.87	0.112
16	Canada	0.19	1.66	0.114
17	Spain	0.18	0.89	0.202
18	United States	0.14	2.64	0.053
19	Mexico	0.09	0.43	0.209
20	Japan	0.08	3.04	0.026
21	Australia	0.06	1.53 (2000)	0.039
22	Finland	0.05	3.19	0.016
23	New Zealand	0.01	1.03	0.001

Source: (for TBP) Technology balance of payments, payments as percentage of GDP, OECD (2001b, 197); (for GERD) OECD (2001) and NSB (2004, 4–51) and own calculations.

The picture seems surprisingly clear from the table. It demonstrates that a quite important number of countries import technologies and technological knowledge instead of using their own R&D and technology base. Countries importing FDI to a relatively great extent, such as Ireland, Belgium or Hungary, seem to have followed this strategy (Portugal may also be considered a similar case).

The consequence of this behaviour on competitiveness seems to be contradictory: on the one hand, these countries can largely benefit from the most advanced technologies if and when they import them and use them for constructing highly competitive capacities for export. On the other hand, this behaviour of R&D-oriented firms of these countries may negatively affect domestic R&D competitiveness since domestic R&D is partly deprived from its most important potential clients in domestic business.

The most advanced economies with the highest GERD/GDP levels are also those which have relatively low FDI imports and expenditures on technology of foreign origin. Such cases include the United States, Japan, Finland and Denmark (Korea and Germany were not included in the figure in order to ensure consistency of the data).

The trend line in Figure 2.1 shows only a few outliers such as Belgium where the TNI is extremely high. The figure, in addition to Table 2.3, seems to confirm our hypothesis of a certain complementarity between GERD and the imports of technology which are not necessarily accounted for in the GERD but significantly contribute to strengthening the R&D base. Imports of

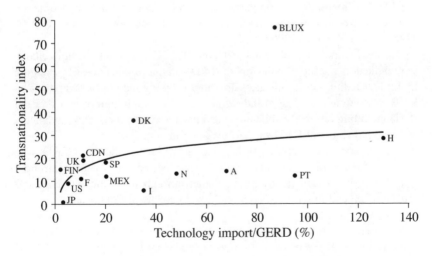

Figure 2.1 Relationship between technology imports/GERD and the transnationality index (TNI)

technology can also improve the R&D competitiveness of an economy which is seemingly (judged only from the GERD) not strongly R&D oriented.

2.4   CONSIDERATIONS FOR MEASURING R&D COMPETITIVENESS

International Comparisons of R&D and Innovation – what Indicators to be Used?

Measuring performance in R&D has a history of no more than 50 years. Godin's seminal article (2003) describes the process of development of not only the tools of measurement of R&D efforts, but also how this development was accompanied by various attempts to measure national R&D performance.

There were two initial directions of such attempts: the first one was undertaken by the American government in order to evaluate strengths and weaknesses of R&D in the country. The first publication by the National Science Foundation, presenting a large number of R&D indicators produced for practical use, appeared in 1973 and was followed by a regular series of statistical publications and analyses called *Science and Engineering Indicators*. This currently bi-annual volume contains international data to an increasing extent, but it still has a main focus on the R&D sector of the United States.

The other direction of work was undertaken primarily by the OECD. The OECD laid a much greater emphasis on assessing indicators potentially useable for international comparisons. Its 1978 report made a distinction between short-term, medium-term and long-term indicators of R&D (OECD, 1978, quoted by Godin, 2003, 684).

The distinction is based upon the degree of stability of the indicators. Short-term indicators are input indicators of R&D – in the first place R&D spending by firms. Medium-term indicators are those showing the use of manpower by R&D institutions. Long-term indicators are for example output indicators of R&D including refereed publications and patent counts, innovation indicators and also indicators of R&D support by governments.

We can add to this approach that one macro-level indicator, GERD, also shows a quite high degree of stability over time, and it is usually strongly linked to R&D financing by governments through the indicator of BERD (business expenditure on research and development). BERD usually changes quite slowly over time.

An interesting rule of thumb can be observed on wide international samples of BERD data. It seems to be true, in general, that the proportion of BERD within GERD (GERD expressing the entire expenditure on R&D within GDP), increases with the level of development of the economy, and also with the strength of linkage between national R&D and export performance. The role of government in financing R&D also counts in the cases of those countries, especially the transition economies, where public financing of R&D has not yet been fully complemented by business spending on R&D. The systemic reasons of the slow changes in BERD might also explain the relative stability of this indicator on the country level over time.

To give some examples: the ratio BERD/GERD was 72 per cent in Japan and 67 per cent in the United States in 1999, whilst only 55 per cent in the European Union (OECD 2001, A.3, and Table A.3.1.). It was the highest in the most developed countries (besides the above, 66.9 per cent in Finland, 64.3 per cent in Germany, 67.8 per cent in Sweden and, in 1995, 67.5 per cent in Switzerland), and the lowest in the least developed countries of the OECD (Czech Republic 52.6 per cent, Hungary 38.5 per cent, Poland 38.1 per cent, Slovakia 49.9 per cent, Mexico 23.6 per cent, Portugal 21.3 per cent). The indicator changed by less than 5 percentage points between 1989 and 1999 in the following OECD countries: Japan, Finland, Germany, Italy, the Netherlands, Spain and the United Kingdom, and less than 5 percentage points between 1989 and 1997 in the following countries from where more recent data were not available: Australia, New Zealand, Greece, and the European Union on the average. Fast changes (over 10 percentage points through 1989 and 1999) occurred in the United States, Austria and Iceland.

The idea of making in-depth international comparisons of R&D emerged in the early 1970s when some European strategists, most of them French, seemed to be obsessed with the idea that Europe was going to lose ground in high-technology industries vis-à-vis the United States.

The American Challenge (Le défi américain), a best-selling, manifesto-type book by Jean-Jacques Servan-Schreiber published in 1967, warned that Europe was threatened by the emergence of a technology gap owing to the concentrated effort of the United States towards increasing its technological dominance over the world, and mainly based on its strategic industries. Servan-Schreiber also attributed the threat to a certain inflexibility of European governments and business, and to the relatively low prestige of innovation in European societies.

Another influential book, *The French Disease (Le mal français)* by Alain Peyrefitte was published a couple of years later (Peyrefitte, 1976). That book focused on the potential development gap threatening France, but the arguments were similar with a more historical flavour and in a long-term approach.

Besides these often cited essays, the problem of Europe's relative technological backwardness was assessed in a number of multi-country analyses by the OECD (for a survey of these see Godin, 2003). The first report (OECD, 1968) used the concept of technology gaps to explore the factors of Europe's lag in development as compared to the United States. This report pioneered the application of some currently used indicators for international comparisons of technological development: R&D spending, innovation, trade performance, production, foreign direct investment and the 'technology balance of payments' were compared for the United States and the member countries of the European integration. The message of the report was clear: the difference in R&D efforts between the United States and the European Community was to be blamed for the widening of the technology gap.

The first in-depth multidimensional analysis of technological and R&D development was prepared by Pavitt and Wald (OECD, 1971, quoted by Godin, 2003). This study was titled *Conditions for Success*, and it used six indicators to measure technological innovation and compare innovative capacity and performance across countries. These six indicators included the number of significant innovations, the country's receipts for patents, licences and know-how, the pricing of technology, the number of patents granted, and the imports and exports of R&D-intensive industries. This was probably the first comprehensive effort to link innovation to some understanding of competitiveness, even if this latter term was not explicitly named.

The question underlying Pavitt and Wald's approach was not so much how countries compete in terms of innovation and R&D, but rather how a country's economy can benefit from innovation and R&D. Ranking countries on the basis of the impact of their domestic R&D on their national economy is however not the same thing as ranking them on the basis of R&D performance as compared to their competitors. A country can have a good R&D performance (for example relatively many publications and patents) in international comparison even if its high-level R&D plays a relatively modest role in its economic development.[26]

Pavitt and Wald identified a number of important R&D indicators for international comparisons, but some of these indicators have been of quite limited use since their analysis was published. The first international comparisons of R&D introduced a number of indicators not widely used before, and only a limited number of them was able to survive.

The reasons include important statistical distortions such as for example in the case of receipts for IP (intellectual property) where transfer pricing might be a factor of distortion. The pricing of technology variable was meant to show how prices of technology-intensive goods are influenced by explicit or implicit trade barriers, but the thorough liberalization of world trade with substantial tariff cuts and the elimination of a number of red tape barriers made these price distortions relatively unimportant in the industrial countries. The exports and imports of R&D-intensive industries have become increasingly independent of domestic R&D, but this was not foreseen by analysts in the early 1970s. They did not expect the globalization process to take place at such a speed, and the multinationalization of R&D within transnational corporations was not yet on the agenda for research.

Godin also surveyed those efforts in the literature which were aimed at compiling lists of indicators to be used in international comparisons of R&D performance, not speaking at all about competitiveness yet. The first such efforts were made in the 1960s by Freeman and Young, and they were 'in fact, far in advance of everybody' (Godin, 2003, 687). Still, the first comprehensive list of R&D indicators was published in the 1970s by the National Science Foundation of the United States. Even the first version of that list contained more than 100 indicators which were classified based on their useability in statistical analysis.

Godin's critique of generally used science and technology indicators emphasizes that most of these indicators are input rather than output oriented (Godin, 2003, 679). We agree with this statement, and the measurement of competitiveness in R&D (in the subsequent chapter) has, as one of its key objectives, the purpose of finding a balance between the input- and the output-oriented approach.

The other element of Godin's critique is that S&T indicators are 'mainly preoccupied with the economic dimension of science and technology' (Godin, 2003, 679). No doubt, but competitiveness is really an economic concept, and this economic orientation of S&T indicators is precisely the main reason why we think that their well-mixed cocktail can serve as a good measurement technique of competitiveness in R&D.

Godin's study is important as a survey of former efforts to assess cross-country differences of R&D capacity and performance, and also to clarify the problem of technology gap. Measuring competitiveness in R&D is however a different issue. It is not about how a country is performing in R&D, but about how some of its inputs into the sector and some of its outputs from the sector, both understood as measures of R&D competitiveness, compare with those of its competitors in R&D and in trade in general.

Godin concludes his study by reproducing the National Science Foundation's list of indicators of science, out of which only a selection are recommended for analysis, and even less for international comparisons (Godin, 2003, 688–90). This list was certainly prepared to be used as a benchmark, and its exhaustive character makes this use possible. It seems useful to comment on this list with a special emphasis on the indicators considered applicable in international comparisons.

The NSF list consists of seven groups of R&D indicators: scientific output measures, scientific activity measures, scientific education measures, attitudes towards and interest in science, manpower measures, extent of new thrusts and international indicators. Some of these groups include indicators that are appropriate for measuring the input or the output side of R&D competitiveness, as for example output and activity measures or international measures. The content of the other groups makes necessary some more detailed clarifications. Only the more important indicators in each group are discussed below as a starting point for our detailed assessment of R&D indicators.

Scientific output measures

Two out of the five indicators listed here are related to scientometrics (number of papers in top-quality, refereed journals and number of referenced articles and citations), and can well be used for measuring not only scientific output, but also one aspect of competitiveness. A third, apparently similar indicator is the number of refereed publications originating from a specific project and the estimated cost per paper. This is however not a good indicator of output or competitiveness, because it tries to express the cost of R&D only as compared to one kind of return, namely the results appearing in publications.

A further output indicator listed here is the longitudinal number of patents per the size of population in the age group 22 to 64 years, that is (supposedly) active population. It remains an open question why exactly the number of patents has to be linked to the size of active age groups, because this could equally be done for other indicators of output.

Still, it is beyond doubt that at least one measure of publications and at least one measure of patents has to be used for assessing the output side of R&D competitiveness. These are however indicators that are able to measure direct output only. Indirect output includes a number of different spillovers such as the impact of R&D on the competitiveness of manufacturing, but indirect indicators of this kind are only sporadically included in the list.

Activity measures: 16 indicators are listed here. Most of them have a structural character. These are related to the academic or industrial background of research, and show the age structure of researchers or the distribution of R&D funding between different sources of support. Some reflect the linear model of R&D and innovation.

These indicators (such as for example the ratio of basic research funds to total investment in R&D) might be of interest rather to national R&D policy-makers. The vast majority of these indicators are input related, and show the distribution of financial resources for R&D among groups of recipients. Only one indicator out of 16, the geographic distribution of R&D, is not an input-related one (albeit it also shows the direct impact of the regional structure of R&D financing).

Science education measures

These nine indicators are, for their major part, input related, but they influence the input side of R&D competitiveness only with a considerable time lag. The number of science and engineering degrees per total degrees in a given year could be a good indicator of the human resources of R&D within a time span when the fresh degree-holders become really productive in R&D – supposedly a foreseeable proportion of these 'outputs' of science education choose career paths in research. In addition to that, differences between national education systems also make education-based international comparisons a quite daunting task.

The reliability of education-related indicators for competitiveness measurement is largely distorted by the uneven increase of international mobility in higher education. For example the recipients of American doctoral degrees in 1999 returned to their home countries in percentages varying greatly according to their country of origin: China 10, India 10, South Korea 37, Taiwan 38, Canada 28, Turkey 41, Germany 35, Mexico 69, Brazil 69, United Kingdom 21 (NSB, 2002, 2–36). For example, only 10 per cent of Chinese recipients of American doctoral degrees in 1999 returned to work in their home country in that year, and presumably many of them took jobs in the United States.

This means PhD programmes in the United States turned out highly skilled R&D manpower first of all for the American economy as far as their students from the Far East were concerned, whilst most of their Latin American students returned home after earning their PhD degrees. In other words, American PhD programmes improved the human resources side of future R&D competitiveness of the US economy much more with their degrees awarded to Chinese students than with the ones taken by Latin Americans or Europeans.

Attitudes towards and interest in science

The three indicators listed here express the level of prestige enjoyed by science in society at large and among students. Such indicators are indirectly related to competitiveness in R&D, because political support (and therefore one component of possible financial support of R&D from the government) for R&D probably depends on public attitudes towards science as well. Such data are not available for most countries of the world.

The relationship between public opinion about science and the government financing of R&D seems however to be far from direct. The main reason is that university-based and other scientific lobbies may be able to exert considerable political pressure on governments in order to increase the public financing of R&D, irrespective of their relative weight in society in general. In any event, the impact of public attitudes towards science on the development of R&D competitiveness needs to be further explored.

Manpower measures

These indicators are used to assess the sectoral structures of manpower employed in different fields of R&D. The overall labour intensity (or labour input) of R&D is not listed here, because it is one of the major indicators of factor endowment of R&D used in international comparisons. The measures of manpower listed here include two indicators, both of a sectoral character. One of them describes the employment of scientists and engineers by sector, scientific degree and field of science, while the other looks into unemployment in science as compared with other areas of professional employment.

Extent of new thrusts

This seemingly cryptic denomination stands for two indicators which might be used for grasping the movement of the frontiers of science and the role of national innovation systems in such movements. This is in general a very important field of analysis for long-term national R&D strategies, but mainly in countries with really ample resources for R&D. These are in fact also the countries which could afford spending on the elaboration of comprehensive long-term R&D strategies.

These could be, in all probability, only the countries on the top of international ranking lists of competitiveness in R&D, and primarily the United States. One of these indicators is called 'major new frontiers of science opened up during a specific year' (Godin, 2003, 689). If however a frontier of science was really opened up in a given year and this can be proven, it is very likely that only a limited number of such really important explorations can be registered for the totality of world science each year.

The other indicator belonging to the measurement of the 'extent of new thrusts' has an infrastructural character. It is about the number of potential major frontier research facilities which are feasible but not under construction yet. The understanding of frontier facilities in this respect is related to the technological frontiers of their construction, and not to the financial ones. Similarly to the 'frontier' indicator referred to above, this one also is applicable only for the countries performing best in R&D. For most if not all of the other countries, the financial frontiers of constructing new research facilities certainly take precedence over the technological ones. The example of CERN can be called in this respect. In that case not only the construction, but also the running and maintenance of such a frontier research facility has been dependent on wide international R&D cooperation.

In any event, the measurement of R&D competitiveness cannot draw much upon the 'extent of new thrust'-type indicators.

International indicators

Most of these are national indicators of input and output placed in an international context. These are in fact the most useful indicators for measuring both the input and the output side of competitiveness in R&D.

The NSF list of these indicators has six elements. It is not entirely clear why these are more international than others which could be used equally well for international comparisons, but a strong statistical reason seems to have prevailed: data on these indicators can be collected on wide international samples with relative ease. This list of six contains output-type indicators along with manpower (input)-related ones, and it is also here that financial inputs to R&D are taken into account.

With regard to this fact, the international indicators could be also called 'indicators applicable in wide international comparisons'. These indicators are as follows (Godin, 2003, 689):[27]

1. Ratio of (US) scientific publications to world total. This indicator is one of the key measures of R&D performance and, in our understanding, competitiveness. It opens up a window towards a whole field of methodology of measuring R&D performance, namely scientometrics.[28]

2. Relationship of R&D per capita to per capita GNP in various countries. This indicator is a derivate of GERD which comes later in the list. In addition to that, it is also important for indicating the equal importance of absolute and per capita approaches in measuring R&D on an international level.

3. Scientists and engineers employed in R&D, across countries. This is an important indicator of the relative endowment of a country's R&D sector with one key factor of 'production' (using classical economics parlance), labour or, more precisely, human capital. It shows, on the one hand, the relative share of skilled human resources of a country employed in R&D, that is the 'employment bias' towards (or against) research. On the other hand, it also indicates how strong the human capital background of one country's R&D sector (or innovation system) is as compared to others. It is not the same indicator as the relative share of R&D personnel in total employment which also includes auxiliary research staff.

4. R&D/GNP in various countries. The currently used version of this indicator is GERD (gross expenditure on research and development) expressed in percentage of the GDP. The difference between the GDP- and GNP-based indicators is linked to the difference between GDP and GNP: GDP summarizes value added in the country's territory (regardless of the nationality of the owners of the factors of production), while GNP is the sum of the services of factors of production owned by that country's firms or individuals (regardless whether these factors of production are located in or outside the country). We believe GDP is more appropriate for evaluating domestic spending on R&D, because that spending goes to domestic research facilities irrespective of their ownership or national background. Furthermore there is a practical and strong argument: modern international comparisons of R&D use GERD exclusively and not

at all its GNP-based counterpart. GERD is also applied as a frame of reference for R&D strategies: the Lisbon Strategy of the European Union has set the target of reaching the 3 per cent level of GERD by the year 2010 (see Rodrigues, 2003).

5. Scientific and engineering personnel per 10 000 population in different countries. This is a less specific indicator than the one showing the number of scientists and engineers employed in R&D. It describes rather the human capital background of science and technology (S&T) in its widest sense, rather than that of R&D. It is however not at all a useless indicator for R&D analysis: it shows whether domestic R&D has an appropriate human capital environment outside the R&D sector itself. If for example human capital is much more available within R&D than outside it, then the domestic R&D sector can suffer from intellectual isolation, would only be able to produce mainly for exports of R&D products and services, and manufacturing would probably have a low R&D intensity.

6. Nobel (and other) prizes per capita won (by US) each year compared with other countries. The fact that this measure has been included in the NSF's list of important international indicators of R&D is quite surprising. The core element of this measure is the Nobel Prize. Others such as the Wolf prize in mathematics and other sciences can be used or rejected by statisticians for similar reasons (see Braun et al., 2003).

Nobel Prize-related data show, of course, the huge superiority of the United States in international R&D, especially if they are expressed in absolute terms. In a per capita approach of the distribution of Nobel Prizes among countries, the US would rank only in the first ten countries of the world, although most Nobel Prizes in science went to US citizens after the early 1990s. The absolute or per capita number of Nobel Prizes is however a very unreliable indicator for several reasons.

*   First, an increasing number of Nobel Prizes have gone to scientists who had moved from one country to the United States, and their research awarded with the prize did not necessarily take place on US soil or financed from American resources. Up to 2001, the number of so-called 'imported Nobel Prize winners' (who were born as citizens of a country other than the one they represented when awarded the Nobel Prize) totalled 103, out of which 61 persons were US citizens as winners of the prize. Out of the total 515 winners of the Nobel Prize, 226 were US citizens but only 168 were American-born (Palló, 2001).
*   Second, the nomination and the selection for a Nobel Prize takes place partly on the basis of individual merit, but also related to the field of

science where progress has been (or had been) remarkable. This may pose problems in the case of larger teams which cannot be awarded as such, and only a limited number of their participants may obtain the distinction.

- Third, the judgement on the validity of a research result can vary with the passing of time. For example a Portuguese winner of the Nobel Prize for medicine of the 1940s (Egas Moniz) turned out later to have reached a discovery in medicine which proved much less important than originally believed.[29] In any event, the Nobel Prize values individual or perhaps team effort, but not the achievements of a country's R&D sector as such.

Except for the number of Nobel Prizes, most of the international indicators listed by the NSF seem to be useful for international comparisons of R&D performance and hence competitiveness, if its measurement is based on an input–output-related approach. Our first approximative analysis of international competitiveness of R&D[30] used two input-side and two output-side indicators. These included GERD and R&D employment for inputs, and patent counts in the United States and the number of refereed publications regarding outputs. Three of these four indicators also figure among the international indicators on the NSF list.

Indicators not recommended by the NSF
To conclude our survey of the NSF list, it is interesting to have a look at the indicators considered but not recommended by the NSF (Godin, 2003). The reasons for including any indicator in this 'negative list' are not given by Godin, but the explanations seem to be quite evident in most cases.

The 'negative list' is surprisingly long, and contains 28 indicators or, to be more accurate, ideas of indicators. Most of them are just vague attempts at measuring something related to science or R&D, but without any clear meaning. For example the 'Nationality of invited speakers at international meetings' is evidently insufficient for describing the international openness of any scientific event or community, or even for showing the real professional value of the R&D sector of any country sending many speakers to international conferences.

The 'Annual average percentage of front-page stories in the *New York Times* that deal with scientific subjects' could reflect nothing else than the taste of the newspaper's editors and perhaps the persuasive power of some PR managers at certain R&D organizations. The 'Subscriptions (per capita) to science magazines and science book purchases' would show, in many countries, not the willingness to and the scientific interest in getting access to up-to-date professional information, but much more the level of R&D financing which is obviously inadequate in many countries of the world.

There are other indicators considered but not recommended which have a higher, albeit still inadequate explanatory power for comparative R&D analysis. The 'Relationship of US scientific papers to world papers as compared with US GNP against world's GNP' might seem to show a certain kind of scientific productivity in an international comparison, but this indicator lacks at least one important element for being considered seriously: the relationship of the cost of producing one scientific paper in the US as compared to the rest of the world.

In a similar manner, 'R&D expenditures per capita for different countries' could potentially show some kind of relative inputs in a comparative approach, but the amount and quality of R&D capacities obtained or obtainable with this spending remains unknown. The differences between the age structures of the populations of diverse countries may cause a considerable distortion in the interpretation of this indicator, since per capita spending (not only on R&D, but on anything) may be higher in countries with higher percentages of active population.[31]

Our survey of former attempts at finding tools for international comparisons of R&D resources or performance has shown that most such comparisons had no more than a partial character. The choice of indicators was in the forefront, and really complex approaches were quite rare on the country level. Perhaps the main challenge for such comparisons is that they should integrate the input and the output side of R&D, and try to establish a relationship between resources dedicated to R&D and the outcomes of the R&D effort. This challenge was not met by any comprehensive analysis before the end of the 1990s, and no complete cross-country assessment of S&T performances was known from the literature either.

Recent years however have brought kind of a breakthrough in this field, at least as far as international comparisons of innovations are concerned. Innovation is a concept broader than R&D, and it is more closely linked to entrepreneurship. This seems to be one of the reasons why it has been more in the focus of policy interest than R&D in a number of countries. Besides this, assessments of innovation systems could hardly ignore the respective R&D sectors as their key elements.

Absolute and Per Capita Approaches

R&D potentials differ across countries more strongly than levels of economic development, and the patterns of both absolute and per capita performance. Trade performance is usually not calculated on a per capita basis (although it could be), neither are market shares as indicators of export competitiveness taken into account with respect to country size. R&D has however a strong qualitative aspect as well, and this is why per capita performance is also an important feature of international competition. Furthermore substitution is often quite weak or inexistent between the fields of R&D, and even small countries can prove very effective and competitive in narrower fields.

We shall also observe that smaller countries have better chances to become key players in world R&D than in world trade, and efficiency has more meaning in measuring competitiveness in R&D than in world trade in general. The linkage between R&D inputs and outputs is quite strong in the best-performing countries, where there is a statistical relationship between national GERD or employment data and scientometric and IP indicators.

The reason seems evident: for example Dutch counts of refereed international publications or the number of Dutch patents registered in the United States are likely to reflect Dutch GERD or R&D employment, because all these measures show inputs and outputs that can be directly linked to the economy of the Netherlands. On the other hand, the market shares of Dutch goods exports might show the impact of Dutch inputs to no more than a limited extent if these exports have only a limited share of value added in the Netherlands.

Our unit of analysis is the nation state which, we believe, is justified for an international comparison of competitiveness in R&D even though this approach would be probably more open for criticism in an analysis of trade performance. We completely accept Laursen's argument (Laursen, 2000, 6), partly borrowed from Nelson (1993): 'institutions such as firm organisation; technological support systems; education systems; financial systems; and university systems are still national, and affect countries' technological and economic performance'.

Laursen's text supports this argument with several references to empirical evidence from the field of the economics of innovation. Out of such empirical analyses, Patel and Pavitt's international analysis of United States patents seems to be the most convincing (Pavitt and Patel, 1991).

International statistics of R&D and innovation also use national frameworks, and migrations of scientists from R&D to industry also mainly take place within the framework of the same NIS (see Zellner, 2003). As has been mentioned before, international competition in R&D can be considered to take place mainly among countries, even if participants of this competition include universities, industrial firms and individual researchers.

Furthermore a number of countries still have NISs with relatively low levels of international openness. As a number of pieces of evidence show from the international literature, there are not only striking similarities between the NISs of European transition economies, but these innovation systems have been very much confined to their respective countries although this seems to be changing (see our subsequent analysis of the roles of National Academies of Science in the transition economies; Biegelbauer, 2000; Aide à la Décision Économique, 2001).

Absolute measures of R&D performance and competitiveness are based on one of the key assumptions of theory of international economics, namely the disregarding of country size.

This principle of international comparisons is used in a number of fields outside of economics. For instance in team sports, where countries are ranked on the basis of the performances of their representatives regardless of any kind of country parameter (size, level of economic development, investment in sports, professional status of the sportsmen and so on). To put it simply, absolute comparisons between countries are the cases where nothing counts but performance, such comparisons however are insensitive to the conditions and the quality of individual country effort.

As opposed to this, relative or per capita comparisons represent such cases where differences in performance are, to be somewhat sceptical, explained with various background parameters of the countries compared. The most important of these explanatory parameters is usually country size. Indeed the relative strength of the R&D capacities of countries competing and cooperating with each other can be quite well demonstrated with per capita indicators of R&D input and performance.

Such kinds of per capita comparisons also raise the question of the international mobility of factors of R&D (the counterpart of the 'factors of production' in conventional international economics parlance). A *post hoc ergo propter hoc*-type false conjecture would be in this respect that factors of R&D are able to perform at the same level in most parts of the world. That is if research team A is able to produce an X number of refereed publications in referenced journals per year in country N, then this performance could be repeated if team A moves to country M. This is however not at all so, since efficiency in R&D is very much conditional upon country- (or NIS-) dependent factors such as national R&D infrastructures, governmental funding schemes or the intellectual potential of universities or scientific communities in a given country.

In line with the methodology of international comparisons in most fields, absolute cross-country comparisons of R&D have to be the first step to assess international competitiveness in R&D. This picture will then have to be completed with per capita comparisons in order to be able to see qualitative differences between countries as well.

2.5 RANKING COUNTRIES

The European Innovation Scoreboard

A comprehensive effort of international comparison of innovation capacities primarily within Europe is the European Innovation Scoreboard (EC, 2003), which has been repeatedly published by the European Commission each year since 2001. This scoreboard uses 28 indicators altogether. We shall review them only briefly and with a methodological focus at this time, because the Trendchart derived from this scoreboard is examined in Chapter 4, and many of the indicators will appear in our subsequent analysis. This in-depth comparison is again about innovation and not R&D. More precisely, it gives information on R&D only to the extent that R&D indicators are a subset of innovation related ones.

The boundaries of this subset are not defined by the authors of the Scoreboard. This means the overall comparison offered by the Scoreboard is only partly overlapping with the international R&D comparison envisaged in the subsequent chapter. A further difference between international comparisons of innovation capabilities or potentials and our comparisons of competitiveness in R&D is that the concept of competitiveness is apparently not present in the Scoreboard and the other innovation-oriented analyses.

The reason seems to be that products or outputs of R&D have a certain kind of international market where they compete (there is competition for the possibilities of publication and, on the basis of this competition, for university tenures, membership rights of national Academies of Science or, in an extreme case, for international scentific awards). It seems to be much more difficult to delineate an international market for innovations since the concept itself is vague for being used in competition analysis. As we shall discuss later, patents express inventions but not innovations, and it is sometimes difficult to identify an innovation competing for being chosen by a potential buyer. What would this buyer pay for – would it be a product, a service or a patent? Probably none of these terms coincides exactly with the term 'innovation'.

The European Innovation Scoreboard (EIS) uses four types of indicators. These are the following:

1. Human resources.
2. Knowledge creation.
3. Transmission and application of knowledge.
4. Innovation finance, output and markets.

Human resources
The five indicators of human resources could be applicable for R&D comparisons only to a limited extent, because they are strongly innovation oriented. Those with some R&D focus include the percentage share of science and engineering graduates within the 20–29 years age class, and the percentage share of people with a tertiary education within the age group 25–64 years.

The problem is analogous to that raised with respect to the duration-of-education based measures of human capital by Mulligan and Sala-i-Martin

(1995, 2): these indicators are insensitive to qualitative differences between different forms of education. For example college-level tertiary education has a different value on the labour market serving innovative firms than graduate-level or PhD-level training.

Further indicators in this group include participation in life-long learning. This kind of learning improves the convertibility of the workforce much more than its useability for innovation-related activities, the employment in medium-tech and high-tech manufacturing (although higher productivity levels in these sectors may tend to lower the level of this employment), and employment in high-tech services. In the latter case as well, productivity differences may considerably distort the picture.

Knowledge creation

The indicators of knowledge creation are a blend of measures of input and output. The input indicators here show spending on R&D (public expenditure: GERD – BERD, and business expenditure: BERD); the output indicators are patent counts. This grouping of indicators under the name 'knowledge creation' conveys a misleading impression. Knowledge is not created uniquely by spending on it, and the amount of knowledge created could be measured, besides patent counts, at least also by scientometric data as well.

> Moreover, Griliches highlighted the fact that patents can be understood, in a longer term approach, also as inputs to the R&D process because current patent statistics offer information about shifts in technological opportunities and influence thereby future patterns of R&D. (Griliches, 1990, 1685)

The patent counts include high-tech patent applications at the European Patent Office (EPO) and the United States Patent and Trademark Office (USPTO), and also patent applications at the EPO altogether and the number of patents granted by the USPTO (all of these four indicators are calculated per million population).

It is obvious that the number of patent applications does not show much of the real value of innovations in their background, and therefore the number of patents granted could be given priority in the measurements. Still, it is not clear why the number of patents granted by the EPO has been omitted from the set of indicators of knowledge creation.

Transmission and application of knowledge

Four out of the six indicators on 'transmission and application of knowledge' are related to the innovation behaviour of small and medium-sized firms (SMEs). This bias of the indicators towards SMEs conveys the impression that the Scoreboard gives relatively more weight to the innovation potential of countries where SMEs are, on the average, more innovative than elsewhere. The problem with this approach is the following. It is not proven that relying more on SMEs in innovation policy improves a country's innovation potential more than if company-level innovation is supported regardless of company size.

The two remaining indicators show innovation expenditures per turnover in manufacturing and in services. Innovation expenditures obviously comprise R&D spending, but it is not clear what their additional elements should be. If the Schumpeterian concept of innovation is used, then a quite broad but probably also rather vague category of expenditures would belong here. Statistical sources (for example Eurostat) are available with a quite accurate definition of data in this category. It still remains an open question how various reporting practices of firms residing in different countries could be used to create a homogenous international database in this respect.

Innovation finance, output and markets
The fourth group of indicators is quite heterogeneous, and its content does not seem to be in full conformity with its title ('Innovation finance, output and markets'). It comprises two indicators of venture capital financing, four indicators of different categories of 'new' products sold by SMEs, three indicators of the 'New Economy' – Internet access, Internet use and information and communication technology (ICT) expenditures – plus the share of manufacturing value added in high-tech sectors and the volatility rates of SMEs. This group of indicators conveys a quite biased impression of innovation, and we can list a number of critical remarks to support this assessment.

Primarily, financing, manufacturing production, the use of information and communication technologies are considered together with certain SME statistics. The priority given to SME statistics again raises the question whether successful innovation is conditional on the presence of SMEs in the process or not (or whether SMEs are inevitable for the success of a NIS). Our answer to these questions could not be fully affirmative.

Secondly, quantitative parameters of the SME sector such as their volatility do not tell us much about developments in innovation, especially if the relative share of innovative SMEs within their total number is not known. Another SME-related indicator here is 'SME sales of "new to the firm but not new to the market" products'. Can a firm be considered innovative if it seems innovative only based on its own standards, but not as measured by the criteria of the market? The answer to this rather philosophical question could not necessarily be affirmative either.

Thirdly, conditions and outcomes of the innovation process are combined in this set of indicators, based on sometimes rather vague and probably not adequately tested hypotheses. For example it is not proven that increasing Internet use and more spending on ICT technologies would directly and proportionally improve innovation performance. Internet use does not necessarily serve innovation only, and higher ICT spending can be the result of an increase of ICT costs.

Fourthly, venture capital is presented here as the exclusive source of the financing of innovation. This might be true for one part (or perhaps the most dynamic part) of innovation, but not for the entirety of innovation activities. The question here is whether the financing of innovation depends solely on the availability of venture capital (VC).

The answer is it depends on the country, because a number of economies boasting very competitive high-tech sectors (for example Sweden or Finland) use only a limited amount of VC-based financing of innovations (Karsai, 2002). Furthermore the definition of venture capital is not the same around the world (for example it includes the financing of acquisitions in Europe, but it does not in North America).

The EU's Innovation Scoreboard uses well-established indicators of innovation together with biased ones which are based on some *a priori* perceptions of the innovation process. Such prefabricated concepts are for example that more people with a tertiary education or more SMEs mean a better country-level innovation performance, and also that more patent applications speak of a higher success rate of innovations. These hypotheses cannot be refuted as such, and they can be stochastically true. Their validity should however strongly vary among countries, and this variation makes the relevance of the ranking lists presented in the Scoreboard questionable to some extent. As a matter of fact, such hypotheses seem reminiscent of 'mechanical' approaches to economic growth and technological development the rigidity of which was one of the factors calling for the new paradigm of evolutionary economics (see Nelson, 1995).

A Ranking Exercise by the United Nations

The United Nations Committee, Science and Technology for Development decided in 2001 to carry out a comparative measurement of the levels of technological development of the widest possible range of countries.[32] This effort is interesting to us for two reasons: (1) its methodological concept is different from the ones surveyed so far; (2) it covers a much larger number of countries than any other survey we know of.

In fact the authors of the UN comparison also tried to measure the level of technological development in such countries which were considered 'no-tech' countries in our approach. In spite of the great effort devoted to the analysis, data could be collected on less than 100 countries. This seems to be in line with the hypothesis that about one-half of all countries of the world are basically outside the sphere of high technology, at least as far as the creation of new (scientific and technological) knowledge is concerned (see Sachs, 2000).

The method used makes it possible to supply comparative indicators for each country in the sample, but it might remain questionable whether this kind of comparison between the most and the least-developed economies of the world really has an acceptable degree of relevance. Our idea of 'fields of competitiveness' is just putting the emphasis on certain groups of countries in the world economy between which comparisons of economic or technological competitiveness are difficult to justify owing to the *de facto* incomparability of their respective microstructures and outputs.

The international comparison of the United Nations aimed at producing a final ranking list of the countries of the world as regards technological development. The UN ranking list is based on three indicators. Two of these are input type ones and the third one is used to measure some kind of output.[33]

The first indicator used was GERD, to measure spending on R&D and also, in a larger sense, to show the scope of the innovation effort in each country. The second indicator was a combined one including the number of technical staff employed in R&D, and the number of students admitted to tertiary education. Its purpose was to serve as a proxy of the stock of human capital in the countries surveyed. The third indicator compared high-tech exports to total exports for each country. Its application is based on the idea that high-tech exports are based mainly on the domestic capacities of R&D and innovation. A number of middle-income countries with high stocks of FDI (foreign direct investment) are not such cases however.

The UN ranking list can be seen from Table 2.4. The list seems to suffer from a number of serious deficiencies if judged from the positions of certain countries. As with most such ranking lists, problems do not appear with entries at its top and bottom which are *grosso modo* in conformity with other sources. On the contrary, the 'midfield' is very problematic at some points. A number of countries with poor R&D performances, sometimes even very weak NISs, are ranked surprisingly high (for example Bolivia fares much better than Brazil), but the fact that Bulgaria is ahead of Slovenia, Guatemala better than Kuwait, or Burkina Faso ahead of Venezuela also makes the value of the list a bit questionable.

A more relevant result of the UN research is that most data used show a remarkable consistency over time. This is in line with information from other sources (for example OECD, 2001, 2002 or NSB, 2004), and important for judging the validity of international comparisons in case they are (as it often happens) based on data four to five years old.

Ranking Lists Commissioned by Governments

A special kind of international comparisons of technological or R&D capabilities or performances are those which were initiated by governments. A

Table 2.4   The UN ranking list of countries based on their levels of technological development (composite indexes of the three indicators listed, 1999)

1	USA	0.7091	45	China	0.1783
2	Korea	0.6894	46	Poland	0.1755
3	Finland	0.6584	47	Brazil	0.1727
4	Japan	0.6509	48	Latvia	0.1718
5	Singapore	0.6426	49	Kazakhstan	0.1696
6	Switzerland	0.6376	50	Romania	0.1670
7	Republic of Ireland	0.5511	51	Macau	0.1654
8	Canada	0.5444	52	Panama	0.1536
9	Belgium	0.5334	53	Armenia	0.1467
10	United Kingdom	0.5299	54	South Africa	0.1454
11	France	0.5115	55	Turkey	0.1414
12	The Netherlands	0.4908	56	Jordan	0.1365
13	Costa Rica	0.4835	57	Uruguay	0.1365
14	Sweden	0.4833	58	India	0.1364
15	Germany	0.4813	59	Azerbaijan	0.1270
16	Australia	0.4810	60	Colombia	0.1147
17	Israel	0.4783	61	Iran	0.1097
18	Denmark	0.4757	62	Egypt	0.0968
19	Russia	0.4362	63	El Salvador	0.0956
20	Italy	0.4216	64	Indonesia	0.0848
21	Norway	0.4040	65	Argentina	0.0733
22	Iceland	0.3863	66	Tunisia	0.0733
23	Austria	0.3831	67	Kyrgyzstan	0.0726
24	Malaysia	0.3673	68	Algeria	0.0696
25	New Zealand	0.3611	69	Peru	0.0684
26	Spain	0.3151	70	Guatemala	0.0654
27	Bulgaria	0.3104	71	Kuwait	0.0646
28	Slovenia	0.2900	72	Mauritius	0.0642
29	Estonia	0.2843	73	Paraguay	0.0628
30	Belarus	0.2780	74	Oman	0.0611
31	Philippines	0.2769	75	Nicaragua	0.0581
32	Barbados	0.2768	76	Uganda	0.0576
33	Bolivia	0.2727	77	Trinidad and Tobago	0.0555
34	Hungary	0.2720	78	Sri Lanka	0.0517
35	Chile	0.2698	79	Zimbabwe	0.0422
36	Lithuania	0.2611	80	Madagascar	0.0353
37	Czech Republic	0.2504	81	Senegal	0.0334
38	Thailand	0.2481	82	Syria	0.0332
39	Greece	0.2470	83	Burkina Faso	0.0298
40	Croatia	0.2375	84	Venezuela	0.0234
41	Portugal	0.2306	85	Togo	0.0218
42	Moldova	0.2156	86	Ecuador	0.0170
43	Mexico	0.2021	87	Tanzania	0.0132
44	Slovakia	0.2004	88	Pakistan	0.0125

Source: compilation by Deli (2004).

simpler version of such comparisons is when already existing ranking lists are used as benchmarks, and their methodologies are developed in order to do the positioning of the country in question, but the only purpose is to obtain comparative data on this country. More complex versions are based on methodologies elaborated for the given international comparison, and the interest of the government commissioning the research goes beyond establishing the international comparative position of just one country (Deli, 2004).

The comparative analysis of R&D in Slovenia belongs more to the first group than the second (Slovenian Ministry of Education, Science and Sport, 2002). The Slovene government built upon R&D benchmarking work in the European Union and the OECD in order to establish the country's position in the international ranking. The indicators selected do not constitute a coherent system though, and it seems that such indicators were given priority which make a favourable positioning of the country possible (Deli, 2004). Four groups of indicators were created: (1) the financing of R&D, (2) the human factor of R&D, (3) R&D activities in business, and (4) R&D output.

The methodologically undemanding character of this survey is demonstrated by the fact that separate ranking lists were set up on the basis of each indicator. For example, Slovenia comes out as No. 18 among OECD countries in the international comparison of GERD levels, but the meaning of this position is not explained in detail. GERD analysis is continued until the country gets a significantly better ranking position (No. 4), based upon the comparison of annual growth rates of GERD. Given that GERD is not a variable following too marked trends of change in time in most countries, this indicator is usually not applied on its own, and very rarely for comparative purposes, because it changes slowly over time in most countries.

The indicators of the human factor of R&D are also used to produce a number of ranking lists. Slovenia is below the OECD average regarding the number of researchers per 1000 population, and has similarly low positions for the relative number of researchers employed by the business sector or the number of the new PhD degrees earned in science and engineering. One indicator favourable for Slovenia is the relative number of researchers in government service, along with other OECD countries such as the Czech Republic or Hungary.

The analysis of R&D in Slovenian business revealed that international R&D cooperation plays a relatively modest role in product development. The international comparison of R&D output shows, similarly to R&D investment, that Slovenia fares better in growth indicators than in annual comparisons of R&D output such as publications, citations, patents or even labour productivity used here as an indirect indicator of innovation.

The value of the international R&D comparisons prepared in Slovenia seems to be negatively influenced by the fact that the different dimensions of this comparisons were analysed using different countries as benchmarks. Such a 'moving target'-type comparison may not be apt for establishing a synthetic ranking position for Slovenia in international R&D, which is in fact not produced in the report.

The analysis of Finland's R&D output was carried out in a much narrower scope, but based on a transparent and consistent methodological approach (Academy of Finland, 2000). This was a scientometric analysis carried out in three dimensions, using both absolute and per capita indicators. Although the analysis was prepared in order to establish Finland's relative positions, some of its findings are interesting in a wider R&D policy context as well.

The three dimensions included: (1) the numbers and growth rates of publications and citations; (2) the numbers of publications as compared to GDP, spending on academic R&D and the number of population, and (3) impact factors. The benchmark used was, in each case, the other member countries of the OECD. The last year of the analysis was 1999.

Finland produced 0.95 per cent of the OECD total number of publications in 1999 (the United States was leader with 35 per cent), in a middle position together with Denmark and Austria, and ahead of Greece, Portugal, Turkey, Ireland, Norway and Mexico.

The growth of publications over time gives a surprising ranking list because emerging economies including Korea, Mexico and Turkey are heading this list, Finland is sixth, and some great powers of R&D such as the United Kingdom, France, Japan and Germany have less-than-average values.

Citation numbers lead to similar conclusions as the analysis of publications both in a static and a dynamic international comparison. Fifty per cent of citations are obtained by articles published by American authors, followed by the United Kingdom (12.1 per cent), Germany (10.7 per cent), Japan (8.3 per cent) and France (6.7 per cent). Finland is again a midfielder here with 1.04 per cent, and the list is tailed by Turkey and Iceland. The growth of citations puts Finland again in the group of leaders along with Germany, Switzerland, Poland, Belgium and Italy.

The next dimension of the international R&D or scientometric comparison is, in fact, about the cost of publications. It was examined with respect to GDP, the budget of academic R&D and population. The number of publications per GDP brings Finland to third position on the international ranking list following Sweden and Switzerland. This result seems to be a proof for the existence of a relationship between high per capita GDP, high GERD and good publications performance. It may be also a sign of the so-called 'European paradox' (European Commission, 1995; Papanek, 2003), which expresses the fact that the R&D output of Europe is increasingly embodied in publications, whereas American R&D is showing a growing interest in producing patents instead of publications.

The number of publications as compared to budgets of academic R&D is the highest in Hungary, Switzerland and New Zealand, with Finland being in only twelfth position, but this result speaks rather of differences in R&D financing than in effective R&D output. In a comparison of the number of publications with the size of the population however, Finland is fourth, overtaken only by Switzerland, Sweden and Denmark, again a homogenous group of countries.

The ranking lists of absolute and relative impact factors are strongly correlated with GERD per GDP levels, and the countries widely considered as leaders in international R&D are on top of these lists as well. The leading position of the United States and of Switzerland is also clear regarding impact factors in diverse fields of science, and Finland belongs to the best performers in almost each such special list.

The Finnish benchmarking analysis of the country's R&D limited itself to one type of R&D output, publications. While strictly observing this limit, it produced valuable conclusions on one dimension of Finland's competitive performance in R&D within one field of competition, the OECD countries.

This analysis gave a favourable picture of the performance of Finland in producing publications with considerable professional impact, but this attempt evidently fell short of offering any kind of comprehensive competitive picture. The analytical perspective has to be made considerably wider, which makes it necessary to take a look at multidimensional assessments of R&D performance, leaving the straightjacket of one-country-oriented analysis, and pursuing methodologically more ambitious goals than just simply comparing different lists of statistical indicators.

2.6   SELECTING THE INDICATORS OF R&D COMPETITIVENESS

Synthetic Models of the Innovative Performance of Countries

In addition to statistical comparisons, there have been a number of encouraging attempts to create synthetic (that is both input- and output-related) models of national innovative performance. These attempts deserve our more in-depth attention for several reasons, in the first place owing to their sophisticated analytical structures. Second, and not independently from analytical sophistication, these models use a number of complicated indicators which call for a number of methodological questions.

The first important effort towards building such a model was undertaken by Porter and Stern (1999). They assessed, using a number of indicators partly appearing also on the NSF list, the innovation potential of 17 OECD countries between 1973 and 1993 in order to give a forecast of the annual number of patents granted to them (or more accurately to their citizens or firms) in the United States. This research was a few years later crowned by the creation of a comprehensive model of national innovation capacities (Furman, Porter and Stern, 2002), which will be referred to with respect to the methods of international R&D comparisons in this text.

The 1999 forecast by Porter and Stern was a very convincing and high-precision one, as pointed out by Faber and Hesen (2004, 193). These authors built upon Porter and Stern's work to a certain extent. Their complex model on national innovation systems as consisting of innovation capabilities and innovation-related performances under the influence of economic, institutional conditions and process variables seems to be the last word pronounced hitherto in comparative NIS research (Faber and Hesen, 2004).

It seems useful to pay more detailed attention to their model. We feel this is the model most in line with our approach based on combining input- and output-related factors of internationally comparable performances in the field of innovation. The parallels between their approach and ours (which is based on a combined use of input and output indicators of R&D in order to produce a synthetic ranking list of R&D competitiveness) have to be stressed in spite of a number of conceptual differences in theoretical backgrounds and techniques of measurement.

Faber and Hesen call their model the 'model of national innovation capabilities' (Faber and Hesen, 2004, 195). Their carefully constructed multi-tier model starts from the firm level, and looks into the input, process and output variables of innovation. The second level is that of input variables determining the innovation capabilities of a NIS. The next level includes a number of so-called contextual variables.

The focus of the authors is on the determinants of the innovation process. This is a focus definitely broader than ours which has a narrower and more clear-cut R&D orientation.

Both levels in the Faber–Hesen model include so-called input, process and output variables. These variables are markedly different from what we understand by the input- and output-related factors of R&D competitiveness.

Their input variables are related to innovation activities. On the firm level, these variables include privately funded R&D activities and total innovation expenditures. On the NIS level, input variables are related to economic, institutional and contextual conditions (there are no output variables on the NIS level). This approach seeks a causal relationship between a number of macro- and microeconomic factors on the one hand, and the innovation performance of the economy on the other.

Therefore the input side of the model does not contain only inputs as they are usually understood, but also a number of framework conditions which are important for a good growth performance but not necessarily for intense innovation activities. This approach reminds us of those models of competitiveness which are based on the assumption that an economy in a good general condition is also highly competitive. In this case as well, the existence of a strong causal relationship is likely but not certain.

Input variables linked to economic conditions are partly structural ones (the distribution of technology inputs, the size distribution of firms, and the innovation orientation among firms), and partly ones expressing market conditions (the size of the national economy, the level of economic prosperity, and the openness of the national economy).

Some of these variables are measured in ways that seem more or less problematic. For example the distribution of technology inputs is measured as the percentage of total industrial value added generated by high-tech and medium-tech industrial firms. This technique of measurement is based on the assumption that technology inputs are distributed in the economy corresponding to the relative share of technology-intensive production within total production. This overlapping of the two structures is however not ensured if there is fast structural change under way in the economy and technology inputs are moving into sectors in which the degree of technology intensity is increasing.

For example the pharmaceutical industry is a sector where R&D and very likely also technology intensity have been growing fast (see Scherer, 1996; Hara, 2003). However, statistics used in such measurements use data with delays up to ten years (the authors cited used statistical information from 1992 and 1996; Faber and Hesen, 2004, 202).

Another quite problematic variable here is the openness of the national economy which is measured by 'the excess of trade exposure'. Trade exposure is defined as

$$\text{Exports/GDP} + (1 - (\text{exports/GDP}))(\text{imports/production} + \text{imports} - \text{exports})$$

(Faber and Hesen, 2004, 202).

This concept of economic openness or exposure is quite logical but it suffers from a potentially serious statistical flaw. The problem is that indicators are compared (exports and GDP) which have different statistical dimensions and are therefore not comparable. GDP is calculated from the amounts of value added generated in the economy (so it is a net indicator). The value of exports shows much more than the exported part of GDP (it is therefore a gross indicator). It includes for example the value of imported inputs (for example the value of engineering exports does not change if less domestic iron and steel is used for the same amount of export-oriented machinery production).

The apparent openness (trade exposure) of the economy can also change if there is terms of trade improvement without any change in the part of GDP that was really exported. To sum up, exports as such are not part of GDP and therefore the export: GDP ratios could be comparable over time and/or in a cross-country approach only if the domestic value added of exports is constant as compared to GDP.

The input variables reflecting institutional conditions indicate: (1) the possibilities of financing innovation projects, (2) the fiscal climate in which firms have to operate, (3) the availability of personnel on the labour market, (4) public R&D spending, and (5) the level of entrepreneurship.

The possibilities of financing innovation projects are approximated in the model with the percentage of venture capital within GDP (as in the European Innovation Scoreboard). International comparisons are quite problematic in this respect, because the importance of venture capital among various sources of innovation financing varies greatly across countries (Karsai, 2002). To complicate the situation even more, international data on venture capital are quite unreliable, since they are collected with the help of enterprise question-naires and the response rates to these questionnaires as well as the techniques used for data collection vary largely across countries (Karsai, 2002).

Available data show important differences in venture capital-based invest-ments among industrial countries: for example, the relative share of venture capital investments within GDP was 2.9 per cent in Israel, 1.5 per cent in Iceland, but around 1 per cent in the United States, Sweden and the UK, and only 0.3 per cent in Finland in the year 2000 (EVCA, 1999–2001, quoted by Karsai, 2002).[34]

The fiscal climate of firms is measured by the percentage of company taxes in GDP. It seems obvious that less taxes means more money for financing innovations, supposing that other sources of financing innovations (such as venture capital) are equally open to firms operating in different countries. We have seen that this latter condition is far from being fulfilled. A further ques-tion here is whether company tax rates are a good approximation of the tax burden of firms. Not necessarily, because lower government revenues from lower corporate taxes might mean higher rates for other taxes (municipality, sales taxes or taxes related to employment) which could indirectly increase the cost burden of the corporate sector and constrain its innovation financing potential.

The average number of years of education of the labour force is a typical case of a quantitative indicator insensitive to qualitative factors.

A comprehensive critique of this indicator is given by Mulligan and Sala-i-Martin (1995). Their main points are: (1) It is assumed that workers belonging to a certain education category are perfect subtitutes for workers of all other categories; (2) It is assumed that productivity differentials among workers with different education levels are proportional to the duration of their schooling – that is someone with 16 years of education is 16 times more productive than another worker with only one year of education, independently from their wage rate differentials; (3) The indicator is calculated based on a constant elasticity of substitution among workers belonging to different educational categories in any possible case; (4) The use of this indicator supposes that one additional year of schooling provides the same amount of skill improvement also in any possible case. All these assumptions are far from reality. Thus they make this indicator an inaccurate proxy of the value of human capital or 'the availability of personnel on the labour market' as in the Faber and Hesen study.

The quality of a country's education system is a complex variable which does not offer itself easily for measurement. On the other hand, such data can be seriously biased if a country's education system is used as a shock absorber for unemployment (that is, additional low-cost education is offered instead of or complementing unemployment support).

Public R&D spending is obviously a good indicator of government financing of R&D, but it is not always complete. For example some countries or the European Union increase the public support for R&D using non-financial policy measures such as increased patent protection or the so-called block exemption system in European competition policy.[35] These incentives to R&D and innovation usually function as tools of leverage additional to governmental R&D spending, but there are no estimates available from the literature on the extent of potential public spending on R&D which might be replaced by such incentives. In any event, the size of public R&D spending is an inadequate indicator of total government support for R&D or innovation in most if not all industrial countries.

Entrepreneurship is measured in that percentage part of the labour force which is officially registered as entrepreneur. This indicator is one of the least convincing within the model, but the reasons of its relative unreliability lie outside of the scope of innovation analysis. The main problem is that the definition of entrepreneur or entrepreneurship is not an accurate one anywhere in the world. According to Wyatt, entrepreneurship is 'more a quality of individuals than of organisations' (Wyatt, 1986, 29). Is, for instance, the manager and minority shareholder of a large company an entrepreneur or not? It would seem more adequate to link entrepreneurship to firm size or firm age, although these indicators leave aside the measurement of individual entrepreneurial effort.

Entrepreneurial activity is more adequately measured by the 'total entrepreneurship indicator' (TEI) of the GEM (Global Entrepreneurship Monitor) Project of international entrepreneurship comparison (Acs, Szerb, Ulbert and Varga, 2002). The TEI is calculated as the sum of two ratios (the data are taken from a representative enterprise survey, but one respondent can be considered only for the calculation of one ratio from the two): the share of new enterprises under creation[36] in percentage of the active population (18–64 years), and the relative share of new firms within the active population. The respondent should be, in the latter case, member of the managenent of the firm considered new, he/she should be at least its partial owner, and the firm cannot be more than three years old.

The country values of the TEI ranged, for the year 2001, between 5 per cent for Belgium and 7 per cent for Germany, to 13 per cent in the United States, the Republic of Ireland and Hungary, to 21 per cent in New Zealand and Mexico with 29 countries surveyed altogether (Acs, Szerb, Ulbert and Varga, 2002, 9).

The TEI indicator has one weak point which it shares with the entrepreneurship index of the Faber-Hesen model, namely that it includes so-called 'forced entrepreneurship'. The GEM project made an additional effort to gauge the size of the problem which has come to the fore mainly in the transition economies and is also frequent in some parts of the Third World.

The problem of 'forced entrepreneurship' can be briefly described as follows, especially as regards the transition countries. Fast-growing budget deficits and political promises towards cutting government employment led to a considerable dwindling of the state sector and a surge of unemployment during the initial years of transition. These changes forced a considerable number of former employees of government agencies and government-owned firms to leave their jobs, whereas their expertise was still needed by the government. They were thus encouraged to create their own small businesses (mainly simple partnership-type ones) in order to be legally able to perform their former tasks, but in a different form, that is not as government employees. In fact this was nothing else than a special kind of 'subcontracting' strategy made not only possible, but necessary by the fact that employment-related government expenditure was severely monitored while the growth of administrative tasks could justify the increase of spending on subcontracting a number of administrative services.

This strategy became widespread also outside the government sector. College teachers created teaching firms to speak to the same student audiences as before, employees of ministries had to establish formal consulting firms in order to obtain contracts based on their former job descriptions (and sometimes even copied from them), and journalists became *pro forma* subcontractors of their journals.

In other cases in transition countries, forced entrepreneurship appeared due to high income taxes and social security payments to be deducted from wages and salaries. Many employees or workers created their own small businesses in order to minimize their tax burdens. Indirect evidence has been provided on this on Hungary by Major (2003), who showed the reasons why small and medium-sized enterprises (SMEs) in that country tend to perform poorly in the financial sense. One of the reasons is that many SMEs are not created based on a long-term strategic perspective of enterprise growth, but rather 'they long for financial enrichment' (Major, 2003, 111) in a short-term approach. We can add that financial enrichment can be also understood in this special case as an escape route from financial marginalization.

The GEM project estimates the size of 'forced entrepreneurship' to be below 1 per cent of the active population in Norway, the Netherlands and Denmark, while it seems to have reached 3 per cent in Hungary, 5 per cent in Poland and 7 per cent in Mexico and India (Acs, Szerb, Ulbert and Varga, 2002, 12). These are not really important orders of magnitude, but they show how difficult it is to estimate the level of entrepreneurship if the entrepreneurial factor of innovation has to be identified in the quantitative sense.

Process variables appear in the Faber–Hesen model only on the firm level. They also belong, in a larger sense, to the group of input variables and could be also called 'non-financial input variables on the firm level' or, in a broader sense, 'systemic variables' because they might be helpful for a synthetic quantitative description of the efficiency of a country's NIS.

The incorporation of such indicators into a complex model of the innovation process means important progress in innovation systems research. It is namely based on the experience that non-financial and systemic inputs (primarily different kinds of professional and managerial information) leading to efficiency improvement in R&D and innovation can partly substitute for the financing of innovation. While the idea of introducing process variables in the modelling of innovation systems and capabilities seems to be path-breaking, the technical realization of these variables still leaves a number of questions open.

The model uses three kinds of so-called process variables (Faber and Hesen, 2004, 201):

The sources of information available to firms are measured with the percentage of industrial firms contacting various sources of information. This is a quite soft variable depending very much on what is understood by 'contacting' (is Internet use for example identical with simply browsing on the Web?) and on what kinds of 'sources of information' are meant? The latter issue has a certain relationship to some methodological problems known from scientometrics: how can different types of sources of information be ranked according to their importance for their users (the scientific/innovation community), and what should be the line of separation between close substitutes (for instance, the Internet and the printed edition of the same journal if the two do not have strictly the same content)?

R&D cooperation between firms is a very important factor for increasing synergies in the innovation process, but it is not at all clear whether its measurement should be based on intents or on facts of cooperation. The model in question uses as a proxy the percentage share of innovative industrial firms within the totality of industrial firms participating in R&D cooperation. Here again, the simple number of firms involved in inter-firm R&D cooperation is a quite rough indicator which is disregarding the qualitative parameters of those cooperation agreements. For example firms carrying out joint R&D with others may get an equal weight in the model with such firms whose R&D cooperation agreements stipulate only a regular exchange of some R&D inputs or information.

Difficulties encountered by firms during innovation projects is again a very important strategic variable, but not exempt from measurement problems. The measure here is a survey-based one: the percentage of such industrial firms which have experienced innovation difficulties.

Our first critical question here would be again on the qualitative aspect of measurement: how are innovation difficulties classified and weighted? Apart from this remark, the 'difficulty' indicator is probably (economic) system specific, because its value can be expected to be much higher for Russia or Ukraine than for the United States or Switzerland. The problem is not this dimension of international comparison, but the degree to which this indicator could be sensitive enough to show tangible differences between countries with similar levels of economic and innovation system development.

The idea of process variables is, in spite of the current technical difficulties of its realization, very important for introducing NIS-related (or 'systemic') variables in the comparative analysis of capacities and performances in R&D. In addition to that, the efficiency of the national innovation system is also a key variable in measuring R&D competitiveness.

In our own research however, the measurement of these systemic variables has been completely omitted. Faber and Hesen used data for OECD countries only, which are usually available on a broad scale and well comparable within the OECD, while we worked with a country sample much broader than theirs. A further reason for this omission was that adequate survey results were not available for most of the transition countries we wanted to include in our international comparison.

Surveying the last group of variables used by Faber and Hesen, we come to a point where the closest similarity can be recognized between their approach and ours. This is the group of output variables which they again use only on the firm level. This limited use of the output variables can be understood if their innovation-focused approach is accepted, since some important outputs on the country level such as refereed publications or other scientometric data simply have no sense on the firm level. Some authors consider the output indicators of innovation to be stronger than the input ones because output indicators are related to innovations that have already taken place (Flor and Oltra, 2004, 325).

Output indicators as patent counts can be used on both the firm and the macroeconomic level. Finally, an important difference between the approaches is that Faber and Hesen measure national innovation capabilities (or, in our understanding, potential) combining firm-level and country-level variables, whereas we worked with country-level variables only.[37] Measuring national innovation capabilities is not the same thing as measuring competitiveness in R&D – in spite of the likely fact that country ranking lists would not be very different as a result of the two kinds of measurement.

Faber and Hesen used only two measures of output which partly coincide with the ones we have preferred (as has been repeatedly said, scientometric data are not perfectly suited for measuring capacities or performances in innovation because such data are strongly R&D oriented). Their two indicators in this field are sales of product innovations by firms, and patents granted.

Sales of product innovations by firms is expressed by the percentage share of 'new and substantially improved products' in the sales of industrial firms. A more accurate definition of products considered here would be welcome for a really in-depth evaluation of this indicator. This indicator is much akin to the macro-level indicator of the relative share of high-tech products within exports. Its major deficiency is also similar: the export pattern of firms exporting from a given country reflects this country's innovation potential only in proportion to the role of domestic innovations in developing that export structure. Both indicators are based on the assumption that a country's indicators of high-tech production or innovation output reflect that country's innovation potential fairly well. This would be true only if the country in question was self-sufficient in terms of innovation or technology development, and it did not produce high-tech goods based on innovations realized abroad.

Patents granted is a relative measure expressed by the ratio of the number of patents granted by the European Patent Office (EPO) to organizations or residents of a country, per GDP of that country at constant prices. This patent indicator takes country (or economy) size into account which is one possible approach to be used along with the one disregarding country size. It will be shown in Chapters 3 and 4 that the best option is the combined use of both approaches.

The source of patent registration is also important, because patent counts can be based on different sources which yield more or less different data. Global comparisons of R&D or patenting activities should probably be based rather on patent registrations in the United States (it is where patents by Latin American or Far Eastern applicants are more frequently registered).

Analyses with a more European or OECD focus should rather use EPO data, since most member countries of the OECD are in Europe. An indirect proof for this is offered by Guellec and Potterberghe (2001, 1259) who have shown that patents filed by European residents at the USPTO have a much more international character (that is are controlled by non-EU residents) than at the EPO, while the opposite is true for American, Canadian and Mexican residents.

We have opted for a third solution. In order to avoid the geographical bias resulting from the use of either American or European patent statistics, we used national statistics in creating our indicators based on patent counts. Also the number of domestic patents granted from the WIPO (World Intellectual Property Organisation) database was available for us for more countries than the patent counts from the USPTO or EPO database.

Considerations for Input and Output Measurement

Our survey of a string of indicators of innovation and R&D has shown that most indicators currently in use are more or less inaccurate for measuring inputs and outputs of R&D and the innovation process. These inaccuracies are, to a not negligible extent, due to the approximative character of a number of indicators, and also for the sometimes blurred line of separation between R&D and innovation.

For example a patent is not necessarily a result of R&D, and obtaining a patent is not the equivalent of successfully concluding the innovation process. Further inaccuracies result from the fact that many such quantitative indicators are used which neglect qualitative inhomogeneities within the groups compared.

Such inaccuracies abound both on the input and the output side. On the input side for example, aggregate indicators of education are used for assessing the quality of manpower employed in R&D or innovation, regardless of the differences in the value of one year spent in different kinds of educational establishments. On the output side, the national character of R&D (mainly if it is government-financed and academic) is often in a sharp contrast with the globalization of innovation within multinational companies. This contrast is expressed, among others, by the fact that the innovative performance of a country is only inadequately measured by the relative share of high-tech products in its manufacturing exports.

There are also indicators which can effectively help assess the R&D competitiveness of any country. These indicators also suffer from inadequacies, and some of them are not exactly R&D related. Still, they express well both the input and the output side of R&D, and their relatively wide availability makes it possible to use them for the largest possible country samples. We have made an effort to avoid their in-depth analysis in the previous part of this chapter, but references to them could not be completely skipped.

On the input side, we assess GERD and related indicators on the one hand, and indicators of employment in R&D on the other. Our output-side analysis will be devoted to three methodological approaches which also mean, in essence, three frequently used indicators. The focus of our attention will belong to scientometrics and the validity of scientometric indicators for the analysis of R&D competitiveness. Technological indicators of export structures will be also assessed, despite their major shortcomings already referred to. Finally, patent counts are also part of the output indicators we have decided to use.

The various outputs of R&D are produced for greatly different markets and are meant to satisfy different demands. The main outputs open for analysis include publications and such research results which have been officially declared as pieces of protected intellectual property (IP) and appear in patent statistics as such. Both ways of earning recognition for R&D results are only well suited for the accurate assessment of R&D performance, but their applicability in R&D competitiveness analysis deserves a couple of footnotes.

GERD (Gross Domestic Expenditure on Research and Development) and its Business Component

GERD is the most widely used indicator for international comparisons of R&D. In a strict sense, it indicates annual amounts of money spent on R&D in a given country. For international comparisons however, it is mostly used as the percentage share of GDP.[38]

The long-term behaviour of this indicator shows a quite remarkable consistency with the trends of national economic development for a wide range of countries. This is probably one of the key reasons for the popularity of the GERD in international comparisons of R&D. It is also frequently used as a benchmark for R&D policies or strategies as, for instance, in the Lisbon programme of the European Union. The Lisbon Strategy has set the GERD/GDP target of 3 per cent on the EU average for the year 2010 (see Rodrigues, 2003).

The GERD was already used as a benchmark for R&D policies in the 1960s (De Solla Price, 1963). De Solla Price described a major increase in American GERD from the early 1950s to the early 1960s, from 1.4 per cent to 3.5 per cent of the GDP (De Solla Price, 1979, 177) which was a level substantially higher than that observed in the late 1990s. In his view, GERD/GDP of 1 per cent should be the minimum value for smaller and less-developed countries (De Solla Price, 1979, 178). Data from the 1990s make it appear that this was a very optimistic way of seeing things, if not a kind of 'wishful thinking'.

Historical statistics of the GERD (see further UNESCO, 1998; NSB, 2002) make a few general trends of its development quite evident (see Table 2.5).

Table 2.5   GERD levels of selected OECD countries as a percentage of GDP

	1981	1985	1990	1993	1997	1998	1999	2000
Canada	1.24	1.44	1.54	1.71	1.71	1.71	1.66	1.94+
USA	2.37	2.78	2.65	2.52	2.57	2.60	2.64	2.71+
Japan	2.13	2.58	2.85	2.68	2.90	3.04	3.04	2.98
Austria	1.13	1.24	1.39	1.47	1.69	1.80	1.80	1.91+
Belgium	1.57	1.63	1.64	1.75	1.83	...	...	...
Denmark	1.06	1.21	1.57	1.74	1.94	1.92	2.00	...
Finland	1.17	1.55	1.88	2.17	2.72	2.89	3.19	3.37
France	1.93	2.22	2.37	2.40	2.22	2.18	2.17	2.20+
Italy	0.88	1.12	1.29	1.13	0.99	1.02	1.04	1.07
Netherlands	1.78	1.97	2.07	1.92	2.04	1.95	...	1.97
Norway	1.18	1.49	1.69	1.73	1.66	...	1.70	1.46+
Spain	0.41	0.53	0.81	0.88	0.82	0.90	0.89	0.97+
Sweden	2.21	2.78	2.84	3.27	3.67	...	3.80	...
Switzerland	2.18	2.82	2.83	2.66 (1992)	2.73 (1996)	...	...	2.64
United Kingdom	2.38	2.24	2.16	2.12	1.84	1.83	1.87	1.85
EU	1.69	1.87	1.98	1.88	1.80	1.81	1.85	1.88

Note: + data from 2001 in last column
Source: OECD (2001), Table A.2.1.1 (for 1981–99); NSB (2004), 4–51 (for 2000 and 2001).

First, the GERD has shown a long-term increase in most OECD countries, mainly from the early 1980s, but with a marked slowdown during the 1990s. One group of countries (latecomers to the OECD including Hungary, the Czech Republic, Poland and Slovakia) has been the only notable exception with a contrary trend: as was referred to in Chapter 1, their R&D sector lost much of its preferential treatment in the national economy during the transition process.

In Hungary for example, the GERD/GDP values of the mid-1980s (see OMFB, 1999) were between 2.5 and 3 per cent, thus similar to those of highly developed industrial nations. In sharp contrast to this, the country has been struggling to reach GERD/GDP levels of 1 per cent since 1993, but without much success (Biegelbauer, 2000; OECD, 2002, Table A.2.1.1; Török, 2002; OM, 2002). The primary reason in Hungary, as in other former socialist countries of Central and Eastern Europe, has been a much lower interest of governments in strategic issues (such as R&D) when a great number of imminent problems had to be solved in agriculture, systems of social welfare, the restructuring of industry or privatization. Another important reason for the fall in GERD/GDP levels has been the low values of BERD, that is a weak interest of domestic business in R&D after 1990. (OMFB, 1999b; Török, 2002)

The second internationally remarkable feature of GERD consists in its strong correlation with the levels of economic development. GERD/GDP data from the late 1990s and the early 2000s make it possible to create four groups of countries based on their respective GERD levels. These groups have shown a surprisingly high degree of stability from the early 1980s on. In general, GERD seems to be an R&D indicator in which major trend changes occur once in a decade for most countries.

The 'leaders' (GERD/GDP > 2 per cent)

These countries are, without exception, those which determine international trends and patterns in R&D. The United States stands out even within this group based on most of its R&D indicators, but not if GERD is considered. The highest GERD/GDP levels worldwide can be observed in two North European countries (Finland and Sweden), but this is not typical for Northern Europe as a whole. Finland has pursued a long-term strategy of R&D based economic growth (see Steinbock, 1998), while the case of Sweden is also special due to the strong role of the Gripen fighter programme in its national R&D strategy. Only one non-OECD country, Israel, belonged to this group with a 2.54 per cent GERD/GDP level already in 1997 (only civilian research, see NSB, 2002, 4–47). According to the latest data available (NSB, 2004, 4–51), the 3 per cent threshold of GERD/GDP has only been surpassed by Israel (the world leader in GERD with 4.43 per cent of GDP spent on non-military research in 2001), Finland, Sweden and Japan. The group of 'leaders' includes the most important industrial economies and Korea with the notable exceptions of Canada and Italy, and also certain industrialized countries from the Far East but outside the OECD such as Taiwan and Singapore (both slightly above the 2 per cent GERD/GDP level in 2000 or 2001; see NSB, 2004, 4–51). This group of countries is also the one where technology can be regarded as a strong endogenous factor of growth in the Romerian sense (see Romer, 1990).

The 'followers' (GERD/GDP > 1 per cent)

These industrial economies are much more present on the demand than the supply side of the market of R&D products. The example of Canada shows it that it is not necessary for a highly developed economy to have GERD/GDP levels above 2 per cent, although this and the Italian example rather belong to the exceptions. A number of examples from Italian industries (ceramics, tiles, leather, luxury goods) shows however that even low-tech sectors can be innovative without much R&D effort (Porter, 1990; Commissione (V) Bilancio, 2000).

Further members of this group are mostly OECD countries, some of which, similarly to Italy, are large exporters of services and/or popular tourism destinations (for example Austria, Norway, Ireland, Australia and New Zealand).

This group includes, furthermore, two advanced transition economies (the Czech Republic[39] and Slovenia). Russia (in certain fields still a 'trend-setter' in R&D) is on the boundary of this group with GERD/GDP rates oscillating around 1 per cent (1.16 per cent in 2001; NSB, 2004, 4–51).

The group of 'followers' is still relatively narrow, with an approximate number of countries roughly equal to the number of 'leaders'. The main common feature of the first and the second group is that these countries have R&D facilities able to set trends in certain fields of science and technology, but the 'leaders' are able to do so on a much wider scale. The existence of such 'trend-setters' is, then, mostly an exception in the third group.

The 'midfield' (GERD/GDP > 0.5 per cent)

Countries belonging here are still players on the international scene of R&D, but they are involved in the application rather than the creation of original R&D results. In fact the first three country groups in our scheme based on GERD indicators include those countries which are integrated in the modern world of high-tech and R&D. Most of their R&D centres and universities are in everyday communication and maintain a regular exchange of students and staff with the leading research centres of the world, and their R&D professionals are, to a larger or a lesser extent, known internationally. The 'midfield' countries are however much more on the 'downstream' than the 'upstream' side of the international flows of R&D information (this means they use new R&D results more often than they create them). Their presence cannot be denied in international R&D, but their influence on its trends is quite limited.

This group of countries is quite large and very heterogeneous. It includes several less-developed OECD countries (mainly in the Mediterranean area including Spain, Portugal and Greece), some of the more performing and advanced transition economies (for example Hungary, Slovakia and Poland),[40] and a number of Third World countries with a fast progress in R&D spending and performance such as China, Brazil, Chile and South Africa (NSB, 2002, 4–47; NSB, 2004, 4–51).

The 'marginals' (GERD/GDP > 0.2 per cent)

These are countries with R&D sectors still worth speaking of, but without any remarkable presence in worldwide R&D cooperation and competition. Some of them have a few internationally competitive R&D centres, but the sector itself has only a marginal importance in their national economy. The fact that many of these countries have competitive manufacturing sectors and some of them are large importers of foreign direct investment (FDI) shows that they are not excluded from modernization. Their technological modernization is however based primarily on knowledge generated abroad, and technology is very likely not an endogenous factor of their economic growth at all. This group of countries includes for example Mexico, Turkey, Argentina, Colombia, Morocco, Egypt, Uruguay, Panama and Malaysia (NSB, 2002, 4–47; NSB, 2004, 4–51).

The remaining countries are at least 100 in number, and they are basically not present in the world's R&D (see our former reference to Sachs, 2000). The 0.2 per cent GERD/GDP threshold is, of course, indicative. It might thus be the case, at least in a theoretical sense, that minimal GERD is used in a very efficient manner, making a low-GERD country's R&D effort a competitive one. Our experience from other data speaks however of a complete lack of such exceptional country cases.

It has to be noted at this point that our sources do not include data on military research. This is the likely reason why nuclear power Pakistan is missing from our above analysis. North Korea is also a nuclear power with some important R&D facilities, but that country has a justified reputation of not supplying any data for international statistical purposes.

Some of the countries not belonging to groups 1 to 4 have (statistically) very low levels of GERD (as El Salvador or Nicaragua), and many others, none at all. This makes no real difference between these countries because they are completely missing from international statistics of R&D output. Therefore these countries cannot figure on the international map of R&D competitiveness.

As we have seen, GERD levels make a fairly clear classification of the actors of the international R&D scene possible. The number of influential players is in the range of 30. Another group of roughly similar size includes those participants of the game who still have a word or two to say in international R&D competition. The rest (40–50 countries) still maintain an R&D sector of some importance, but their influence on international trends in this sector is negligible even in an optimistic approach.

The interpretation of GERD/GDP levels may create some confusion with respect to the sources of R&D spending. The rapid decrease of the GERD/GDP levels of the transition economies around 1990 was often attributed to the partial withdrawal of their respective governments from the financing of R&D (see Biegelbauer, 2000; OMFB, 1999b; Müller, 2001, 198–9; Tamási, 2001, 215; Kukliński, 2001, 229; Zajac, 2001, 249.). This is however only one side of the coin, and an at least equally important factor of the decline of GERD/GDP in the transition economies consists in the reluctance of the corporate sector regarding the financing of domestic R&D.

An important and often key component of GERD is BERD (business expenditure on research and development). Privately financed research is often regarded as a substitute to publicly funded research, but a comprehensive survey of publications on the relationship between public and private R&D has shown that there is no widely acceptable evidence on either the substitutive or the complementary character of this relationship (David et al., 2000).

It is more likely that the more developed an economy (and a NIS) is, the better incentives public R&D funding can provide for private R&D in that country (see Furman, Porter and Stern, 2002). Therefore it can be supposed, in general, that government spending on R&D is a partial substitute of business spending on R&D in less-developed economies due to the general lack of business interest in domestic R&D. At the same time, public R&D spending offers clear and positive incentives for private R&D (by partly also justifying it) in more advanced countries and it is thus supporting the increase of the BERD.

There are however major differences regarding the incentives provided by public spending on R&D on the sectoral level between the world's leading technological powers. As Giesecke has shown, the role of American government spending on R&D in biotechnology has been rather positive in providing the right incentives, whereas the German government was less successful in this respect (Giesecke, 2000).

The ratio of BERD to GERD shows a remarkably consistent pattern across countries with regard to their level of economic development, and also to their respective GERD levels (see Table 2.6).

It can be observed even from our limited sample that higher GERD levels usually mean proportionally higher BERD values. The rate of BERD to GERD is, in the group of the 'leader' countries, around two-thirds, and it tends towards one half in the 'followers'. It is down to about a third in most 'midfield' countries, and may be even lower in those 'marginals' where business shows practically no interest in domestic R&D.

Table 2.6 shows only a few exceptions to this rule. Out of the 21 countries observed, only four have shown patterns different from the one expected. France has an unusually low BERD rate for a 'leader' which could be partly explained by the French government's open political ambition to keep the country's status as a world power; hence a high degree of government financing of R&D spending. Spain behaves less as a 'midfielder' than as a 'follower', but that country's GERD/GDP levels have been approaching the 1 per cent threshold in recent years. Moreover Spain also stands out with respect to its level of economic development as compared to the other 'midfielders'.

Turkey is a similar case in the group of the 'marginals': its GERD/GDP data have fallen short of the threshold of 0.5 per cent only to a minimal extent, and the Turkish economy has reached a level of development (measured in per capita GDP on a purchasing power parity basis) equal to that of Lithuania and Latvia, new member countries of the EU (Brandsma et al., 2002, 12).

Finally, Czech BERD data are unusually high for a 'midfielder'. This can be explained by the relatively low speed of Czech privatization (see Brandsma

Table 2.6   The BERD/GERD ratio in selected OECD countries and years

Countries	1991	1995	1999	2001
'Leaders'				
USA	0.57	0.60	0.67	0.68
Sweden	0.62	0.66	0.68	0.68
Japan	0.76	0.72	0.72	0.72
Korea				0.72
Finland	0.56	0.59	0.67	0.70
France	0.43	0.48	0.54	0.54
Germany	0.62	0.61	0.64	0.67
'Followers'				
Austria	0.50	0.46	0.39	0.40
Denmark	0.51	0.45	. . .	0.58
Norway	0.44	0.50	0.51	0.50
Netherlands	0.38	0.46	. . .	0.50
United Kingdom	0.50	0.48	0.49	0.49
Italy	0.45	0.42	0.44	. . .
Canada	0.38	0.45	0.45	0.42
'Midfielders'				
Czech Republic	. . .	0.63	0.53	0.51
Greece	0.23	0.24	. . .	0.24
Poland	. . .	0.36	0.39	0.33
Portugal	0.24	0.19	0.21	0.21
Spain	0.49	0.44	0.49	0.50
Hungary	0.56	0.38	0.38	0.38
'Marginals'				
Mexico	. . .	0.16	0.23	0.24
Turkey	0.28	0.34	. . .	0.42

Source: own calculations from OECD (2001, 2002). Data for Italy in 2001 were not available from NSB (2004), 4–52, either.

et al., 2002, 28–9). If an economy still has a high share of state-owned firms, BERD comes from the state sector to a large extent and it is therefore not the result of really independent business decisions. This is probably also the reason why internationally comparable BERD data are not available for the former socialist member countries of the OECD for the years prior to 1995.[41]

Our analysis of the GERD and one of its main components, BERD, could probably give a quite comprehensive picture of the size of financial inputs to the R&D sectors of a number of important countries in the world economy.

The survey of these two indicators may have also helped to obtain a first impression of international competition in R&D due to the fact that GERD levels, and especially the interest of business in R&D expressed by the BERD, are primary factors of competitiveness in R&D.

This first look at the international map of R&D competitiveness of course makes only general remarks possible, such as for instance the key role of the 'leaders' in international R&D – but this can be considered common knowledge not necessitating any in-depth research. We have been able to observe however that:

- business spending on R&D is a key factor in reaching high GERD levels,
- GERD generally increases with the level of economic development, and
- the BERD/GERD ratio tends to increase if GERD/GDP increases.

GERD and BERD show the level of financial inputs to R&D which corresponds to the capital intensity measures used in HOS-type models of comparative advantages. Neoclassical comparative advantages analysis also uses labour intensity measures which play a key role in the input-side assessments of competitiveness. Our critical survey of former international comparisons of innovation has shown that the reliability of most measures of human resources of innovation and R&D is limited.

Employment in R&D

Neoclassical trade theory makes a marked distinction between measuring factor endowments and factor intensities, and this distinction is necessary for calculating comparative advantages for different branches of industry. Regarding R&D however, this distinction can be avoided if it is supposed intuitively (but based on much empirical evidence completing the theoretical arguments) that R&D is a labour-intensive, more accurately a skilled labour-intensive, activity (see Simon, 1999; Furman, Porter and Stern, 2002).

If the high skill intensity of R&D is accepted as a fact, then measures of employment in R&D can be used as measures of factor (skill) endowment. Higher levels of employment in R&D would then mean better factor endowments and also better conditions for competitiveness improvement in this respect.

International comparisons of R&D employment as such are less widespread than comparisons of GERD, because their statistical background is less accurate and national data on R&D employment may have diverse contents. Moreover R&D employment seems to correlate quite strongly with GERD in the most industrial economies, while its behaviour is more haphazard in less-developed countries.

The usual indicator of R&D employment is the number of researchers per 10 000 labour force, because researchers are considered the central element of the R&D personnel (OECD, 2001). The definition of researchers is somewhat imprecise because it refers to such professionals who are engaged in creating new knowledge, products, processes, methods and systems (Frascati Manual, 2002). It is also a requirement that a researcher should be directly involved in the management of projects (OECD, 2001, A.9.2). R&D personnel is always calculated on an FTE (full time equivalent) basis in order to ensure the correct statistical coverage of part-time employment.

It is a daunting task to establish precisely whose involvement in R&D projects has a direct character, and the statistical delineation of researchers varies greatly across countries. In advanced industrial countries however there seems to be no great diversity in interpreting the content of this term. It is more of a problem elsewhere, especially in countries where there is a lack of reliable national R&D statistics or the boundaries of the national R&D system cannot be sufficiently identified.

Such countries often use the number of university graduates as a proxy of R&D employment. This is of course a rough indicator not useable in international comparisons of R&D, but it is applied in some countries based on the assumption that the percentage share of R&D personnel within the total workforce changes in parallel with the change in the number of university graduates.

A brief survey of R&D employment in the OECD measured by the number of researchers per 10 000 labour force shows a picture quite similar to what has been seen with regard to GERD. Based on this experience, it can be considered likely that countries with lower GERD/GDP levels (basically those under 0.5 per cent) also have marginally small numbers of researchers. Sporadically available comparable data from Third World countries confirm this assumption (UNESCO, 1998), very likely because a substantial part of GERD is necessarily spent on personnel.

The structure of great geographical aggregates in R&D employment within the OECD is quite similar to the geographical breakdown of GERD. Both the European Union and Japan have a relative share of the OECD's total R&D employment equal to their share in the total GERD of the OECD. The American shares in R&D employment and in GERD are markedly different from each other due to methodological problems in delineating military R&D with respect to spending and human resources.

Comparably to the international comparisons of GERD levels, the OECD countries can also be put in quite homogenous categories with respect to their indicators of R&D employment. The group of 'leaders' consists of countries with more than 60 researchers per 10 000 labour force. Japan, Finland, the United States and Sweden belong in this group along with Norway and Australia (the latter two only 'followers' in terms of GERD/GDP).

The 'followers' as regards R&D employment to a large extent overlap with the parallel group of countries in the GERD/GDP ranking list. This means all the other advanced industrial economies of the OECD including for example Germany, France, the UK, Canada, the Netherlands and Austria. Their R&D employment indicator is above 30 in each case.

The 'midfield' (between 30 and 10) here is less densely populated. The only surprise here is Italy, other members of the group being the other Mediterranean EU countries plus the former socialist countries from Central and Eastern Europe. The poor condition of some of the R&D sectors of these countries is indicated by the fact that the density of researchers is close to 10 in Hungary, Poland and the Slovak Republic.

In fact, analyses of recent developments in their R&D sectors (see Biegelbauer, 2000; OMFB, 1999b; Müller, 2001; Tamási, 2001; Kukliński, 2001; Zajac, 2001) also speak of kind of an exodus from R&D in these countries after 1990. Biegelbauer's data illustrate this sometimes shocking trend for a number of transition economies for the first years of the transition process (1991 to 1994): the loss of R&D manpower was in the range of 54 per cent for the Czech Republic, 25 per cent in Hungary, 19 per cent in Slovakia and 17 per cent in Slovenia (Biegelbauer, 2000, 161).[42]

The reasons for the exodus, dramatically affecting the R&D sectors of several transition economies, have been multiple. poor financial conditions of research (including both salaries and financial means of obtaining instruments, materials and literature), modest domestic career perspectives, and also attractive scholarship and promotion possibilities abroad. The exodus from R&D had, in contrast to the development in China, a partly domestic character in the transition economies of Europe where business was able to attract skilled people from the academic world on a large scale, but only to a modest extent to R&D jobs.[43]

In any event, data on researchers reflect trends parallel with trends of the GERD in most OECD countries. The relative number of researchers is used less in international comparisons than GERD/GDP because numbers of R&D personnel do not tell us anything about the quality and the productivity of that personnel. This is along with GERD/GDP, still the best and the most widely used indicator of R&D input, and also of R&D competitiveness in the input-side approach.

Both GERD/GDP and the relative number of researchers (and, due to the inflexibility of labour markets in many industrial countries, especially the latter) have an additional advantage for R&D analysts. These indicators show a relative stability in time which, to some extent, offsets the problems caused by the frequent lack of recent international R&D data. This lack is regularly observed for many OECD countries, and it is typical for most other countries of the world.

Imports of Measurement Equipment

This input to R&D has not been given much attention by literature thus far. Its use in our measurement of R&D competitiveness is based on the assumption that higher inputs of measurement equipment as one important technological factor of R&D may mean higher competitiveness. In addition to that, the international statistical coverage of this input of R&D is one of the widest among the indicators we have used.

This is of course a quite *ceteris paribus* type of assumption because a significant number of countries are likely to manufacture domestically most of the measurement equipment used by their R&D sector. The import of measurement equipment has to be treated with care also because from the aggregate country statistics we do not know (and cannot even estimate) the portion that is actually used by the R&D sector of a country. Opposed to this argument – and based on our experience with trade statistics – it has to be noted that most measurement instruments are built by very specialised manufacturers and even researchers from highly developed countries could possibly need a quite large amount of imported measurement equipment.

Publications: an Assessment of Scientometrics

While the measurement of GERD and R&D employment as main elements of R&D inputs seems to be a routine statistical exercise, measuring the most important output-side indicators of R&D has almost become a field of science in its own right. This is especially true for scientometrics[44], the technology for assessing the number and comparative value of publications produced by the R&D sectors of countries. Scientometrics is the quantitative analysis of scientific production, productivity and efficiency, and it is based on indicators of publications and citations.

Scientometrics can cover and register only such R&D results which (1) have been submitted for publication; (2) have been recommended by their referees, and (3) have been accepted by a prestigious professional journal. The fulfilment of each and all of these three conditions does not depend on the quality of the result only. This is why results of scientometric analysis are proxies of scientific production to some extent.

Firstly, any researcher able to publish his or her results would not necessarily decide to do so if incentives for publication (in the first place academic career and promotion) were weaker than incentives for withholding the result from publication. These latter incentives can be linked for example to efforts to keep the result secret from competitors, or to concerns about finding an appropriate channel for publication in the case of an absolutely new result. Publishing an R&D result may pre-empt its becoming the starting point for a successful innovation. This is the case for example when a company researcher is not allowed by his firm to publish his or her results, because the firm wants to avoid any leakage of information that could influence the success of an innovation process under way.

Secondly, the refereeing process of scientific articles is impartial in the vast majority of cases, but journals relying too strongly on referee reports in their editorial policy may run the risk that, on a final account, the profile of the journal is marked by the referees almost as strongly as by the editors and the authors. It is well known among researchers that the appropriate choice of a journal may well improve the chances of publishing an article. The reason is that one author's knowledge of the editorial policy and the thematic preferences of journals in his or her field may make that author's choice of a journal close to optimal from his or her point of view, while another author less prepared in this respect could fail to take such a good decision with negative consequences for the future of his or her article.

> Some recent publications (Coupé, 2003; Simonovits, 2004) evoke the possibility that the playing field could be somewhat tilted instead of being completely level as supposed by many. They are very keen on avoiding any definitive conclusion of this kind, and only mention a few statistical facts on apparently biased editorial policies of some leading academic journals in economics. The most interesting case is that of two highly quoted professional journals each of them published by one prestigious American university. The professional views expressed by leading exponents of these universities are sometimes contradicting each other. Interestingly, the analysis of the institutional affiliations of the authors of articles accepted by the two journals for publication shows a biased structure: the probability that an author can publish an article the journal edited by in his/her university is significantly higher than their chances of publication in the journal of the other university. (Simonovits, 2004)

Thirdly, access to internationally recognised journals is not guaranteed for scientists unfamiliar with the techniques of submitting competitive publications, unable to write appropriately in English, and/or lacking even the modest financial resources sometimes needed for submitting a publication in journals with high impact factors.

In spite of the elements of uncertainty listed above, scientometrics are generally recognized as a reliable toolkit for the analysis of publication performances. We first give a short overview of the present stand of the field and try to offer a comprehensive picture of international competition in the 'market' of publications. Following this, an overview of a recent *Methodenstreit* and its assessment is provided.

The term 'scientometrics' has its origins in Russia – Nalymov and Mulchenko (1980) explain the genesis of this term by considering science as a process of information, and the original idea underlying their book was to develop an information-based model of the development of science (Nalymov and Mulchenko, 1980, 19). Their book (originally published in Russian in 1969) dealt, along with several fundamental problems of scientometrics, with a number of political issues with a surprising amount of intellectual courage given the political circumstances then prevailing in the Soviet Union. For example they mentioned the lack of regular exchanges with foreign researchers as one of the primary reasons for the low number of citations of Soviet articles in international scientific literature (Nalymov and Mulchenko, 1980, 233).

A few pieces of early scientometrics-related analysis are known from literature (for example Lotka, 1926), but the term and the field of science itself gained worldwide recognition only after the second edition of the classical work of De Solla Price on the history of science (De Solla Price, 1961, 2nd edition 1975) was published. His second major book (De Solla Price, 1963) can be regarded as a path-breaking work for modern R&D policy analysis. The Russian scientists defined scientometrics as quantitative methods which deal with the analysis of science understood as generating and processing information (Nalymov and Mulchenko, 1980). This conceptual approach is still enjoying widespread acceptance 35 years later, but the term 'scientometrics' has lost its monopoly position. On the other hand, new attempts at defining scientometrics are more careful about using the terms 'science' and 'R&D' in a really accurate way.

Pritchard (1969) also introduced the term 'bibliometrics' in the late 1960s with the underlying idea that the statistical analysis of bibliography data can yield interesting insights into the production of scientific results. Still, the bibliography-based approach has a somewhat limited character because it focuses on information generated by R&D as opposed to scientometrics, which is interested more widely in the measurement of scientific production.

Scientometric analyses can be carried out in structural, dynamic and evaluational dimensions (Braun et al., 2003, 1183). The first and the third dimension carry only a limited interest for international R&D competitiveness analysis. Structural scientometrics deals with the analysis of structures in R&D teams or communities, in sets of scientific products, or with conceptual issues with relevance for wider fields of science.

Dynamic scientometrics is based on the quantitative analysis of the behaviour in time or in space of a number of elements or products of R&D. Such analyses may cover dynamic processes implying authors, publications or even citations.

Evaluational scientometrics has a narrower scope, since it is interested in the players constituting the R&D community, such as countries, regions, institutions, journals, research teams and individuals. This is the field of scientometrics which tries to dig deeper than the other two in attempting to identify the factors of R&D performance.

Evaluational scientometrics is also pioneering methodological (or technical) development in a number of fields of scientometrics. It has three levels of investigation, similarly to what we have outlined regarding the levels of relevance of R&D competitiveness analysis:

- the macro level (countries, but also the wide fields of research belong here);
- the middle, 'mezzo' or interface level including institutions and journals, that is the levels which play a role of transmission between society or science in a large sense and the individual researcher;
- the micro level is that of the basic building blocks of the R&D system, the micro level consists of small research units or teams and the individual researcher.

The application of the analytical tools of scientometrics has a very important ethical requirement (Schubert, 2003). Scientometrics has to be used as 'antidiagnostics': that is it should not help to identify negative or unhealthy phenomena in scientific production (this would be diagnostics), but should rather be used to point out positive developments.

This requirement is based on the recognition of the fact that scientific merits based on scientometric data doubtlessly exist, but the lack of scientometric information on an individual, or a team or even a country does not necessarily mean the lack of valuable scientific production in that case. In other words, scientometrics is applied with the underlying assumption that it is not and cannot be the exclusive method of measuring scientific production.

A recent publication in *Scientometrics*, the leading journal in the field, gives an in-depth assessment of the scientific production of the world's 32 countries most productive in science (Glänzel et al., 2002). Data series covered the time period 1990 through 1998 for the articles published, while citations were registered for an article during the year of publication and the two subsequent years.

The data used for the article by Glänzel et al. were taken from the Philadelphia Institute for Scientific Information (ISI) Science Citation Index (SCI) database. This database was recently replaced by the Web of Science / Science Citation Index Expanded Database, which makes scientometric comparisons difficult for time series expanding beyond 1998.

Articles were attributed to countries according to information on the institutional affiliation of the authors displayed in the running head of each article. Co-authored articles were registered as one article for each co-author.

All these rules of scientometric analysis are in full conformity with the standards generally accepted in the profession. We shall see shortly however, that these standards are being questioned. If this *Methodenstreit* is concluded in favour of the challengers of the existing rules of the game, the messages of comparative analyses of innovative performance and R&D competitiveness would necessarily change to some extent.

Three cumulative international ranking lists were elaborated for the years 1990 to 1998 by Schubert (Schubert, 2003), based on the methodological toolkit presented in (Glänzel et al., 2002). The first list is about the total number of publications by country. The second list indicates the average impact of publications from a country indicated by the ratio of citations per publication – this is the indicator with the most qualitative character of the three. Glänzel et al. used a third indicator called RCR (relative citation rate), which is obtained from dividing MOCR (mean observed citation rate)[45] with MECR (mean expected citation rate)[46] (Glänzel et al., 2002). This indicator measures whether the publications of a country or institution attract more or less citations than expected on the basis of the impact measures, that is the average citation rates of the journals in which they appeared. Since the citation rates of the papers are gauged against the standards set by the specific journals, RCR is largely insensitive to the big differences between the citation practices of the different science fields and subfields. It should be stressed that in this study, a three-year citation window to one source year is used for the calculation of both the numerator and denominator of RCR (Glänzel et al., 2003a).

The three lists are reproduced in Appendix A in Tables A.1 to A.3. The first list shows the supremacy of the great powers in international R&D, with the United States, the United Kingdom and Japan in the first three positions (two of them English-speaking countries). The top of the second list is almost identical, with the Netherlands taking the place of Japan as Number 3. The third list however is markedly different with countries arriving on top of the list which excel in the quality rather than in the quantity of scientific output. Switzerland appears as the best performer here, the United States comes twelfth and the Netherlands sixth.

This third list confirms, on the one hand, that R&D in the United States plays a decisive role in world science from both a quantitative and a qualitative viewpoint, in spite of the fact that this is only one aspect of measuring R&D output. On the other hand, it creates a correct impression of the competitive advantages of other economic powers in the mass production of science (mass production meaning in this sense that certain minimum but still quite rigorous quality standards are observed in any event), and of the competitive advantages of small, open and highly developed economies if the quality of the best pieces published also matters in the assessment of a country's scientific production.

These conclusions of course still have a preliminary character because they assess outputs without regard to inputs. They show however that the application of scientometrics can lead to surprisingly diverse conclusions if the differences between its main methods are not adequately clarified.

A quick comparison of the three indicators most often used in scientometrics offers some insight into a couple of methodological problems of the measurement of scientific output and also R&D competitiveness. The total number of publications per country is a typical absolute indicator in which neither country size nor the quality of publications matters. It would be interesting to examine if there is any correlation between the absolute number of publications originating from a country and the number of referenced journals published in that country.

The existence of an asymmetric information situation can be assumed here: authors from countries with a higher level of concentration of editorial offices in their universities would be potentially better informed on the journals' requirements (and, not to be too sarcastic, of the tastes of the possible referees) than authors from countries where such information is not similarly detailed and available.

Furthermore language could also be a factor of competitive advantage because English has almost become the sole language of international science (other languages as German or French play a certain role only in special fields of science such as history, history of art, international law or archeology, but all these fields belong to the realm of the social sciences), and authors from English-speaking countries obviously have less difficulty in preparing publications meeting the standards for submission.

The total number of citations per country would be also an absolute indicator without any reference to the inputs used for producing the publications and the amount of publications generating the given number of citations. This indicator was used only as an input in the international comparisons by Glänzel et al. (2002), but neither they nor Schubert (2003) produced separate ranking lists based on them. Such macro-level citation indicators may have shortcomings which may influence the reliability of measures developed on their basis.

The number of citations divided by the number of publications is a special kind of productivity indicator if publications (usually considered as outputs of R&D) are considered the 'inputs' of citations,[47] and citations themselves are the 'outputs'. This indicator shows the international impact of publications produced by the R&D sector of a given country. The side effects which are created by the different citation patterns of scientific fields, adverse citations, cyclical citation of collaborative groups, large number of co-authors, and international collaborations are averaged out in cross-country comparisons of scientometric indicators.

Country performances indicated by this ratio can still be much influenced by the structures by fields of science of the R&D sectors of countries. As calculations by Schubert (2003) have shown, countries with very active R&D in biology or medical sciences can expect better positions in cumulative lists since the total number of referenced international publications is four to five times higher there each year than in physics or engineering sciences.

An interesting conclusion from the ranking lists based on citations per publication and the RCR is that very small or, from the point of view of international R&D, not too relevant countries such as Iceland (general and internal medicine), Vietnam (organic and supraorganic biology), Senegambia (medical biology, non-internal medicine), Uruguay (general biology and genetics), Azerbaijan (agricultural and environmental sciences), Romania (neuroscience and behavioural sciences), Costa Rica (engineering sciences), Tanzania (physics) or Moldova (mathematics) can arrive at very high or even top positions.

This is obviously not due to their 'mass production' of high-quality R&D results, but rather to the fact that their limited number of publications included one piece or perhaps two containing highly relevant scientific information. From the 12 fields of science surveyed in Glänzel et al. (2002), most other RCR-based ranking lists show Switzerland in the top position. This is also a small country, but obviously a decisive player in several quality-sensitive segments of world R&D.

The scientometric comparison of R&D outputs[48] gives a many-faceted picture of one important aspect of international competitiveness in R&D, namely that part of scientific output which has been made a public good by those who produced it and also by those who own it. From all the scientometric indicators surveyed, first of all publication counts will have to be included in our quantitative analysis, because citations-based indicators suffer from a number of shortcomings.

For example it would probably lead to enormous technical difficulties to try to register citations obtained by a given publication for post-publication time spans significantly longer than two or three years. Even so, most really seminal contributions to science can be identified as such only if they are still cited more than 50 years after they were published. Mathematics is a science where important findings are regularly cited even decades after their publication (Csörgő et al., 2003).

Most results in economics are quoted only for a few years after their publication, except for path-breaking, fundamental theoretical results. Yet, publications of lasting scientific influence (to name just a few, and even without evident references to Adam Smith and David Ricardo) include Cournot (1838), Fisher (1925) and Coase (1937), all of which have obtained a significant number of citations still many decades after their publication (and Coase received the Nobel Prize more than 50 years thereafter).

The currently used 'mainstream'-type methods of counting publications give a quite reliable picture of the international production of science, but the important question marks in this regard cannot be neglected either.

The usual tools of scientometric analysis have different levels of relevance for the various fields of science. This is why they should be used only with a great degree of caution for comparing performances or aggregating them across scientific fields. Such comparisons are made difficult for example by the fact that the occurrence of co-authored articles is different across fields of science.

There seems to be a tendency toward the increase of the percentage share of co-authored articles in overall scientific production (see Papp, 2004). This is also proven for articles in economics by Coupé (2004) who demonstrates that the percentage of co-authored articles increased from 18 per cent in 1970 to 47 per cent by the year 2000 in a fixed sample of 88 journals. He cites a similar development in biology based on Laband and Tollison (2000).

The *raison d'être* of the strategy of increasing the number of co-authored articles is provided by the principle widely used in current scientometrics and also applied by Glänzel et al. (2002): co-authored articles count as one article by each co-author. As was referred to earlier, the principle of mutual favours might well work in increasing the number of citations obtained.

The well-known dilemma of how co-authored articles could be correctly registered for scientometric measurement cannot be simply overcome by considering an article as one single piece of publication. Co-authors of such a publication would get their respective percentage shares from the scientific merit attributed to that article. The problem has multiple aspects. Alas, there are also reasonable arguments in the defence of the principle 'one co-author = one publication'.

First, contributions of authors working in real-life teams cannot necessarily be expressed in quantitative terms if their research effort was a joint and indivisible one.

Second, even a contribution unimportant in quantitative terms (for example a simple idea towards taking a new path of research) can have a disproportionally large influence on the success of an article.

Third, the otherwise not completely ethical principle of 'one co-author = one publication' may also protect the interests of those co-authors whose low bargaining power could not be adequately offset by their proportionally large research effort towards producing a successful article. Such 'weak' co-authors could be also omitted from publication teams if the number of authors were strictly limited.

Fourth, sophisticated specialization patterns within research teams in fields of science such as chemistry or biology make co-authored articles not only necessary but also inevitable. In such specialized teams however, the measurement of the individual research efforts and contributions can pose a real difficulty if these efforts were made in completely different fields (for example IT, diagnostics and theoretical medicine) without any common benchmark of performance and measurement.

Most scientometric analyses, including the benchmark publication in the field (NSB, 2002 and 2004) stick to the principle 'one co-author = one publication'. This could be explained, besides the arguments we have listed above in favour of this principle, by some kind of inertia: former time series of scientometric data would become practically useless, and the value of some scientific careers could even become questionable *ex post* if this principle was given up. But it is also evident that the unlimited application of this principle cannot prevent the mushrooming of multi-author publications with all the distortions in judging the real value of scientific performances that this mushrooming could entail.

Compromise could be sought in such a way that the principle 'one co-author = one publication' would remain in use for publications with a number of authors not exceeding a normal number for a small team, say three or four. Above that threshold, preferably up to the limit of ten authors, each co-author would be entitled to count his contribution as a '50 per cent publication'. Between the author numbers 11 and 20 each co-author would be considered a '25 per cent author', and above 20 the virtual percentage share of each co-author would remain at the level of 10 per cent.

All these limits and percentage shares would apply, of course, only in such cases where no member of the research team makes public his or her real contribution to the publication also in percentage terms. If, however, one or more such declarations accompany the article submitted, all the virtual percentage shares listed above should be adjusted accordingly for the remaining members of the team.

The last methodological difficulty which makes the use of citations as a tool of measuring scientific performance somewhat problematic is the large diversity in the frequency of citations across different fields of science. One can recognize the relevance of the term 'entry barriers' borrowed from Industrial Organization theory, and we consider it apt for the description of the following problem.

Two kinds of entry barriers can be considered. The first is the science-specific character of most journals publishing articles from a given field of science: a journal of medicine would be quite open to articles produced by biologists, less so to articles from chemistry, and probably not open at all to articles from geology or architecture.

This is analogous to the problem of 'limited substitution' known from Industrial Organization theory. The chances of market access are higher for those 'products' (in this case articles) whose market niches are larger and which are less threatened by the entry of substitutes to their respective market niches. Therefore those researchers have a greater chance of having a high count of refereed publications in referenced journals who work in fields with relatively great numbers of journals and whose fields are not very open to entry of authors from other fields of science.

The second entry barrier is specific language or notation. Those fields of science are more open to entry from outside which use less specific language and which do not have too narrowly defined notation requirements. The development of such special tools of communication within a given field of science may facilitate the flow of ideas between the representatives of that field but can also act as an entry barrier to competition from outside.

The fact that entry barriers are erected in science was observed by De Solla Price (1979, 111). He noted that publications are increasingly aimed at narrow, specialized professional audiences, and only the inertia of tradition means that wider readerships are sometimes also targeted.

One possible solution to the problem of entry barriers between different fields of science is the emergence of interdisciplinary journals (as for example the *Journal of Law and Economics* in social sciences). It remains to be seen whether articles published in such journals can earn a degree of reputation for their authors similar to articles published in flagship or general interest journals of their respective fields.

Patents

Patent counts as indicators of innovative or R&D performance are not subject to much debate in the literature. It seems to be widely accepted that patents belong to one of the three key but indirect indicators of technology: (1) the inputs to technological development are shown by R&D indicators, (2) the outputs can be measured in terms of patents, and (3) the effects of technology are reflected by higher productivity (Keller, 2004, 757).

It has been demonstrated that the efficiency of a country's patent protection system acts as an incentive for R&D investment (Scherer and Ross, 1990; Varsakelis, 2001). The latter study has also shown that the United States has the strongest patent protection system in the world (based on a sample of 50 countries: Varsakelis, 2001, 1062). Patent counts are the simplest kind of patent-based indicators, and more sophisticated ones such as the number of innovations based on patents and the number of patent citations have been introduced to complement them (Flor and Oltra, 2004, 325–6).

The United States Patent and Trademark Office (USPTO) runs a quite rigorous patenting system which functions as kind of a filtering mechanism for innovations coming from less developed countries (LDCs) (Da Motta, 2000, 1042). This ensures that only the best innovations patented locally in the LDCs are submitted for patent protection in the United States, and even some of these are not found original enough by the US patenting standards. Available evidence suggests that this patenting function is exerted by the USPTO for many developing countries (Da Motta, 2000), but most LDCs are in general unable to appear with really competitive innovations on the world market.

The development of the American patent protection system and the extension of protection generated an explosion of patents granted by the USPTO from the late eighties, but this is not generally considered as an appropriate proof of a similar increase of innovations in the United States (Jaffe, 2000). A micro-level analysis of US patents in the 1990s identified a string of factors underlying their impressive increase, but its focus is rather on changing geographical and company patterns of patent activities in the United States than on the relevance of patents as the main indicator of innovation (Hicks et al., 2001).

More conclusive in this respect and also from the point of view of our methodological interest is the study by Acs, Anselin and Varga (2002). They used patents as a measure of regional innovation activity (or, as they say, the production of new knowledge) and found this measure quite reliable in the given case. They are also more accurate than many of the authors on measuring R&D or innovation. They consider R&D expenditure and patent counts proxies of innovation activities, and express their preference for so-called literature-based measures of innovations (such as for instance the analyses of cases of innovations appearing in literature – Acs, Anselin and Varga, 2002, 1070).

These are micro-level measures with both the clear cost and methodological advantages that they are based on publicly available information instead of material obtained from firm surveys.

Firm surveys are usually difficult and time-consuming to carry out, and their outcome and statistical relevance depends largely upon the response propensity of firms. This has become outstandingly evident from our own experience obtained in a transition economy (Hungary): response rates in enterprise surveys on R&D have decreased from around 50 per cent in the mid-nineties to less than 15 per cent by 2003.

One measure of innovation obtained from public sources is based on sampling the new product sections of trade and technical journals. This indicator is however also quite biased: it has been shown that larger firms spend proportionately more on advertisements than smaller ones (Acs, Anselin and Varga, 2002, 1070).

A further reason for such a bias can be a type of market behaviour described by antitrust policy literature. This behaviour is called 'Predatory Product Pre-Announcement' and the kind of still non-existent products announced this way 'vaporware', at least in the software industry (see Scherer, 1996, 277;

Fleischer, 1997). Obviously if this kind of predatory behaviour prevails then literature (or press) information on new products and technologies is not really a reliable source for microeconomic research on innovation and R&D.

This kind of literature-based indicators of innovation suffers from certain deficiencies as outlined above, therefore we should return to the analysis of the perhaps most frequently used 'proxy' of innovation, patent counts.[49] The idea that the most commonly applied indicators of innovation are just proxies is in fact quite well in line with our approach to assessing competitiveness.

Standard Industrial Organization literature builds the economic analysis of patents around the 'patent race' model (Tirole, 1988, 394–6). This model is microeconomic in character. It is based on the assumption that a firm's innovation (or patenting) capability is strongly dependent on its current R&D expenditure, but not at all on its past innovation or R&D record.

Hagedoorn and Cloodt point out the fact that R&D expenditure of companies is not only an input indicator in a narrow sense, but also a good measure of their innovation capacities, mainly in high-tech industries (Hagedoorn and Cloodt, 2003, 1368). It remains an open question at the moment whether this extension of the relevance of R&D expenditure as a capacity and therefore indirectly an output indicator could be also proposed for country-level measurements of R&D performance.

To make the picture more complex, recent research has also quite convincingly shown that patents result much more from investment than just creativity (Kingston, 2001, 421). This is reminiscent of the 'linear' model of innovation which considers R&D spending as an input and patents as an output in a 'tunnel-like' process. The 'patent race' model however identifies R&D too strongly with innovation, and the results of the innovation process too much with patents.

A critique of the 'patent race' model (Dasgupta and Stiglitz, 1980, quoted by Tirole, 1988, 396) emphasizes for example that competition in R&D (inter-firm competition in this case, but inter-country competition as we understand it) involves choices between different R&D technologies[50] with respect to their risk structures.

For example, in an extreme and simplified case, there might be a choice between R&D technologies (procedures) A and B. Technology A leads safely to the patent envisaged, but applying that technology takes four years with a 100 per cent probability. On the contrary, technology B promises obtaining the patent in two years with a 50 per cent probability, or in six years (50 per cent probability again). It is clear that the choice between A and B depends mainly on whether the innovator adopts a risk-averse strategy (choice A) or a risk-taking one (choice B). The two strategic choices are, however, not really equivalent.This would be the case only if the value of the patent on the market showed a linear change with the passing of time, so that its value in year 4 (supposing the application of technology A) would be equal to the average of its values in years 2 and 6 (supposing the application of technology B).

Therefore patent registrations on the basis of an R&D project are achieved not only in function of R&D spending, but also as a result of better, good, bad or still worse choices of R&D technology. This idea gives further support to the 'proxy' argument: patents are such outcomes of the innovation process which are not really in a direct relationship with the financing, the quality and the size of the R&D effort.

Another standard description of the problem of patents emphasizes their role as incentives to R&D and innovation (Scherer and Ross, 1990, 621–6). Patents help innovators monopolize the sales of new products, and this poses the problem of the optimal size of incentives. Monopoly rights lead to losses of consumer welfare which can be potentially offset by such gains in consumer welfare which occur owing to the faster introduction of a new product (for example a new drug or hardware).

The problem is again related to measurement. Losses of consumer welfare could be calculated by comparing the 'monopoly' price of the new product with its 'competitive' price, which is difficult to be established since there is no competitive product on the market, but close substitutes could be identified. However the welfare gain is much more difficult to measure. To give one example from the pharmaceutical industry: let us suppose the new drug used for the treatment of the same disease as its predecessor on the market can be purchased at the same market price, and it prolongates average life expectancy from five years obtained with the use of the old drug to eight years with using the new one. How could welfare gain be measured in this case?

The reliability of patents as measures of technological innovation output is widely debated in literature (see Griliches, 1990; Patel and Pavitt, 1995). A frequently used argument against giving it too much weight in innovation analysis is that it measures inventions rather than innovations (Griliches, 1990, 1671; Flor and Oltra, 2004, 326; on the economic analysis of inventions see Wyatt, 1986). No doubt inventions represent just one intermediate step in the innovation process, and many inventions do not become successful innovations. Patents may give a positively distorted picture of innovations, since it is not at all guaranteed that all patented inventions will lead to or become commercially viable innovations.

Another problem with patent counts is that they give equal weight to inventions or innovations representing very diverse scientific and/or commercial values. The economic value of patents can be measured with approximative methods only, since there is only a very limited market for them, and their replacement value is practically incalculable.

One of the methods of patent value approximation is extensively reviewed by Griliches (1990, 1679–82). The apparently best method to establish not the value of individual patents (this would be practically impossible), but the aggregate value of different patent groups is based on observations on patent renewals. The underlying assumption is the following: the more times a patent is renewed, the higher the interest for the invention (or innovation) protected by it is on the market.

This approach is however a bit simplistic. To begin with, this method of calculation is not easily useable in international comparisons due to significant cross-country differences in patent renewal fees. Moreover this measurement is biased against company sizes. The reason is that smaller firms (primarily SMEs) tend to be less able to pay regular renewal fees, first of all for patents whose economic benefit is still only an expectation for smaller and medium-sized firms with weaker financial potentials.

The main argument developed against patents by Scherer and Ross is of a much more general character and it is aimed basically at the scope of patent protection: 'because of diverse real-world complications, the patent protection given an innovator may be too little, too much or of the wrong kind' (Scherer and Ross, 1990, 624).

This means that many patents did not really provide the expected incentive at the time the book by Scherer and Ross was written (its first edition was published in 1980). The patent legislation system of the United States has been since amended in several successive steps (on the analysis of the Bayh-Dole Act of 1980 and the subsequent legislative changes see Coriat and Orsi, 2002). The essential feature of these legal changes was a strengthening of patent protection taking the special features of different fields of new technology (for example biotechnology or the software industry) into account, and making innovation and intellectual property a field of investment where the interests of investors enjoy a better protection. Representatives of the American biotechnology industry explicitly noted that a more watertight patent protection system largely increased investors' confidence in the sector (Coriat and Orsi, 2002, 1501). Further improvements in the patent protection system have been suggested by Kingston (2001).

In spite of the recent regulatory changes in American patent legislation, the necessity of further changes has implications for our deliberations on patents as one kind of the outputs of the innovation process. If patents have a role of protection from competition as their primary function then they are submitted for registration not necessarily in order to protect new, innovative outputs of R&D, but rather to protect pieces of intellectual property with a stronger focus on property rights than on technological novelty.

Let us suppose an innovation is not threatened by imitation and other kinds of IP protection are less expensive.[51] In such a case, the innovation process will not be concluded with patent registration, and the patent-based measurement of innovation output yields an imperfect result.

Patents are, in spite of all the measurement difficulties referred to above, widely used as an indicator of the innovation performance of companies (for a review of this literature see for example Hagedoorn and Cloodt, 2003, 1368). In his (still in recent years) widely quoted paper Griliches stressed that 'patents are a good indicator of differences in inventive actitivity across different firms' (Griliches, 1990, 1702). This is a very accurate formulation: patents reflect firm-level inventions quite well, but it is not sure at all that inventions become innovations.

High-tech Exports

This indicator of R&D output also used in our measurement of R&D competitiveness has been explained in detail before. As we have stressed, this indicator is a good proxy of R&D output in the case of countries which use domestic R&D and innovations extensively for export production. This is true for most advanced industrial economies, but notable exceptions are such recipients of massive foreign direct investment (for example Ireland, Hungary or Slovakia) where exports of high-tech goods are based on R&D and innovation activities carried out abroad by the multinational firms producing these export goods in such countries. This fact may cause a massive bias on the level of the individual countries in question, but the behaviour of the international sample would probably not be distorted by it.

2.7   ASSESSING SUCCESS AT THE END OF THE INNOVATION PROCESS

Performance in R&D or innovation is also strongly conditional upon the degree of how inputs are converted into measurable outputs. This is, in a broad sense, an issue related to the entire NIS of a country, but the relationships between inputs and outputs of R&D have to be observed on the micro level, taking into account individual R&D teams or projects. Ultimately the success of R&D is reflected by the acceleration of productivity growth (Keller, 2004, 757), but measuring the impact of R&D effort on productivity on the macroeconomic level poses a serious econometric challenge due to the complexity of the transmission mechanism between R&D, innovation, market performance and, at the end of this not fully causal link, productivity.

We could think in terms of a 'steam engine' scheme of the development of a scientific idea from the research and development stage through invention to the final stage of innovation. This process is called the 'path analysis' of knowledge production by Griliches (1990, 1671), but his scheme is different from what we understand by the steam engine. The steam engine metaphor is used because not all R&D results obtain patent protection (some of them take the publication path and may become patented later in a revised form, others are not patented due to high patent costs or the lack of fear of imitation), and not all patented inventions become commercially viable or successful innovations.

This metaphor is applied because steam engines are similar to the innovation process in the sense that each step of transmitting energy to the next involves a substantial loss as compared to the initial amount of energy, and the final percentage of energy really used by the steam engine is only around 10 per cent of its consumption of energy.

There can also be cases when inventions are 'hijacked' and become innovations at other firms. This hijacking might mean a simple theft of intellectual property, but also that the patent owner is unable to finance the innovation process and sells the patent to another firm, sometimes in the framework of a market-sharing agreement.[52]

The 'steam engine' scheme shows that R&D can have at least three kinds of outputs and comparisons of these are very difficult (see Figure 2.2). The mainstream path goes from R&D through invention to innovation, and the result of this kind of R&D effort can be estimated based on patent statistics. There seems to be a transmission problem here: as the 'steam engine' demonstrates, only one part of R&D output takes the innovation direction.

There are two kinds of transmission loss at the first step in this direction: (1) not all inventions are submitted as patent applications, and (2) not all patent applications are accepted. The second step also involves an important transmission loss: not all patents granted end up as successful innovations.

We have described a scheme of 'transmission of energy within the steam engine' so far, that is the path R&D $\Rightarrow$ invention $\Rightarrow$ patent $\Rightarrow$ innovation. We

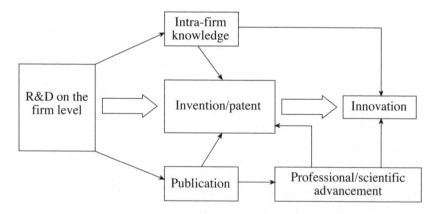

Figure 2.2   The 'steam engine' scheme of the R&D process

prefer not to call this path a chain. The reason is that any parallel with the linear model of innovation should be avoided at this point. The linear model describes a one-way stream of new knowledge, while we speak here of successive steps potentially resulting in innovation, but not inevitably leading to it.

There exist two other, to some extent secondary paths of moving from R&D potentially, but not necessarily to innovation. R&D can take the scientific path where success is measured by standards other than patents or innovation. On the scientific path, success is closely linked to the extent of impact on the research of others and, in more general terms, the scientific community.

The output to be evaluated here is publications, and this kind of impact is measured by the tools of scientometrics which have been discussed. Depending on how scientific impact and success are assessed, good performance on this path may lead to such recognition in the global (or the local) scientific community as a Nobel Prize or a tenured professorship.

The scientific path does not necessarily end at this point. It has been demonstrated by scientific career research that high scientific awards may vastly improve the prestige of a researcher, but it can also be extremely helpful for the fund raising potential of his or her[53] employer (Hargittai, 2001). Such successful scientific careers may create 'loops' within the 'steam engine' scheme which speak against its linear character: the same R&D output leads to scientific advancement and, with some delay, also to innovation which then improves the financial background of the research centre or team. At a later stage of the process the R&D output will, if leading to commercial success, improve the welfare of the country from where financing was obtained for the project.

Teams including or headed by highly rated researchers might have above-average chances to obtain better financing. R&D by a team may have publication success with a research result which (or a part of which) preserved from public attention could be channelled back to the transmission path, perhaps become a patent, and later become a successful innovation.

The other alternative path from R&D to innovation leads through the upgrading of intra-firm knowledge. Taking this path supposes that the intra-firm information system is watertight (for example researchers are strictly requested to have their conference papers or posters authorized by their company before presentation, and all outgoing information is rigorously screened). Patent protection may be deliberately avoided, also because that would also possibly mean some kind of leakage of technical information, at least regarding the direction of the research. Innovation can be generated entirely within the firm in such a way that the innovation comes as a complete surprise to competitors. In such a case, patenting can potentially follow the introduction of the innovative product or service to the market, and patent counts are not a correct indicator of inventions or innovative activity in a given year any more.

3. R&D competitiveness measured

Balázs Borsi and András Telcs

Previous chapters in this book showed that nations do compete and a substantial part of this competition is played out in the technological R&D and innovation arena. The game is a dynamic and global one, but can we shoot pictures of it that help us understand it better? The answer is a contingent yes. We believe numbers to be reliable yet cross-country R&D statistics undoubtedly carry an amount of uncertainty. Nevertheless in this chapter we would like to present methodological approaches to determine the R&D competitiveness position of countries. The problem of multivariate ranking and efficiency is discussed with the help of three well-known methods: principal component analysis, non-parametric ranking and Data Envelopment Analysis (DEA). After a brief introduction into the database compiled the ranking methods are explained for the year 2000 in section 3.2. Beyond ranking R&D efficiency is also a discussion problem for which section 3.3 introduces the DEA method. Section 3.4 extends the analysis to two points in time and section 3.5 presents the conclusions.

3.1 COLLECTING THE INDICATORS

Ranking and positioning emerged with biological evolution. Species, races and even biomes are competing for survival for which mixed strategies of cooperation and competing are needed. Dominance is a key concept in competition: the dominant species or race has better access to food, water, shelter and the chance of reproduction. The question arises: can we talk about dominant strategies in R&D? If so, how can we describe dominance?

When there are more than two competing entities pairwise comparisons can show dominant positions which can be ordered and then extended to the whole population of entities. Full, ordinary ordering[54] is simple and easy to interpret. The information coded in the order might be vital: it shows the ranking of species in a colony, and the subordination level of a given specimen or race or country.

In our modern era ranks are very common. Magazines that prepare and publish ranks of company results, wealth of individuals, bonds and shares are just one example. Such ranks might orientate investors. Similarly general macroeconomic or sectoral performance indicators are inputs for governmental policy formulation. For the lack of full information and understanding of the underlying processes the only possibility to compare is to use aggregate indicators and ranks to learn which entity performs better than others. Though it is an indirect way to explore complex economic relations, it has proved to be very fruitful.

If we want to rank countries by their R&D competitiveness, they must be described by a number of attributes of differing nature that are linked in some way to their success in R&D competition. The simplest set of appropriate attributes can be statistics; however there are two fundamental problems:

- even if we manage to consolidate the term 'R&D competitiveness', it is very unlikely that we can collect the appropriate statistics;
- if we manage to collect some statistics, they might not be appropriate and might not describe 'R&D competitiveness'.

There is no need to go into details about competitiveness as other chapters in this book deal with the issue. Without providing a definition for R&D competitiveness and analysing the complex knowledge processes in depth, it needs to be emphasized that:

- R&D and innovation are among the main driving forces in the modern economy;
- the efficiency of R&D in bringing value added and increased quality of life is crucial in improving the competitiveness of the economy;
- such efficiency attracts 'capital' (that seeks only profit) thereby aiming to strengthen the competitiveness position (for that profit sought).

The efficiency of R&D referred to above is directly related to R&D competitiveness. If we manage to understand the R&D positions of countries and capture this efficiency we come closer to understanding R&D competitiveness. We collected indicators as shown in Table 3.1 to test ranking and efficiency measurement methods for the widest possible pool of countries.[55]

Certainly, analysing the data in Table 3.1 separately may lead to debatable results. However by applying and testing the reliability of multivariate methods, we may prove that these data can describe R&D competitiveness positions. In particular:

- the 'absolute' numbers can describe a country's position interpreted as a 'weighted point' on the globe;

Table 3.1   Statistical data for R&D and innovation

	Input	Output
	statistics	
'Absolute' indicators	Number of researchers GERD* (US$) Import of measurement equipment (US$)	Patents granted to residents Scientific publications High-tech export (US$)
'Relative' indicators	GERD/GDP (%) Researchers per million inhabitants	Publications per million inhabitants Patents per million inhabitants

Note: *Gross Domestic Expenditure on R&D

- the 'relative' numbers can position the general state of R&D of countries;
- the relative size of 'absolute' input and output statistics describe efficiency of R&D systems of the different countries.

The sections that follow provide detailed discussion of the three topics outlined above. Individual country statistics can be found in Appendix A.2.

3.2   HOW TO RANK?

If we have a look at the statistical data in Table 3.1 we may have eight different ranks of the countries. For instance if absolute input type of statistics are taken, Brazil is the seventeenth according to the number of researchers, thirteenth if GERD is considered, twentieth for the imports of measurement equipment. The ranks are 24, 17 and 26 for domestic patents, publications and high-tech export respectively. But what is the actual position of Brazil if all the absolute figures are taken into account?

Obviously Brazil is somewhere between 13 and 26 on the world map of R&D if absolute size is considered. However the same issue can be raised for all the countries and separately for the 'relative' indicators. To provide a sound solution to the problem, we must aggregate the information and obtain a master list so that the smallest possible portion of information is lost. A straightforward option is to assign weights to the variables,[56] compute a 'mix', an 'average' indicator and rank the countries. It is a nice and simple solution but we have to explain why we prefer one weight system and not another.[57] Two further methodological questions emerge:

- For the set of n R&D indicators, can $m < n$ aggregate indicators be constructed so that the vast majority of information is carried forward to the aggregate indicators, that is 'enough' variance of the n indicators is explained by the $m < n$ aggregate indicators?
- Can we obtain a system of weights which is not subjectively pre-defined so that it produces a statistically consistent master ranking list?

The mathematically exact answer to the first problem was presented by Pearson (1901) and some 30 years later Hotelling (1933) developed further the so-called 'principal component analysis'. We can and will use the classical principal component analysis technique to construct ranks. To the second question we would like to show an answer using the rank correlation coefficient of Spearman (1904) in a heuristic method, the so-called 'genetic algorithm'.

The principal components are the weighted averages of the variables but the weights are not voluntary: they are combinations of the original variables so that all the variance is explained. However in practice only a few principal components have significant explanatory power, and if we are lucky[58] only one principal component will explain most of the variance in the R&D indicators. The countries can then be ordered and their respective ranks determined.

The other method proposed to determine rankings does not explain the variance of the original variables, but directly searches for an optimum rank, which is the closest to the ranks defined separately for all the variables (so a rank number between 13 and 26 is chosen for Brazil in such a way that it best reflects Brazil's position). The weights can be selected in an iterative way.

Let us imagine that we construct a composite indicator using $w_1, w_2, \ldots w_6 = 1/6$ as weights for the original six 'absolute' indicators. Then we compute the ranks for the countries and the rank correlation coefficients of the original indicators and the mixed one. By changing the $w_1, w_2, \ldots w_6$ weights, the rank correlation will change and can in practice be maximized. In contrast with the principal components approach, this 'non-parametric ranking' approach is insensitive to large values: only the order in ranking counts.

Let us now imagine that the weights represent genes in a population. Different species of the population correspond to different weight sets and these species compete, which produces a higher simultaneous rank correlation with the original indicators. The most successful species (set of weights) have the chance to multiply and/or go through mutation and become members of the next generation. Less successful species drop out from the formation of the next generation. The iteration of this procedure is the evolution of the population, which yields a nearly optimal solution.

The novelty in the non-parametric ranking approach is purely technical. In earlier times, the optimization of weights was almost impossible. Currently however, substantially increased computer power makes it possible to run genetic algorithms.[59] The task is to find those optimal weights which maximize the simultaneous rank correlation between the composite indicator and the original ones. This problem has no exact solution, which is why a good numerical estimate is needed.

The non-parametric ranking method can be used by itself, but a particular gain can be realized if we compare the ranks produced with the two methods. We use the example of the six 'absolute' variables for the year 2000, which can be amalgamated into one principal component (so that nearly 87 per cent of the total variance is explained). However constrained our database is, this one principal component represents the absolute size of R&D activities in the countries in 2000.

Similarly, using genetic algorithms a composite ranking list of countries was computed so that the rank correlation between the individual ranks and the composite rank was maximized (the Spearman rank correlation coefficient was between 0.8 and 0.95). The results are presented in Table 3.2.

At first sight the ranks are very similar and differences in ranking positions are very small for most of the countries. A difference of 4 or higher, and particularly above 6, shows that the position of the given country in one or more 'individual' rank does not align well with its position in other 'individual' ranking lists.

From Table 3.2 we can see that the non-parametric method is unfavourable for a certain group of countries. Singapore is the first example: according to the principal components method, Singapore is the tenth, but in the list computed by genetic algorithms it is only the twentieth. The difference is caused by the 'trade' indicators: Singapore is the fifth exporter of high-technology goods and the tenth importer of measurement equipment, but all the other individual lists have Singapore after the twenty-fifth position.

Similar conclusions apply for Mexico, Malaysia, the Republic of Ireland, Thailand, Indonesia and to some extent Hong Kong and Hungary. The countries that are valued higher according to the method of genetic algorithms are those that have less substantial differences between their positions in the 'trade' indicators based and other ranking lists. These are Denmark, Norway and Argentina, but to some extent Brazil, Poland and Greece as well. Thus for nine countries at least, the ranking lists produced with the genetic algorithm method clearly change the picture we get if we think intuitively of the countries' positions in 'absolute' R&D effort and performance. To put it differently,

Table 3.2 Ranks computed from the six 'absolute' indicators using principal components and the difference caused if non-parametric ranking was used

Rank	G*	Rank	G*	Rank	G*	Rank	G*	Rank	G*
1 USA	0	11 Italy	2	21 India	3	31 Indonesia	-9	41 New Zealand	3
2 Japan	0	12 Netherlands	1	22 Ireland	-10	32 Hungary	-4	42 Slovakia	-1
3 Germany	0	13 Mexico	-6	23 Finland	0	33 Turkey	3	43 Venezuela	-1
4 UK	0	14 Malaysia	-15	24 Hong Kong	-4	34 Norway	7	44 Chile	2
5 China	-1	15 Spain	2	25 Austria	3	35 Czech Rep.	1	45 Bulgaria	0
6 France	1	16 Sweden	4	26 Israel	5	36 South Africa	3	46 Colombia	0
7 Korea, South	0	17 Australia	3	27 Ukraine	1	37 Argentina	6	47 Iceland	0
8 Canada	0	18 Switzerland	3	28 Thailand	-11	38 Portugal	1	48 Panama	0
9 Russia	-1	19 Belgium	2	29 Poland	4	39 Greece	4	49 Cyprus	0
10 Singapore	-10	20 Brazil	4	30 Denmark	6	40 Romania	-1		

Note: *this column shows how many positions are given to or taken from the given country according to non-parametric ranking.

for these nine countries the 'trade' indicators are not in accordance with other R&D indicators and this fact can be shown if the two ranking lists are compared.

We then hypothesized that the two ranks must be very similar if the 'trade' indicators are taken out. This was exactly the case: the ranking lists obtained with the principal component extraction approach and the genetic algorithm method were basically the same (this means differences between the two ranks were less than 4 for the vast majority of the countries). There were only two exceptions: China and Indonesia. Both countries were 'punished' (that is, they obtained worse ranking positions) by the genetic algorithm method for the same reason: the number of researchers is outstanding in both countries compared with the other indicators. China is punished by 4 positions (it is not necessarily a substantial difference) and Indonesia by 17 positions.[60]

The ranks can similarly be computed for the 'relative' indicators. We may even hypothesize that the GERD/GDP ratio, the number of researchers per million inhabitants, domestic patents granted per million inhabitants and scientific papers per million inhabitants together represent variables that describe the 'general R&D culture' in a country.[61] The two methods produce nearly the same ranking list[62] (see Table 3.3). Only Singapore is 'punished' by the genetic algorithm approach: the reason is the country's very high 'density of researchers' that places the country fifth on the individual list according to the number of researchers per million people.

To sum up, both the principal component analysis and the non-parametric ranking method are based on a simple idea, replacing the multivariate space with a univariate one. The principal component analysis uses LSM (least squares method) while the second minimizes simultaneous rank correlation. Non-parametric ranking is a good complement to the principal component ranking, which is sensitive to absolute values. A further advantage is that it helps us to see which entities carry statistical information that is not in accordance with the others.

It is important to note that the weights are self-selected in both cases, because the criticism that the choice of weights is ad hoc always has solid grounds. The ranks presented above are mathematically optimal in a given sense, and they coincide well with the overall picture expected or ranks constructed using other methods as these were surveyed in earlier parts of this text. However we must also be aware that any simple linear ranking of multivariate data has a cost of losing information as well. In other words a multidimensional scenario cannot be fully reconstructed from its one-dimensional projection. If we do not forget that the information loss has taken place, multivariate ranking can be very useful to understand the internal factors determining the relative positions.

Table 3.3 Ranks computed from the four 'relative' indicators using principal components and the difference caused if non-parametric ranking was used

Rank		G*	Rank		G*	Rank		G*	Rank		G*	Rank		G*
1	Japan	0	11	Norway	-1	21	Russia	0	31	Poland	0	41	Cyprus	0
2	Sweden	0	12	Netherlands	2	22	Ireland	0	32	Hong Kong	0	42	India	0
3	Finland	-3	13	Singapore	-5	23	Spain	0	33	Bulgaria	0	43	Mexico	0
4	Israel	-1	14	Australia	0	24	Czech Rep.	-1	34	China	-1	44	Panama	0
5	Switzerland	1	15	France	2	25	Italy	-1	35	Brazil	-1	45	Venezuela	0
6	United States	3	16	Canada	0	26	Ukraine	2	36	South Africa	2	46	Malaysia	0
7	Iceland	-4	17	UK	2	27	Slovakia	-1	37	Romania	-1	47	Indonesia	0
8	Denmark	-1	18	Belgium	-1	28	Hungary	1	38	Argentina	1	48	Colombia	0
9	Korea (S)	2	19	New Zealand	2	29	Portugal	0	39	Chile	0	49	Thailand	0
10	Germany	2	20	Austria	0	30	Greece	0	40	Turkey	0			

Note: *the positions given to or taken from the given country according to non-parametric ranking.

3.3   DATA ENVELOPMENT ANALYSIS: AN INSIGHT INTO EFFICIENCY

The principal component analysis and the non-parametric ranking method differ only in the distance used to measure the difference between the optimal mix of indicators and the individual indicators. By constructing one-dimensional ranks we lose not only statistical information, but also the possibility of finding similar countries that have similar 'R&D policies'. To further refine the picture, an efficiency measurement method is applied. It is called Data Envelopment Analysis (DEA).

The DEA method makes extensive use of the fact that the variables are grouped as input indicators (number of researchers, GERD) and output indicators (publications and patents).[63] One may argue that especially the output indicators are not appropriate, because the main output of R&D is primarily new technologies and products (innovation).[64] However we had to make a compromise and use these indicators, which can be accepted as proxies for R&D results.

When we have inputs and outputs, the basic economic question can be posed: how efficient is one country compared with another? The DEA method will be used for such cross-country comparison.

Data Envelopment Analysis is a relatively new non-parametric method rooted in multi-objective decision analysis or operations research originally proposed to measure production efficiency. It was originally proposed by Charnes et al. (1978) (see Färe et al., 1994a for a comprehensive review). The recent literature of the topic is enormous and the method should be well known by non-expert economists as well, so we omit the technical introduction. For the interested reader some conceptual introduction is given in the context of the present study deviating from the usual terminology.

A country is considered as a production unit which uses inputs (GERD and researchers) to produce outputs (publications and patents). Referring to R&D competitiveness, a country will be more attractive (to an investor) if it produces more output using less input, or simply if it is more efficient. This can easily be quantified if only one input (for example GERD) and one output (for example publications) is considered. The cheaper a country produces a scientific paper, the more efficient it is in a strictly economic sense, that is without considering the paper's real impact on research (not even its impact factor can be considered as a proxy for the real impact).

If only these two dimensions of R&D are taken into account, the ranking list is interesting. The developed industrial countries produce very expensive papers. Someone could possibly be tempted to come up with the obvious interpretation that a few good but poor countries offer something at low cost, but they are obviously not the flagships of international R&D.

Given the complexity of the R&D activity it is appropriate to take more indicators into consideration. The DEA method measures the relative positions of countries (the objects) with respect to peer countries based on their production of a mix of R&D results (p publications and q patents) given a mix of inputs (r researchers and s GERD dollars). The countries are placed in a multi-dimensional space of variables or indicators.

In the so-called output-oriented model[65] the goal is to maximize output based on given inputs (mix). So the DEA algorithm normalizes on the input mix used and produce an envelope of the country set in the multidimensional space. This envelope contains the best-performing countries, also called efficiency frontier. The best-performing countries are the reference level of efficiency. It may happen that a less efficient country has a different mix of inputs than the best ones, but we can 'mix' the efficient countries to get a virtual country which is also efficient and uses the same mix as the investigated one. This is the target or reference point on the efficiency frontier for the given country and its efficiency is the production rate relative to the virtual, so it is always between zero and one.

Scale invariant (constant returns to scale, CRS) and scale dependent (variable returns to scale, VRS) efficiencies can also be distinguished. In the 'scale free' approach, efficiency of a country that uses 2 units of input to produce 2 units of output equals to that of another country with 1 unit of input and 1 unit of output. In reality absolute values count (for example the law of diminishing rates of return in economics). In general however, efficiency might depend on the absolute values (scales) of inputs and outputs. In this case literature uses the variable return to scale terminology, and a modified way to calculate efficiencies. To gain a full picture it is worthwhile to run the DEA using both assumptions (VRS and CRS) and compare the results.

To see how multi-object comparison works, efficiency and relative positions are depicted for the two inputs and one output case. Let us call the countries on the maximum efficiency level peer countries.[66] On the surface they span each country has a reference point, which is their virtual optimum. For instance if we are seeking for output optimization for country B the point B'' in Figure 3.1 indicates what the efficiency would be of the peer countries if they use the same mix of inputs as B.

The CRS frontier defined by the points $G, C, D,$ and F lies on it as well. So points A, B, E and Q are not efficient if CRS is assumed yet A and E are efficient if VRS is applied. Thus points B and Q are not efficient, they are below the VRS frontier. Their virtual optimum on the VRS frontier are B' and Q' and B'' and Q'' on the CRS frontier.

Let TE_{CRS}, TE_{VRS} denote the technical efficiency in the CRS and VRS models. Pure technical efficiency is measured by $TE_{CRS} = OB''/OB$ while VRS technical efficiency is $TE_{VRS} = OB'/OB$. It is natural to assume that R&D

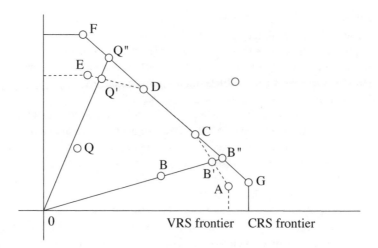

Figure 3.1   The frontier of objects with maximum efficiency

is very scale sensitive and only the VRS approach is adequate. On the other hand it is worth studying both on the same data set. In doing so one can decompose efficiency into pure Technical Efficiency and Scale Efficiency. One can also observe that in the CRS model fewer countries are efficient than in the VRS. This is normal, because size or capacity is not taken into consideration in the former while in the latter it might turn out that on a less advantageous level of scale some countries are very efficient.

Let us denote Scale Efficiency by *SE*. $SE = TE_{CRS}/TE_{VRS}$ and it can be interpreted as the loss (or gain) in efficiency due to the non-proportional scaling. A country can not change its size, so it has no option to improve the efficiency by changing the scale of operation, which is a possible option for enterprises. A country can modify its GERD or number of researchers to some extent, and this limited room for manoeuvre is a critical issue of policy debates but cannot change the scale position of the country in a drastic way.

There are three regions with respect to scale efficiency. The constant region is where the output is proportional with the input, the increasing region where the output–input ration is increasing, and correspondingly the decreasing region is where the ratio is decreasing. If we run not only the VSR model for the countries but also the CRS, then we can determine individual scale efficiencies as well as pinpoint if the countries are in the decreasing returns to scale or in the increasing returns to scale region.

Now let us return to the two inputs (researchers, GERD) and two outputs (publications, patents) analysis.[67] Although diagrams cannot be constructed, the DEA method works the same way. Both CRS and VRS efficiencies have been calculated as well as scale efficiency. It turned out in the VRS model that

Bulgaria, Hong Kong, Israel, Korea, New Zealand and Ukraine are on the efficiency frontier (see Table 3.4). The reasons in our framework are:

- Bulgaria and Ukraine produce patents and publications very cheaply.
- Researchers in both Hong Kong and Israel publish many scientific papers per capita; further, in Hong Kong the 'GERD price per paper' is fairly low and Israeli researchers are also granted many patents.
- South Korea is the patent champion: researchers produce many patents and they do it cheaply.
- New Zealand is in the first seven in all aspects: it produces many patents per researcher at reasonable price and the same holds for publications.

The reference countries are all efficient, they represent different policy mixes of R&D. In their direction in the four-dimensional space, there are no more efficient countries than those on the frontier. All other countries are positioned in relation to their efficiency coordinates in the four-dimensional space. The reference countries are efficient both in the CRS and the VRS models.

Different combinations of the reference countries can be used to construct the virtual optimum for the less efficient countries. The non-efficient countries, which form heterogenous groups, will be presented according to their CRS reference countries.

The first group represents developed countries, and their references are Israel, South Korea and New Zealand (see Table 3.5). If VRS is taken into account, Japan, the Netherlands and the United States are also efficient countries. With the exception of Japan and the United States, New Zealand is the most important reference country in this group.

Weights of the reference countries show how the virtual optimum can be composed using the reference countries. In this virtual country $TE_{CRS} = 1$ and

Table 3.4 R&D input and output data for the reference countries (2000 or latest available year)

Country	Patents per million GERD $	Publications per million GERD $	Patents per thousand researchers	Publications per thousand researchers	TE_{CRS}, TE_{VRS}
Bulgaria	217	1205	15	85	1
Hong Kong	5	228	9	411	1
Israel	8	93	50	549	1
Korea (South)	187	55	212	62	1
New Zealand	95	411	66	287	1
Ukraine	1681	749	47	21	1

Source: computations using the statistical data in Appendix 2.

Table 3.5   R&D input and output data (2000 or latest available year). Reference countries: Israel, South Korea and New Zealand

Country	DEA statistics				Ref. countries and weights			Patents per million GERD $	Publications per million GERD $	Patents per thousand researchers	Publications per thousand researchers
	TE_{CRS}	TE_{VRS}	SE	I/D*	IS	KO	NZ				
Japan	0.85	1.00	0.85	D	0.39	0.61	0.00	79	34	173	74
Netherl.	0.84	1.00	0.84	D	0.21	0.01	0.78	39	145	69	257
Switzerl.	0.75	0.87	0.87	D	0.33	0.01	0.67	21	111	52	272
Austria	0.65	0.67	0.97	D	0.24	0.02	0.74	32	102	60	191
France	0.62	0.85	0.74	D	0.23	0.03	0.74	36	96	64	171
Sweden	0.59	0.69	0.86	D	0.29	0.01	0.70	22	90	48	194
USA	0.58	1.00	0.58	D	0.49	0.07	0.44	32	62	76	147
Germany	0.57	0.79	0.72	D	0.25	0.04	0.70	36	80	66	145

Note: *increasing (I) or decreasing (D) return to scale.
Source: computations using the statistical data in Appendix B.

relative efficiency is given in the TE_{CRS} in Table 3.5. As an example France has $TE_{CRS} = 0.62$, its virtual optimum would be the mix of Israel, South Korea and New Zealand with weights 0.23, 0.03 and 0.74 respectively. This means that basically it is the mix of the first and the third reference country and it is much closer to New Zealand than to Israel in its indicator composition.

The second group also contains developed economies and again it has three reference countries: Korea is replaced by Hong Kong (see Table 3.6). If VRS is assumed, then the United Kingdom and Italy are also efficient and Hong Kong is their most important reference.

The third group contains two developing and three transition countries (see Table 3.7). Russia – as a cheap 'producer' – is VRS efficient and Romania and Poland are also very close to the VRS efficiency.

The next group is a heterogeneous one, because the two reference countries are quite different: Bulgaria is a cheap producer of 'scientific-technological goods' as patents and papers, and New Zealand is not only cheap but very productive as per researcher at the same time (see Table 3.8). Under VRS assumptions, Hungary, India and Spain are also efficient (and for the former two, Bulgaria is more important as an efficiency reference). In general we can see that New Zealand is basically the reference target to the more developed countries of this group.

The last group also contains very different types of countries (see Table 3.9). The reference countries are Hong Kong and New Zealand: the former is a cost-effective and productive publication producer while the latter is efficient in general. Chile has the same mix as New Zealand, while Panama is more similar to Hong Kong. Finland or Mexico can be described as a balanced mix of the reference countries. Within this group Australia, Cyprus and Panama are efficient on the VRS frontier.

Although the DEA analysis with two inputs and two outputs is not suitable for obtaining a single ranking list, it definitely enriches the possibilities of studying the phenomena embraced by the ranking methods. It must also be added that the DEA is very sensitive to extreme values. Interpretations of DEA results will primarily depend on whether the reference countries represent clear efficiency directions in the multidimensional space.

In our case for 2000 the reference countries seem to have captured representative directions, because – with the exception of the last group – more or less similar countries belong together based on the reference country 'mix'. Ranking has a meaning within the country groups where output efficiency is measured in the same direction (DEA implicitly assumes that one patent equals one publication – an assumption we do not want to assess in this chapter).[68]

In order to understand the efficiency envelope 'graphical interpretation' is also possible if we use a single input that produces publications and patents as

Table 3.6 R&D input and output data (2000 or latest available year). Reference countries: Hong Kong, Israel and New Zealand

Country	DEA statistics				Ref. countries and weights			Patents per million GERD $	Publications per million GERD $	Patents per thousand researchers	Publications per thousand researchers
	TE_{CRS}	TE_{VRS}	SE	I/D*	HK	IS	NZ				
UK	0.68	1.00	0.68	D	0.62	0.06	0.32	16	150	26	252
Italy	0.66	1.00	0.66	D	0.95	0.01	0.05	5	150	10	264
Denmark	0.57	0.69	0.82	D	0.74	0.08	0.18	8	109	17	224
Belgium	0.47	0.56	0.83	D	0.31	0.11	0.58	15	100	25	162
Norway	0.40	0.42	0.96	D	0.37	0.06	0.57	15	98	21	137

Note: *increasing (I) or decreasing (D) return to scale.
Source: computations using the statistical data in Appendix B.

Table 3.7 R&D input and output data (2000 or latest available year). Reference countries: Bulgaria, New Zealand and Ukraine

Country	DEA statistics				Ref. countries and weights			Patents per million GERD $	Publications per million GERD $	Patents per thousand researchers	Publications per thousand researchers
	TE_CRS	TE_VRS	SE	I/D*	BG	NZ	UA				
Romania	0.94	0.96	0.98	I	0.40	0.27	0.34	626	568	42	38
Russia	0.72	1.00	0.72	D	0.73	0.08	0.19	527	571	29	31
Thailand	0.68	0.74	0.92	I	0.21	0.74	0.05	98	302	35	107
Poland	0.65	0.94	0.69	D	0.77	0.23	0.00	85	409	17	82
China	0.21	0.32	0.65	D	0.41	0.46	0.13	60	108	91	17

Note: *increasing (I) or decreasing (D) return to scale.
Source: computations using the statistical data in Appendix B.

Table 3.8 R&D input and output data (2000 or latest available year). Reference countries: Bulgaria and New Zealand

Country	DEA statistics				Ref. countries and weights		Patents per million GERD $	Publications per million GERD $	Patents per thousand researchers	Publications per thousand researchers
	TE_{CRS}	TE_{VRS}	SE	I/D*	BG	NZ				
Hungary	0.93	1.00	0.93	D	0.67	0.33	47	524	12	136
Slovakia	0.84	0.84	0.99	I	0.89	0.11	63	661	8	87
India	0.69	1.00	0.69	D	0.70	0.30	26	400	6	97
Czech R.	0.65	0.66	0.99	D	0.30	0.70	40	292	20	145
Greece	0.63	0.64	0.99	D	0.22	0.78	0.4	277	0.2	151
Spain	0.57	1.00	0.57	D	0.02	0.98	33	233	23	160
Turkey	0.51	0.58	0.89	D	0.09	0.91	2	216	1	138
S. Africa	0.43	0.45	0.97	D	0.49	0.51	0	211	0	78
Argentina	0.42	0.44	0.96	D	0.33	0.67	12	189	5	89
Portugal	0.40	0.41	0.99	I	0.28	0.72	6	179	3	90
Colombia	0.28	0.34	0.84	I	0.53	0.47	14	141	5	49
Indonesia	0.16	0.39	0.39	I	1.00		0	197	0	2

Note: *increasing (I) or decreasing (D) return to scale.
Source: computations using the statistical data in Appendix B.

Table 3.9 R&D input and output data (2000 or latest available year). Reference countries: Hong Kong and New Zealand

Country	DEA statistics				Ref. countries and weights		Patents per million GERD $	Publications per million GERD $	Patents per thousand researchers	Publications per thousand researchers
	TE_{CRS}	TE_{VRS}	SE	I/D*	HK	NZ				
Australia	0.61	1.00	0.61	D	0.30	0.70	22	211	20	190
Canada	0.58	0.91	0.64	D	0.80	0.20	8	149	12	217
Chile	0.54	0.56	0.97	I	0.00	1.00	8	223	6	156
Cyprus.	0.52	1.00	0.52	I	0.08	0.92	0	203	0	152
Ireland	0.42	0.43	0.99	I	0.71	0.29	3	114	4	151
Malaysia	0.40	0.44	0.92	I	0.22	0.78	18	145	15	122
Finland	0.34	0.43	0.80	D	0.58	0.42	1	99	1	116
Panama	0.34	1.00	0.34	I	0.87	0.13	0	83	0	129
Mexico	0.33	0.34	0.98	D	0.35	0.65	5	111	5	105
Venezuela	0.31	0.34	0.93	I	0.25	0.75	3	111	3	96
Singapore	0.30	0.31	0.99	I	0.46	0.54	2	95	2	99
Brazil	0.28	0.38	0.74	D	0.55	0.45	6	82	7	93
Iceland	0.18	0.26	0.70	I	0.73	0.27	1	49	1	66

Note: *increasing (I) or decreasing (D) return to scale.
Source: computations using the statistical data in Appendix B.

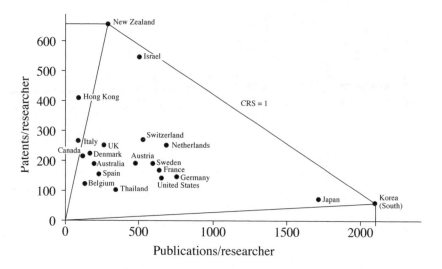

Figure 3.2   Patents and publications per thousand researcher: the
efficiency frontier (CRS = 1)

outputs. First we take the example of researchers as the input. The most efficient countries are shown in Figure 3.2 (but we must remember: these efficiencies are not the same as the ones presented above for the two inputs, two
outputs model). This is the direction of New Zealand and Korea, two important reference countries for the developed world. The third was Israel, since it
was an efficient country in the four-dimensional analysis; now it is not efficient, although it is very close to the two-dimensional frontier as well. We
have to emphasize again that the figures show CRS frontiers and efficiencies,
which penalize large and/or rich countries to some extent.

Figure 3.3 contains less efficient countries. In our example one can follow
how the countries are located relative to the sub-efficiency frontier with 0.24
efficiency.

Similarly to 'researcher productivity', 'cost efficiency' can also be plotted.
In this dimension Bulgaria and the Ukraine are the reference countries (Figure
3.4 depicts the GERD usage in 2000 by the most efficient countries).

The countries with lower efficiencies are plotted in Figure 3.5.

The figures not only visualize the efficiency differences, but they also
group the countries again in relation to their reference countries (that is how
they produce the output mix given a single input). Countries are clustered
according their efficiency as well as how their output is divided between publication and patent production.

The DEA method enriches the picture drawn by the ranking methods.

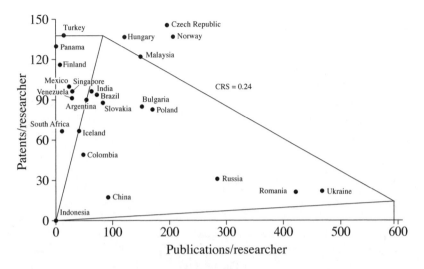

Figure 3.3   Patents and publications per thousand researcher: the efficiency frontier (CRS = 0.24)

While the presented ranking methods are one-dimensional, DEA provides some insights into efficiency shifting the analysis to higher-dimensional space.

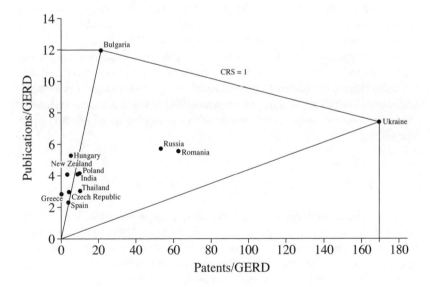

Figure 3.4   Patents and publications per million GERD dollars: the efficiency frontier (CRS = 1)

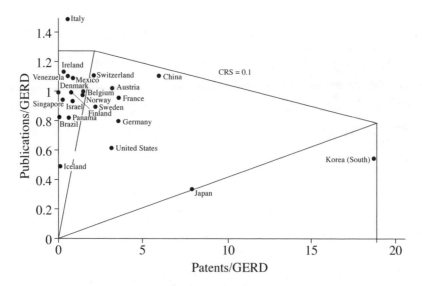

Figure 3.5   Patents and publications per million GERD dollars: the efficiency frontier (CRS = 0.1)

Of course we cannot 'see' more than three dimensions, but by using tables illustrative and meaningful projections can be given and interpreted. Still, if we want ranks, the two input, one output models can be used whereby one input, two output charts can be drawn showing the efficiency frontier.

The grouping of countries according their reference countries seems to be a powerful tool (it is widely used in benchmarking the performances of different corporations for instance). Nonetheless in the present context positioning and repositioning can be much more meaningful if R&D policies, systems of education, cultural backgrounds and so on of the peer countries are thoroughly studied.

3.4   CHANGES BETWEEN 1995 AND 2000

Until this point our focus has been exclusively cross-sectional. Less reliable data did not cause fundamental problems, because R&D statistics change fairly slowly over time and we could rely on 1999 publications data for instance. Although the methods presented are more or less sensitive to small changes, the general cross-country comparison of R&D positions and efficiencies did usually meet the *a priori* expectations. In an ideal case the ranking techniques and the DEA could be repeated on annual statistics to explore smaller changes – given the unreliability and unavailability of indicators however, it cannot be done.[69] Therefore we limit our discussion to the comparison of 1995 and 2000 data (see Figures 3.6 and 3.7).

As far as the ranks of countries according to their absolute sizes of R&D are concerned, rather robust lists can be constructed both for 1995 and 2000. Besides stability in the position of the first and last three countries some remarkable trends can also be shown:

- in the first ten countries, Russia is slowly sliding down whereas South Korea is catching up;
- in these five years all transition countries lost position;
- South-East Asia is a more and more important player in the world's R&D;
- the developed countries show a mixed picture.

Further interpretations of the list can also be drawn, although we have to warn the reader that the 2000 statistics, and so the ranks in general, are much more reliable and consistent than the 1995 ones.

The composite ranks of 'relative' R&D indicators are also consistent, but these ranks reveal greater fluctuations. This is not surprising, because the frequency distribution of the 'relative' R&D indicators is usually skewed and has positive kurtosis so relatively small changes can cause large moves in the rankings. Less sound but eye-catching changes and tendencies can be shown in this case as well:

- despite its economic depression, Japan's first place was not challenged;
- South Korea shows an outstanding performance here again;
- the transition countries either kept their position or slid down;
- many of the developed European countries lost position.

The comparison of composite ranks for two points in time confirms that the ranking problem can be handled provided there are more or less reliable statistics. With the help of genetic algorithms that maximize the rank correlation between the composite rank and individual ranks, even extreme values cause little trouble. Before extending the DEA to the time interval discussed, we must be aware that this efficiency analysis is based on the evolution of frontiers, and since DEA is an extreme value method it is very sensitive to small changes of the peer objects (see Färe et al., 1994b). Nonetheless it is interesting to compare the change of mix and efficiency gain or loss in the scale free model. This might lead to a better understanding of the optimal composition of 'mainstream R&D' and to the formulation of catching up policies.

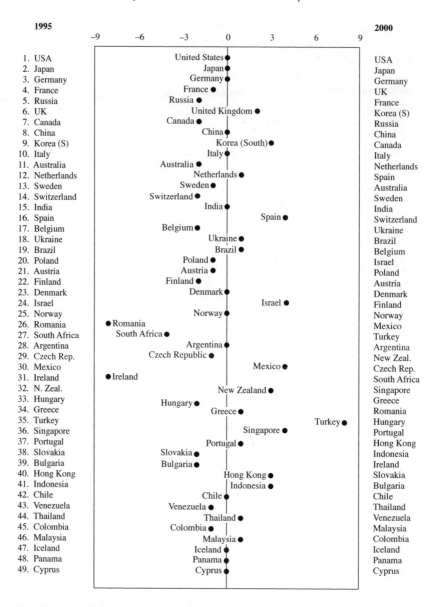

1995

2000

	1995	2000
1.	USA	USA
2.	Japan	Japan
3.	Germany	Germany
4.	France	UK
5.	Russia	France
6.	UK	Korea (S)
7.	Canada	Russia
8.	China	China
9.	Korea (S)	Canada
10.	Italy	Italy
11.	Australia	Netherlands
12.	Netherlands	Spain
13.	Sweden	Australia
14.	Switzerland	Sweden
15.	India	India
16.	Spain	Switzerland
17.	Belgium	Ukraine
18.	Ukraine	Brazil
19.	Brazil	Belgium
20.	Poland	Israel
21.	Austria	Poland
22.	Finland	Austria
23.	Denmark	Denmark
24.	Israel	Finland
25.	Norway	Norway
26.	Romania	Mexico
27.	South Africa	Turkey
28.	Argentina	Argentina
29.	Czech Rep.	New Zeal.
30.	Mexico	Czech Rep.
31.	Ireland	South Africa
32.	N. Zeal.	Singapore
33.	Hungary	Greece
34.	Greece	Romania
35.	Turkey	Hungary
36.	Singapore	Portugal
37.	Portugal	Hong Kong
38.	Slovakia	Indonesia
39.	Bulgaria	Ireland
40.	Hong Kong	Slovakia
41.	Indonesia	Bulgaria
42.	Chile	Chile
43.	Venezuela	Thailand
44.	Thailand	Venezuela
45.	Colombia	Malaysia
46.	Malaysia	Colombia
47.	Iceland	Iceland
48.	Panama	Panama
49.	Cyprus	Cyprus

Note: *computed by the genetic algorithm.

Figure 3.6   The composite rank of 'absolute' R&D indicators in 1995 and
            2000 and position changes as compared with 1995*

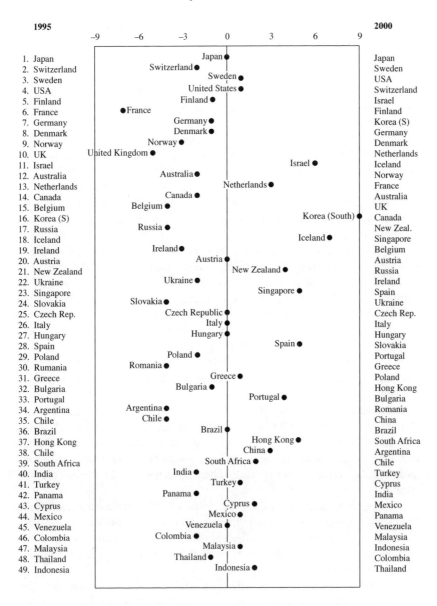

1995 | −9 | −6 | −3 | 0 | 3 | 6 | 9 | **2000**

1. Japan — Japan
2. Switzerland — Sweden
3. Sweden — USA
4. USA — Switzerland
5. Finland — Israel
6. France — Finland
7. Germany — Korea (S)
8. Denmark — Germany
9. Norway — Denmark
10. UK — Netherlands
11. Israel — Iceland
12. Australia — Norway
13. Netherlands — France
14. Canada — Australia
15. Belgium — UK
16. Korea (S) — Canada
17. Russia — New Zeal.
18. Iceland — Singapore
19. Ireland — Belgium
20. Austria — Austria
21. New Zealand — Russia
22. Ukraine — Ireland
23. Singapore — Spain
24. Slovakia — Ukraine
25. Czech Rep. — Czech Rep.
26. Italy — Italy
27. Hungary — Hungary
28. Spain — Slovakia
29. Poland — Portugal
30. Rumania — Greece
31. Greece — Poland
32. Bulgaria — Hong Kong
33. Portugal — Bulgaria
34. Argentina — Romania
35. Chile — China
36. Brazil — Brazil
37. Hong Kong — South Africa
38. Chile — Argentina
39. South Africa — Chile
40. India — Turkey
41. Turkey — Cyprus
42. Panama — India
43. Cyprus — Mexico
44. Mexico — Panama
45. Venezuela — Venezuela
46. Colombia — Malaysia
47. Malaysia — Indonesia
48. Thailand — Colombia
49. Indonesia — Thailand

Note: *computed by the genetic algorithm.

Figure 3.7   The composite rank of 'relative' R&D indicators in 1995 and 2000 and position changes as compared with 1995*

The first constraint of the DEA method is that it was not designed to provide such comparison. The method compares all the efficiencies to the efficient frontier, the changes of which heavily affect comparison. The change in a country's efficiency position is a result of its own change and in the overall change of the efficiency of the countries observed. There is a method to separate the two effects using the Malmquist index (see Färe et al., 1994b). Fortunately however, we do not need it in the present context, because we can assume that there are no big changes in the technology, so there is no dramatic technological change expected in the overall patterns of producing publications or patents. This means that changes in the efficiency-based ranking lists may reflect the rearrangements of R&D competitiveness of countries well.

The second constraint is a methodological one. The output side (patents, publications) of R&D competitiveness is two-dimensional and as we have mentioned it cannot be said that one patent equals one publication. However if the outputs are separated, publication efficiency ranking lists and patent efficiency ranking lists can be constructed. In doing so, we still assume that GERD and the number of researchers are both used solely for producing publications or patents and only the combinations of output differ as per country.[70] These preconditions can still be debated; however we constructed the corresponding ranks to test the ranking ability of the DEA method. Table 3.10 lists the countries by their 2000 CRS ranking.

Figures 3.8 and 3.9 contain the countries ranked by their 1995 CRS and VRS efficiencies from top to bottom and the change in the rank is plotted horizontally.

It is interesting to observe that changes are more frequent in the midrange than on the end of the 1995 ranking scale. On the other hand the VRS rankings show higher stability. This is not surprising, taking into consideration that VRS compares the countries on their own scale, reference counties are more similar, much closer to each other, consequently the moves are less erratic.

We then considered a similar comparison of patent production efficiency. Ranks and changes can be plotted in a similar way for both CRS and VRS efficiencies. Position changes in this case are greater than in the case of publications; probably due to the much smaller number of the patents, the variability is relatively large.

The simultaneous use of the different methods results in a rich picture. The absolute and relative composite indicators and the DEA method give different ranks and this has an obvious interpretation. The patterns for individual countries coincide in a number of cases, while the directions of changes deviating from these patterns are particularly interesting and worth further investigation.

Table 3.10 Publication efficiency

	2000		1995			2000		1995	
	TE$_{CRS}$	Rank	TE$_{CRS}$	Rank		TE$_{CRS}$	Rank	TE$_{CRS}$	Rank
Bulgaria	1.00	1	1.00	1	Austria	0.46	26	0.22	39
Hong Kong	1.00	2	1.00	2	Sweden	0.46	27	0.27	30
Israel	1.00	3	0.70	6	South Africa	0.43	28	0.34	23
New Zealand	1.00	4	0.70	5	Ireland	0.42	29	0.24	36
Hungary	0.93	5	0.91	3	France	0.42	30	0.20	42
Slovakia	0.84	6	0.84	4	Argentina	0.42	31	0.31	25
India	0.69	7	0.52	10	Belgium	0.41	32	0.20	41
Czech Republic	0.65	8	0.62	9	Portugal	0.40	33	0.29	28
Italy	0.65	9	0.33	24	Malaysia	0.40	34	0.36	22
Poland	0.65	10	0.70	7	Norway	0.37	35	0.25	35
Greece	0.63	11	0.69	8	Germany	0.35	36	0.16	44
United Kingdom	0.63	12	0.43	16	United States	0.34	37	0.25	34
Netherlands	0.63	13	0.36	21	Finland	0.34	38	0.30	26
Switzerland	0.63	14	0.21	40	Panama	0.34	39	0.24	38
Ukraine	0.62	15	0.24	37	Mexico	0.33	40	0.37	20
Australia	0.61	16	0.45	14	Venezuela	0.31	41	0.38	19
Thailand	0.61	17	0.26	33	Singapore	0.30	42	0.26	31
Canada	0.58	18	0.50	12	Colombia	0.28	43	0.12	46
Spain	0.57	19	0.51	11	Brazil	0.28	44	0.13	45
Chile	0.54	20	0.41	17	Iceland	0.18	45	0.30	27
Denmark	0.53	21	0.29	29	Korea (South)	0.18	46	0.07	48
Cyprus	0.52	22	0.45	15	Japan	0.17	47	0.08	47
Turkey	0.51	23	0.47	13	Indonesia	0.16	48	0.06	49
Russia	0.47	24	0.39	18	China	0.15	49	0.17	43
Romania	0.47	25	0.26	32					

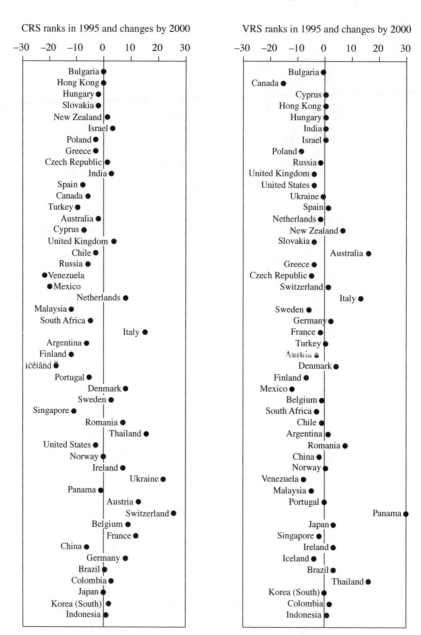

Figure 3.8   Publication efficiency

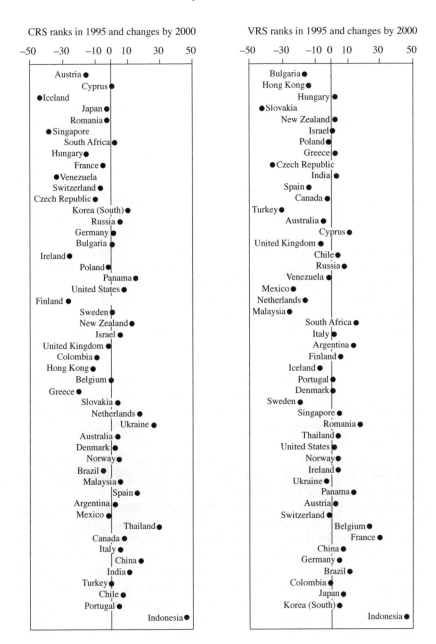

CRS ranks in 1995 and changes by 2000

VRS ranks in 1995 and changes by 2000

Figure 3.9   Patent efficiency

3.5   CONCLUSIONS OF MEASUREMENT

The aim in this chapter was to develop tools for quantitative analysis of positioning R&D competitiveness of countries. Although we may encounter problems both with finding appropriate statistics (see Appendix B) and with linking the existing indicators to the abstract concept of R&D competitiveness, our experiment does give several results relevant both in the methodological and the policy sense.

Foremost, the absolute and relative indicators selected for this analysis statistically correlate with each other, thereby strengthening the a priori hypothesis that they do describe a common phenomenon, whether it is called R&D competitiveness or not. We have also assumed that the ranking methods presented in this chapter can only be used if there is an acceptable level of (linear) correlation relationship between the variables subject to study (correlation coefficients of the indicators used are shown in Appendix B).

Having built the database, two ranking methods could be tested in which weights of the indicators were not predefined and the only difference was how they optimized the distance between the composite rank and the individual ranks of the indicators. A single principal component was extracted for both the absolute and the relative indicators to explain the majority of variance, whereas the genetic algorithm was used to maximize rank correlations between the composite rank and the individual indicators rank.

Both rankings gave a balanced and consistent picture. However for the absolute indicators a very favourable property of the genetic algorithm method showed its advantage, namely not being sensitive to extreme values: a group of countries, in which there was no accordance between trade indicators (high-tech exports and the imports of measurement equipment) and the more conventional R&D indicators (GERD, researchers, patents, publications) was 'punished'. Without the trade indicators however, the composite ranking lists constructed by the two methods are statistically the same.

Since the bias caused by trade indicators touched upon quite a large group of countries, these variables were taken out from further analysis.

In the ranking methods used, we did not differentiate between output and input indicators, because there were no substantial differences between the composite input and composite output ranks (only some of those countries were positioned differently and with less consistency, which were also 'picked' by the genetic algorithm, for example Singapore but not Hong Kong). To compare input and output against one another, we experimented with the Data Envelopment Analysis (DEA) method that is conventionally used for efficiency measurement in operations research.

The DEA method gives very valuable insights beyond simple ranking. Although the ranking lists constructed seem to convey an important message at first sight, they do not answer the question why some countries are more competitive in R&D than others. If we accept that the four-dimensional space determined by GERD and the number of researchers as inputs and domestic patents granted and scientific publications as outputs provide a 'true and fair enough' picture of the world's R&D at the country level, the DEA method will tell an important side of the story.[71]

By providing points in space which are vigorously efficient (reference countries), the R&D policy mix of less-efficient countries can be analysed in light of the position of the given country. To understand some country positions better, diagrams that depict the three-dimensional efficiencies may help the analysis, but in this case not only CSR and VSR efficiency rates change, but some information (the fourth dimension) is also lost.

Unfortunately the DEA is even more sensitive to extreme values or variables that stand out as compared with other variables of the same country. This in general would not be a problem: however quite often we will have countries that have smaller 'absolute' R&D capacity as reference countries where – beyond fluctuating statistics such as in South East Asia – especially the propensity to patenting can change from one year to another. Therefore as long as there is no perfectly reliable R&D data, the Data Envelopment Analysis should rather be used to understand one year's 'static' pictures (cross-sectional analysis) instead of trends in time, for which the ranking methods seem to be much more reliable.

Although we had to omit it from this chapter, it must be mentioned that we tested the DEA method for the six absolute variables case (trade indicators included) as well. Beyond the (partial) unsuitability of the omitted metrics, in the six-dimensional case we basically got lost in details. As a result, in future analysis we recommend running DEA only with four variables when countries are compared.

Beyond the methodological options to position the R&D competitiveness of countries, the quantitative approaches shown carry important policy messages.

For instance comparing the composite ranks of the 'absolute' and 'relative' R&D indicators we have seen that four countries appear in the first ten on both lists: the United States, Japan, Germany and South Korea. Furthermore South Korea is efficient in any approach, but the other three countries are also efficient under variable return to scale conditions. At the turn of the millennium these economies really seem to be the great powers in the world's R&D.[72]

The R&D competitiveness position of a given country can also be analysed in such a way that all possible competitors are taken into account. We would take Spain as an example. In 2000 this country was between the thirteenth and fifteenth positions, if absolute R&D indicators were taken into account. If the individual indicator ranking lists are considered, we will find that Spain's competitive strengths are patents and publications, whereby high-tech exports lag slightly behind.

As far as the composite relative indicator ('the general state of R&D within the Spanish economy') is concerned, Spain is twenty-third in the world. Its spending on R&D as a part of GDP (GERD) is below its competitors. Nonetheless it is efficient in its size group (VRS efficiency = 1) while it is close to its main reference country, New Zealand (CRS efficiency = 0.57). Whether or not this efficiency is reflected in increased R&D investment, the Spanish situation can be described by in-depth studies, which can also investigate whether or not the example of New Zealand is relevant for the Spanish R&D policy (for Spain, New Zealand is the efficiency reference country).

Details about the efficiency of Spanish R&D can be read from the input utilization diagrams. Spanish researchers produce papers and patents with 0.33 efficiency in an input mix close to Israel, which is basically the reference country. Spain is in good company in this comparison: Belgium, Canada, Denmark, Australia and Sweden have very similar positions. Spain's efficiency in GERD utilization is 0.19 which seems low, but this value ensures fourteenth position to the country in international comparison.

Spain's neighbours in this comparison are Greece, the Czech Republic and Hong Kong. Trends can also be surveyed. Spain advanced to the twelfth position in the composite rank of 'absolute' R&D indicators by 2000 jumping four ranks in five years and improved by five positions on the 'relative' composite rank. These changes and the country's respectable position as compared with its competitors confirm it is likely that Spain's R&D competitiveness will improve in the future. This observation is supported by Spain's VRS efficiency in producing publications. In the VRS model Spain was efficient in 1995 and in 2000 as well. On the other hand in the CRS ranking Spain was eleventh and fell back to nineteenth position. Taking the list of countries overtaking Spain shows that not the strong competitors pushed it down, but it seems that it lost some from its publication efficiency during the five years.

There are many further issues to investigate. For the longer-term applicability of the methods it would be desirable to have a more reliable and wider data set over a long time series, which could provide a firm base for trend analysis. In addition to that, domestic patents were considered in our present analysis while from the point of view of international competitiveness internationally registered patents (USPTO, JPTO, EPO patents) would be more relevant.

In the long run the composite ranks developed may serve as guidelines for positioning the R&D of countries particularly if the self-adjusting weights prove to be stable over time or at least show small and consistent changes. Thus a periodic repetition of the same measurement would contribute to the consolidation of the methodologies applied.

R&D productivity could be described in a more articulate way if besides the number of patents and publications their innovation relevance (as analysed in other chapters of this book) can also be taken into consideration. However this would require innovation surveys based on an internationally harmonized methodology, which in the short run will not be possible to carry out in many countries.

The relationship between technological and economic development and R&D indicators also needs detailed analysis. From the input side, education as an input to R&D is also an essential factor, yet harmonized measurement is even more problematic in this case. Depending on national statistical systems and structures of R&D financing, a given part of GERD is channelled into higher education, and thus education is implicitly contained in the analysis to some extent. It is obvious however that the role played by education systems in R&D competitiveness deserves an in-depth analysis, but it is beyond the framework of the present study.

4. Policy conclusions for the transition countries and the developing world

Mainstream NIS analyses have usually covered advanced economies where the 'triple helix' concept is an adequate tool for describing the institutional framework of R&D and innovation policies, and the picture seems to be quite clear from the viewpoint of evolutionary economics as well. This means more or less transparent and evident relationships between R&D, innovation, productivity and GDP growth, and last but not least the systemic, more specifically institutional framework of the NIS.

Other models (such as the 'random' approach) can be used for analysing the NISs of less-developed countries, but there are many cases not covered by any of these models known from the literature. The most important among such cases have an intermediate character: they belong to countries which have the chance to catch up with the developing world regarding R&D competitiveness, but the deficiencies of their R&D and innovation systems also make it possible that they will fall back to the level of poorly performing Third World countries. These intermediate or atypical cases are such countries which are currently more or less directly behind the advanced industrial economies on our ranking lists. These countries include the transition economies of Central and Eastern Europe as well as a quite small number of successfully industrializing developing countries.

4.1 ECONOMIC TRANSITION, R&D AND NISs: SYSTEMIC AND INSTITUTIONAL CHARACTERISTICS

We have included transition economies in our international comparisons, but they have been given only sporadic attention in international R&D policy and NIS related literature so far. In addition to this, it has to be explicitly stressed that only a few publications, mostly not available in English, have dealt with some general problems of evolutionary economics in these countries. No such analytical attempt is known to this author however, in which the toolkit of evolutionary economics would have been used to address the implications of NISs for the economic and institutional development of these countries.

Both available literature and our comparative results seem to speak of a number of special characteristics of NISs in transition economies. The possible paths of developments of their NISs can take two directions: some of them may join the club of international leaders in R&D competitiveness, while others could have NISs with characteristics described by the 'random' model, and performances similar to the poor performers regarding R&D competitiveness, the vast majority of which belong to the Third World.

Transition countries analysed in the international R&D literature include China (Liu and White, 2001; Liu and Wang, 2003), Bulgaria (Tchalakov, 2001), the Baltic republics (Lankhuizen, 2000), and Hungary, the Czech Republic and Poland in country studies of the OECD (1999) or in OMFB (1999b), Biegelbauer (2000), Tamási (2001), Kukliński (2001), Müller (2001), Zajac (2001).

Besides these publications, literature on the problems of innovation and R&D in the transition economies has been far from comprehensive. The quite rare exceptions include Török (1994), Biegelbauer (2000), Gorzelak et al. (2001), Aide à la Décision Économique (2001), Török (2002), but no recent comparative analysis of R&D development and policies in transition economies including the totality of former socialist countries is known to this author.

The separation between R&D and innovation was quite evident in most socialist economies before the political and economic transition that started in the years 1989–90 (except perhaps pre-1990 Yugoslavia on the NIS of which the case analysis of Slovenia from Biegelbauer, 2000 gives a quite comprehensive picture). Most countries had three different networks of research centres, and interaction between these was far from systemic. The three networks included:

- the Academy of Science of each country
- universities and establishments of higher education
- centres for applied research financed and supervised by sectoral ministries.

These networks enjoyed a great degree of independence from each other, while each of them strongly depended on the government from both a political and a financial point of view. These were quite rigid structures showing only few signs of evolution even in times of accelerated economic growth. The Academies of Science maintained extensive networks of institutes for basic research, and the universities were focusing (with the partial exceptions of Poland and Hungary) on higher education rather than research (see the country studies from Gorzelak et al., 2001).

The sectoral centres of applied research and development were supposed to serve the state enterprises in their respective sectors. The research profile of such centres was usually narrowly defined (for example the Research Institute for Construction Materials or the Paper Industry Research Institute), therefore one sectoral ministry had to supervise several research institutes and supply them with work. This meant that within the framework of the planned economy, state enterprises were asked to determine their R&D targets and the sectoral research institutes were expected to produce the corresponding R&D results. The relationship between R&D targets and results remained obscure in a great number of cases, and the contribution of institute-level R&D to enterprise-level competitiveness was mostly not evident either.

To complicate things even further, a certain confusion reigned regarding names and functions of R&D organizations. Some university-level institutions of technologically oriented higher education were called institutes in the Soviet Union or schools in Poland or East Germany. The name 'university' was reserved for institutions with traditionally broad scopes of research and education including humanities, law, medicine, natural sciences and, in some cases, even agricultural and technical sciences.

A notable example was Hungary where (perhaps as a sign of lasting path dependency) the former German practice of maintaining technical universities was kept in spite of the fact that these universities had no really universal profiles. Some technical universities in Hungary had really narrow scientific scopes, such as for example the Veszprém University of Chemical Engineering, the University of Heavy Industry at Miskolc or the University of Forest Engineering and Wood Industry at Sopron. The higher education reforms of the 1990s added new faculties to these universities, most of which then took on a more general character and started to play the role of an intellectual hub in their regions.

4.2   ACADEMIC RESEARCH IN THE TRANSITION ECONOMIES

The Academies of Science have a double character in most former socialist countries. They are a body of distinguished scholars elected by secret ballot,[73] and also an administrative superstructure of a network of research institutes covering most fields of basic research in humanities, social and natural sciences.

Origins of these research institutes go back to the 1950s. There was a relatively short period of (in the given circumstances) lavish government financing for them until the early 1970s. This meant basically safe jobs for a quite large number of researchers, and also some funds available for the development of research infrastructure. This availability of funds was however not necessarily a sufficient condition for obtaining scientific information from the West.

When macroeconomic difficulties set in for most socialist countries in the 1970s, the institutes generally became underfinanced by the government and could offer only deteriorating conditions of existence and work to their researchers. In return, requirements of performance were not too high either.

Before 1990 there were two exceptions to the practice of underfinancing academic research :

1. Additional financing could be obtained from the government if research was considered helpful to the economy or for strategic or military purposes.
2. Relatively liberal countries such as Poland or Hungary made it possible for their research centres including academic institutions to seek additional financing from grants abroad, and also from business.

This latter modest liberalization of academic R&D helped in keeping human capital in the sector. As an additional consequence, the focus of academic research shifted towards projects of a more applied character, and the profile of the research institutes maintained by the national Academies became more dependent on business needs.[74]

The network of research institutes of the Academies of Science underwent major reforms in most Central and East European countries after 1990. Their substantial downsizing implemented by the government was preceded by a loss of research staff owing to the fast widening of the income gap between business and academic research.

In Hungary for example, the nominal monthly wage of a research fellow with a PhD increased about twenty-four fold between 1988 and 2003, whereas the similar wage increase of a head of department in a ministry from approximately the same age group was about thirty fold or more, and still higher for a person with comparable qualifications employed by a multinational firm.[75] Most academic research institutes in the region had to bear a dramatic loss of qualified staff (Biegelbauer, 2000; Gorzelak et al., 2001).

This exodus was the most serious in the former Soviet Union where emigration to the United States and Israel literally decimated most research centres of the Academies of Sciences, mainly in the natural sciences.[76]

In other countries such as Poland, Hungary or the Czech Republic the exodus of highly skilled labour from academic R&D was also considerable. It was rather directed towards better-paid jobs within the country, but not at all necessarily in research and development in the business sector. The reason is that business R&D in these countries has been quite marginal with BERD[77] less than one-third of GERD[78] as opposed to the roughly two-thirds average level of industrial countries (OECD, 2001a). This explanation has a much weaker relevance for the countries of the former Soviet Union. In countries such as Russia or the Ukraine, well-paid domestic R&D jobs at firms were rare (since multinational firms were also not strongly present in those economies in the early 1990s), while many researchers had quite strong personal contacts in the academic world abroad.

National R&D statistics confirm the mentioned loss of highly skilled S&T manpower. In the Czech Republic for example, the number of people employed in R&D went down from 88 000 to 23 000 between 1991 and 1999. The FTE (full time equivalent) number of R&D employees in Hungary declined from 36 384 in 1990 to 21 329 in 1998 (Lányi, 2002).

A crucial and highly political issue of the institutional system of academic R&D in the transition countries was the role of their Academies of Science in formulating R&D policy. These Academies were widely regarded as survivors of old-time structures of R&D policymaking with their institutional portfolios limited to basic research and mostly isolated from real-world business. It was obviously true that the Academies had not been exempt from political influence from Communist governments at all and, mainly in social sciences, some scholars not really accepted by the international academic community became members of the Academies.

However the reference to almost exclusive Soviet influence on the systems of Academies of Science and their models of functioning in the transition economies (sources expressing this opinion are cited by Biegelbauer, 2000) was mainly true for the 1950s and the 1960s.[79] Countries like Poland, Hungary or even (East) Germany had their Academies founded in the eighteenth or nineteenth century[80] and, already at the time of their foundation, had roles and structures very similar to the Russian Academy of Sciences founded by Mikhail Lomonossov in 1755.[81]

In countries such as the Russian Federation, Poland, Hungary or Romania, no political screening of the academicians took place after 1990. This was decided in order to avoid unnecessary political intrigues and tensions with the tacit assumption that time would bring a quite fast rejuvenation of the membership of the Academies of the region.

Such a shift in the age structures of the Academies has taken place to a certain extent, and some Academies were able to gain certain political influence in shaping the R&D policies of their respective countries. On the other hand, their relative shares within the GERDs of their countries have become relatively low. The main reason is more business and innovation-oriented funding schemes of R&D are gaining ground in transition economies which creates an increasingly unfavourable environment for basic research.

The former debate on the *raison-d'être* of the Academies of Science is yielding ground in the transition countries to the debate on whether relatively poor countries could afford financing basic research or not. Leaving basic research to more prosperous countries would certainly raise the problem of free-riding, but such a government decision has not been taken in any of the transition economies yet.

The Soviet occupation of these countries in 1945 did not bring a completely new Soviet-type structure of science policy to them, but only a partly new application of an older institutional framework more or less shared by all countries of the region. Interestingly however, the only new Continental member country of the European Union which (as part of Yugoslavia) had managed to stay clear of the Soviet zone of control or influence after the Second World War, Slovenia, has had an Academy of Sciences organized in a way differently from other transition economies in the region. It is also a society of distinguished scholars, but its research role is confined to culture and history, and its direct influence on S&T policymaking is strongly limited (Biegelbauer, 2000, 176).

Reformist zeal in and after 1990 to destroy or substantially downsize the Academies of Science in East and Central Europe was based on a certain degree of neglect regarding the role of these institutions in preserving national cultural identity,[82] and also on a kind of disregard for their traditional role not only in the institutional framework of R&D as narrowly defined, but also in the broader system of cultural institutions in these countries.

Still, the argument of strong Communist presence in the membership of the Academies based on political rather than scientific merit had to do with reality. Political wisdom was needed to take balanced action after 1990: liberating the Academies from any kind of political influence while offering them a well-specified role in national S&T policymaking on the one hand, and solving the problem of 'pre-transition' membership on the other. This latter problem was all the more complex in that a great number of valuable and internationally recognized scientists had joined the Communist Party in order to promote their own scientific careers. There were very few extreme cases of 'pure scientists' and 'pure Communists'. It would have been very difficult to distinguish between those academicians who had been elected due to their political affiliation but had real scientific merit, and those for whom their pseudo-affiliation had been a precondition for unfolding their own research potential.

Comparable data are not available, therefore Hungarian statistics are used to show the relative importance of the Academy of Sciences in R&D. Its percentage share within the country's spending on R&D is less than 20 per cent, while universities obtain more than 25 per cent of research funding. The role of universities is slowly changing towards the 'research university'-type model usual in the United States and increasingly frequent in Western Europe. This is a good sign of systemic evolution but there is still a quite long way to go if a complete transition to Western models of S&T policy and structure is envisaged. It is still an open question in a number of transition countries whether universities are full-fledged parts of the NISs of these countries or not.

The higher education system of the Czech Republic was, at least until the end of the 1980s, unprepared for doing quality research on a mass scale, even less so than Polish or Hungarian universities (Müller, 2001, 189). The pre-1990 research capabilities of Hungarian universities are given a relatively favourable assessment by Biegelbauer (2000, 93), but both authors emphasize that the fast increase of student enrolment along with a stagnation of the number of teaching staff during the 1990s has made it very difficult to Czech or Hungarian universities to switch to the model of a research university.

Some representatives of foreign investors in the transition countries have expressed their concerns about the poor supply of skilled workers and technicians and the so-called overproduction of graduates in these countries (HEBC, 2003; see also Tamási, 2001; Kukliński, 2001; Müller, 2001; Zajac, 2001; and Aide à la Décision Économique, 2001, 124–6.). Such assessments also say that policies of higher education still tend to inflate student numbers and push the system towards a model of mass education in several transition countries.

The statistical picture is however a bit less clear. It is true, on the one hand, that student numbers have grown at a fast pace in these countries since 1990 and the capacities of higher education have not followed this development (Gorzelak et al., 2001). International comparisons of higher education lead, on the other hand, to a slightly different assessment: the percentage of holders of first university degrees or 'short cycle' or bachelor's degrees in science and engineering degrees in the 24-year-old population is markedly higher in a number of European transition countries than in a number of countries in the EU-15 or Asia, and even not too low by American standards (see Figure 4.1).

The data cover only a limited number of countries because only the number of 'long'-cycle or master's degree holders was given for other countries. Still, the relative position of most transition countries of Europe shown in the graph stands comparison with the EU-15 or the United States, and above all China, if the relative numbers of science and engineering degree holders are considered. The data cited do not inform us about the quality of education, which makes the quantitative comparison somewhat unreliable. The inflation of student numbers is still an argument against the higher education policies of the transition countries. This argument is not supported by our international comparison of limited scope.

Furthermore this argument cannot be subscribed to if there is widespread acceptance of the fact that also the societies of the new member countries of the EU have to move in the direction of knowledge-based society in line with the Lisbon Strategy of the EU. The accelerated growth of their stock of human capital is a necessary condition for the evolution of these economies. This growth helps increase the number of firms not only competitive on the short

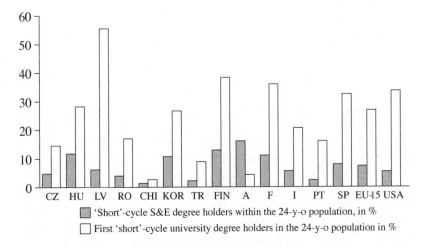

■ 'Short'-cycle S&E degree holders within the 24-y-o population, in %
☐ First 'short'-cycle university degree holders in the 24-y-o population in %

Source: NSB (2004), Appendix Table 2–33, A2–67.

Figure 4.1   The relative share of tertiary degree holders within the 24-year-old population, in percentage (2000)

run, but also fit to apply the routines required by the competitive environment of the mature market economies (see Nelson, 1995, 68).

4.3   SYSTEMIC CHANGES IN THE S&T SECTORS OF THE TRANSITION ECONOMIES

At least two transition economies of Central and Eastern Europe, Poland and Hungary, have had R&D sectors quite open to the West since the early 1970s (see Biegelbauer, 2000; Kukliński, 2001; Tamási, 2001). Biegelbauer's analysis of the Hungarian S&T system describes a number of transitions within Hungary's S&T policy paradigm (Biegelbauer, 2000, 12).

His periodization of the main paradigms and the major foreign sources of influence can be regarded as more or less typical for other countries of the region as well, except for what he believed the influence of American S&T policymaking in the 1970s and 1980s. He specifies four time periods in the development of Hungarian S&T policy based on the paradigms applied and the policy examples followed. This model can be regarded as valid for Poland as well (except for the fact that the country regained its independence only after the First World War). We briefly comment on Biegelbauer's periodization of S&T policy development in transition economies (Biegelbauer, 2000, 12), with an emphasis on its implications for R&D and innovation systems.

The first stage of development lasted from the 1870s to the late 1940s. The main paradigm underlying the system was the 'science push' model, that is scientists themselves enjoyed a considerable degree of freedom in determining the targets and scopes of their research. Inspiration came mainly from Germany and Austria, and the language of scientific communication was mainly German.

During this early period, the Academies of Science in Central Europe were not too much institutionalized. They had only very small administrative staff, and basically no research institutes at all. They were bodies of distinguished scholars working mainly at universities or in the government. The role of Academies of Science was an advisory one in R&D policy issues, but such policies played only a very limited role in the governments' strategic portfolios. Scientific production was widely regarded as something similar to literature or arts – contributing to national prestige and improving the quality of life, but without much direct influence on the economy.

The second period (the 1950s and the 1960s) was still based on a 'science push' model, but R&D was isolated from industry, corresponding strictly to the Soviet structure. Not only was the unique source of S&T policy inspiration the Soviet Union, but the international S&T relations of Central and East European countries were, with sporadic exceptions, limited to partnerships with Soviet research organizations. The language of international science was, in this part of the world, partly Russian with a strong role for German in social sciences and medicine, and English mainly in the natural sciences.

The Hungarian Academy of Sciences underwent an in-depth restructuring after the Communist takeover of power, in 1949. A thorough political screening of the Academy was followed by the exclusion of most of its members (to be accurate, formal exclusion was replaced by the creation of a 'consulting member' status for those declared unwelcome politically, but such 'consulting members' had no voting or other rights linked to membership). The Academy became kind of a Ministry of Science with its network of initially two, and later even close to 50 research centres, a central administrative staff and a president in the rank of a government member. The Academy was under strong political control, but it had no real influence on policymaking. Some elements of S&T or R&D policy in the modern sense started appearing in the early 1960s, but some links between science and economic policy were created only after 1968.

The third stage of development covered the 1970s and the 1980s. 'Demand pull' (that is directions and topics of research partly determined by the needs of the economy) became the main pattern and, at least in Biegelbauer's approach, the leading source of inspiration was the S&T policy of the United States. During these years, English became the language of science in Central and Eastern Europe as well, relegating Russian to the second position even in the communication between Soviet and Polish, Czech or Hungarian researchers.

The emphasis on American influence is understood in strictly technical terms by Biegelbauer. Institutional changes brought Hungarian R&D somewhat closer to industry, and research centres, including those supervised by the Academy of Science, obtained a certain freedom of entrepreneurship. They became free to get additional funding with contracts from industry, and researchers were granted a certain degree of freedom in maintaining contacts with colleagues from non-Communist countries and travelling abroad. The organizational structure of the Academy was not changed to a great extent, but its institutes were given a limited ground for action. They were, for example, quite free in determining their own research strategy but, along with this, they were increasingly pushed towards exploring alternative resources of financing. Most research institutes of the Hungarian Academy of Science had to earn a certain part of their financing from government grants or commissioned research. This meant that their complete financial support from the state budget ceased to be formally granted. In spite of all these positive changes, it is an exaggeration to consider the Hungarian S&T reforms of the 1970s and 1980s as an effort towards establishing an American-inspired S&T policy structure. Certain steps were taken in the right direction, but the entire system kept most of its former characteristics of an inefficient and oversized network of research centres isolated from the real world of innovation.

The fourth phase, initiated in the late 1980s, followed the 'innovation process' paradigm of S&T policy according to Biegelbauer, and the sources of inspiration apparently came from the United States and Germany. R&D spending was drastically cut in the late 1980s when the budgetary realities of the market economy had to be accepted by the government. The scaling down of GERD from levels comparable to those of the leading industrial countries (between 2.5 and 3 per cent) to practically Third World levels, below 1 per cent, was not a reform by itself, although it meant substantial changes in the Hungarian NIS. Similar developments occurred in then Czechoslovakia, Poland or Romania, and the outcome was, in each of these cases, a substantial decrease of GERD in percentage of the GDP.

So-called 'sectoral research centres' with a narrow industrial profile of applied research and development subordinated to the respective sectoral ministries were closed down during the first years of the 1990s in all countries of the region. This strategy was meant to streamline R&D in industry before its privatization, but the result was overkill. The number of enterprise-level research centres was only 98 in 1992 (7.6 per cent of all research units in Hungary,[83] down from a more than 30 per cent share ten years earlier).

The process of aggressive dismantling of R&D capacities in state-owned or non-private industry was not a specialty of Hungary. One of its unwanted by-effects was characterised in a telling way in one interview taken by Biegelbauer in Slovenia: 'instead of shedding fat, industry sheds brains'. (Biegelbauer, 2000, 176)

The Hungarian government understood that, besides making the Academy- and the university-based R&D system more competitive, a third, more busi- ness-oriented branch of the NIS was needed as well.[84] In practice however, the Hungarian government took a slightly different direction of institution-build- ing in 1991, following again the German path of building and maintaining R&D institutions.

It started to set up the Hungarian counterpart of the German network of the Fraunhofer Institutes, the Zoltán Bay Foundation Institutes for Applied Research. Their financial basis was an endowment by the government, but only three such institutes were established before government funding of the endowment had to be discontinued as part of the financial austerity package of 1995. The Bay network still existed in 2004, but it is far from being a substan- tial element of the Hungarian NIS and its presence cannot be considered as a proof that the Hungarian NIS is approaching the German institutional model of R&D.

Biegelbauer calls the not Academy-related, but still in part centrally financed R&D institutions 'intermediary' ones (this category corresponds roughly to what we call 'R&D diffusion organizations'). He points out that there has been one transition economy (the most advanced of all, by the way), Slovenia, where the establishment of such institutions has been a marked success (Biegelbauer, 2000, 176).

4.4   THE NISs OF THE TRANSITION COUNTRIES

The ultimate question with respect to the development path taken by the national innovation (or S&T) systems of the transition economies is whether these systems could survive in the competitive environment of European inte- gration or not. In all likelihood they would, but it is beyond doubt that most of them are lagging behind the European Union average, especially if pre-EU accession data are assessed.

The most recent assessments prepared on the innovation capacity and performance of the new member countries of the European Union use the 'scoreboard' method. This method consists in composing simultaneous lists of indicators considered of relevance for a correct description of the NISs of the countries listed. The scoreboard method poses a number of methodological problems. In spite of those problems, scoreboards offer a good first sight of the condition of the NISs and the R&D sectors of some transition economies, first of all the ones already members of the European Union.

The first attempt to prepare a scoreboard had a rather experimental character (Aide à la Décision Économique, 2001). It covered only those six candidate countries for EU accession which had been considered prepared for EU membership by the European Commission in 1997 (Cyprus, the Czech Republic, Estonia, Hungary, Poland and Slovenia). Further four countries (Latvia, Lithuania, Malta and Slovakia) were added to the group of 'first-round' candidates from Central, Eastern and Southern Europe in 2000, but this extension came too late to change the list of those six countries on which the first attempt to set up an innovation scoreboard was made.

Two new member countries of the EU (Cyprus and Malta) are not transition economies and they can boast of quite high levels of economic development as compared with the Central and Eastern European countries. Their NISs are, however, not too considerable in size and, at least based on the few available indicators, they do not seem to be comparable in quality to those of the most advanced transition countries.[85]

This first attempt was not a full success, for reasons other than the limited number of countries compared in it. The authors originally wanted to work with 17 indicators, but no country selected for this comparison could produce more than 10, and two countries could give data for only five indicators each. In general, most of the six countries surveyed had R&D- and innovation-related indicators below the EU-15 average. Only Slovenia could come up with a respectable statistical performance with three indicators above the average of the EU-15 (Aide à la Décision Économique, 2001. 84).

The overall picture from this first scoreboard experience already shows a number of such characteristics of the NISs of the transition countries, due to which the S&T sectors of this group of countries appear as special blends of quite good R&D and innovation potential and rather poor performance. Most of these characteristics were also described or referred to in other analyses of the NISs of transition countries (OMFB, 1999b; Biegelbauer, 2000; Török, 2002).

The strengths of the NISs of the transition countries surveyed include (Aide à la Décision Économique, 2001, 84):

- a good potential for catching up on the basis of new technologies;
- a relatively high ICT intensity (measured by the percentage of ICT-related spending within the GDP) for some more advanced transition countries, although these differences may only have a short-term character; and
- a relatively favourable skills structure of human resources.

The weaknesses are more significant in number (Aide à la Décision Économique, 2001, 84–5):

- important gaps in the transmission and application of knowledge, and weak connections between the different participants of the NIS;
- weak demand for R&D by domestic business;
- a limited number of innovative small firms; and
- a poor ability to generate financing (mainly venture capital financing) for innovation.

This scoreboard filled its sometimes serious gaps in statistical data with additional mainly enterprise survey-based information, and offered a concise and realistic analysis of the NISs of some transition countries.

It was however still short of a comprehensive statistical analysis which was published by the European Commission in 2003 with the extension of the European Innovation Trendchart to the new member countries joining in 2004. The three membership candidates after the 2004 enlargement (Romania, Bulgaria and Turkey) were also included, so that the Trendchart gave a quantitative picture of the NISs of ten transition and three Mediterranean countries.[86]

The ten indicators used in the Trendchart can be divided in five groups without any in-depth evaluation of the indicators themselves. The five groups are: (1) education indicators, (2) indicators of spending on innovation and R&D, (3) patent indicators, (4) indicators of high-tech employment, and (5) an indicator of ICT development.

The Trendchart data speak of a serious lag of the transition countries behind the EU-15 in almost every element of their NISs. This picture is of course somewhat misleading because it does not show the relative position of the EU-15 countries with respect to the same average, and some of them may also have considerable development lags. It is however quite telling that several transition countries are also in weak positions considering such S&T indicators which do not directly depend on the financial strength or the level of economic development of the country in question. These indicators should rather be regarded as describing key elements of the institutional evolution of the NISs of the transition countries in a narrow sense, but also of their entire economies facing a continuously growing competitive pressure as well.

Education

Quite interestingly, most of the 13 countries are lagging behind the EU-15 average as regards the relative share of young holders of graduate science and technology degrees, the relative numbers of people in active age participating in continuous education, and the relative share of people with graduate-level education. Depending on the indicators considered, only the Baltic republics, Slovakia (for the indicator of continuous education) and Cyprus (for the

Table 4.1 Selected innovation indicators for new member and candidate countries of the European Union, 2002 or latest available year (in percentage if not otherwise indicated)

Indicator	EU-15	BG	CY	CZ	EE	HU	LT	LV	MT	PL	RO	SL	SK	TR
Scid	11.3	7.9	3.3	5.6	7.3	3.7	13.1	7.6	3.3	7.4	4.9	8.2	7.4	5.5
Grad	21.5	21.1	29.1	11.8	29.6	14.1	44.0	19.6	7.0	12.2	10.0	14.8	10.8	8.9
Cont	8.4	1.3	3.7	6.0	5.2	3.3	3.3	8.4	4.4	4.3	1.1	5.1	9.0	3.2
Serd	0.69	0.37	0.22	0.52	0.53	0.57	0.49	0.28	NA	0.43	0.15	0.69	0.22	0.36
Berd	1.30	0.10	0.05	0.78	0.26	0.38	0.20	0.16	NA	0.24	0.25	0.94	0.45	0.27
USpt	80.1	0.6	2.6	3.0	2.2	7.3	1.4	0.8	5.1	1.1	0.5	13.1	0.7	0.4
EUpt	161.1	2.1	14.5	10.7	11.0	19.0	2.4	7.6	10.2	2.5	0.8	40.7	6.1	1.1
Ehti	7.41	5.34	1.11	8.94	3.41	8.50	2.64	1.97	7.14	7.54	5.50	9.28	8.21	1.19
Ehts	3.57	2.66	1.90	3.09	2.87	3.05	1.69	2.26	3.05	NA	1.57	2.35	2.83	NA
Eict	7.0	3.8	NA	9.5	9.6	8.9	5.9	7.9	4.1	5.9	2.2	4.7	7.5	3.6

Notes: Countries: BG = Bulgaria, CY = Cyprus, CZ = Czech Republic, EE = Estonia, HU = Hungary, LT = Lithuania, LV = Latvia, MT = Malta, PL = Poland, RO = Romania, SL = Slovenia, SK = Slovakia, TR = Turkey.

Indicators: Scid = percentage share of holders of graduate science and technology degrees in the age group 20–29, Grad = percentage share of holders of graduate degrees in active age (25–64), Cont = percentage share of participants in continuous education (25–64), Serd = government expenditure on R&D in percentage of the GDP, Berd = business expenditure on R&D in percentage of the GDP, USpt = USPTO patents per 1 million inhabitants, EUpt = EPO patents per 1 million inhabitants, Ehti = employment in high-tech industries, Ehts = employment in high-tech services, Eict = ICT expenditure in percentage of the GDP.

Source: Balogh (2004), 47; European Innovation Scoreboard (2003).

percentage share of graduate degree holders within the active population) are ahead of the EU-15 in these indicators.

Contrary to some widely shared beliefs, the transition economies do not have an adequate supply of highly skilled manpower for their NISs. This can be observed at the same time as their systems of secondary vocational education and apprentice training are underperforming (at least in Poland, Hungary, the Czech Republic and Slovakia, see Tamási, 2001; Kukliński, 2001; Müller, 2001; Zajac, 2001; Aide à la Décision Économique, 2001, 124–6.).

Spending

The levels of both government and business spending on R&D reflect its underfinancing, but from different aspects. Government spending on R&D (GERD minus BERD) as expressed in percentage of the GDP reaches the EU-15 average only in Slovenia, while it is less than half of the EU average in Cyprus, Latvia, Romania and Slovakia (no data were provided on Malta for spending on R&D). It has to be noted at this point that the EU average means a significantly higher level of GDP, but the really discouraging picture can be seen from the BERD data.

Except for Slovenia, and to a certain extent the Czech Republic, all the new member and candidate countries of the EU surveyed suffer from an evident lack of interest of domestic business in R&D.[87] Government measures aimed at providing incentives for business spending on R&D have repeatedly failed in these countries. This is a quite interesting development from the point of view of evolutionary economics. It speaks of the fact that these economies are becoming increasingly performing and competitive without any corresponding development in the innovational competences and capabilities of the firms. Domestic innovation is not pulling economic development to any significant extent, which seems to represent, at least from an R&D and innovation-oriented approach, a quite special pattern of development without evolution. It is very questionable whether such a pattern could be maintained on the long run or not.

As a kind of last resort solution, the Hungarian government introduced in 2004 an R&D tax levied on the turnover of each firm above a certain level of employment, but even this measure could not be expected to raise BERD to a significant extent. It can be said without exaggeration that the most problematic issue of the NISs of transition countries is why business is turning its back on domestic R&D (and R&D in general).

The weakness of institutional links between R&D organizations and business is a symptom rather than a cause. Explanations are better related to the low capacity of technological development for most firms in the transition countries, their concentration in low-tech industries, poor marketing, and the rare presence of firm strategies aimed at shaping consumer needs rather than trying to adapt to them.[88]

Patents

None of the countries listed reaches more than 25 per cent of the EU average, and this 'local maximum' is the EPO patent count for Slovenia. The reliability of patent counts as measures of innovative performance has been discussed in an earlier chapter, but the backwardness of most transition countries is strikingly evident in this respect. On the other hand, differences within their group are also quite visible. Regarding the EPO patent count for example, the relative gap between the EU-15 and Hungary is as wide as between Hungary and Lithuania. Slovenia's EPO patent indicator stands approximately midway between that of the EU-15 and the Czech Republic. This is also quite surprising considering the fact that the Slovene and the Czech economies are at comparable levels of development.

Those patent counts which are only fractions of Hungarian or Czech values speak of a strong isolation of the NISs of some South East European countries from international networks of innovation. Three such countries can be distinguished: Bulgaria, Romania and Turkey, all of which are still waiting for their admission in the EU. Their (sometimes long prolonged) candidate status is not directly linked to their poor innovative performance, but both things could probably be ascribed to backwardness in economic development to a certain extent.

It seems likely that the NISs of these three countries bear more similarities to those found in the developing world than in Europe. On the other hand, the Baltic countries have R&D parameters mostly well ahead of theirs. Still, the potential of Latvia, Lithuania and Estonia of developing modern NISs competitive with those of industrial countries is regarded rather sceptically by Lankhuizen (2000).

High-tech employment

The indicators of the transition economies may create quite favourable impressions in this respect, with several new member countries being ahead of or close to the EU-15 average. In fact, the best-performing transition countries here are those which were able to attract the most FDI (foreign direct investment) and, not unrelatedly to this, are the most prosperous among the new Continental member countries of the EU (Hungary, Poland, the Czech Republic, Slovenia and Slovakia). Relatively high employment levels in their high-tech sectors are due to massive inflows of foreign direct investment much more than to domestic efforts to encourage R&D and innovation.

ICT

A sole, expenditure-related indicator is used here, and this is the one which seems to show the best picture of the innovative capacities of the transition countries. Indeed a well-developed ICT sector is a prerequisite for having a good R&D potential in any country. Relatively high levels of ICT expenditure speak, on the one hand, of the considerable efforts of transition countries to reach the levels of industrial countries in this field. Data of Internet access, host density and the number of PCs per population have reached the EU-15 average or come close to it in Slovenia and Estonia, and partly also in the Czech Republic and Hungary.[89]

Realistically however, high spending on ICT may speak of both a consistent effort to develop the ICT sector and relatively high prices of ICT services. Former and recent international comparisons (Kiss et al., 2000; Petrenko, 2003; Kulikov, 2004) have shown that countries where the telecom sector was privatized without a corresponding strength of anti-monopoly measures tend to suffer from disproportionately high telecom and Internet tariffs:

> Most countries of Central and Eastern Europe have had this experience. For example, the average cost of local telephone calls in countries with comparable levels of economic development ranged between 0.13 USD per 3 minutes in Hungary, 0.09 USD per 3 minutes in Brazil, 0.07 USD per 3 minutes in Poland, the Czech Republic and Thailand, and 0.02 USD per 3 minutes in Croatia and the Republic of Korea. (data from the World Bank, cited by Kulikov, 2004, 37)

The Trendchart data speak of a significant gap in R&D between the EU-15 and all the new member and candidate countries. The case of the transition countries shows NISs in quite contradictory situations with an array of institutional and organizational problems aggravated by chronic underfinancing, but with a number of important assets. These assets put some of these countries in an intermediate position between industrial and developing countries as far as R&D is concerned. This finding is in line with our analysis of the R&D competitiveness of transition economies, several of which are direct followers of the developed industrial economies on our ranking lists.

4.5   NISs IN THE THIRD WORLD

Our survey of non-mainstream NISs is completed with a survey of some typical characteristics of NISs, mainly related to R&D input and output, in the Third World. Literature on the NISs of developing countries does not offer a wide coverage of the most important country cases, but the R&D map of this extremely heterogeneous country group is really varied. About 10 to 15 developing countries are currently quoted as having well-performing R&D sectors and NISs, whereas at least 60 countries have only marginal R&D capacities or none at all.

Mani's estimate is a bit more optimistic: he reckons that based on data from 1994, 98 per cent of R&D spending, 95 per cent of the total numbers of scientists and engineers employed in the world and 99 per cent of the patents issued by either US or EU patent offices belonged to 50 countries (Mani, 2002, 40). Out of these, 24 were considered developing economies by the author.

Mani's list includes at least five countries, which could be squeezed into this statistical category only with some effort. Korea has been a member of the OECD since 1996, Singapore and Taiwan have highly developed industrial capacities and powerful R&D sectors, and Brunei is a small and rich oil-exporting country with GDP per capita levels matching those of many OECD countries. China is a case apart: it can be regarded a developing country for its per capita GDP levels, but it is also an example of gradual economic and social transition, and one of the stars in the transition-related literature.

China's R&D system shows several specificities of developing countries. Its growth of total factor productivity (TFP) is largely conditional upon foreign direct investment (Liu and Wang, 2003), although the authors cited have also shown that domestic R&D in China is also an important factor in TFP improvement. This finding is even more important because their data come from the mid-1990s when both the competitiveness improvement of the Chinese economy and the inflow of FDI (foreign direct investment) to it were less spectacular than in the early 2000s. This is in marked contradiction with the experience of European transition economies (including the relatively advanced ones of the region) where the impact of domestic R&D on economic growth has been negligible in most cases.

The contrast between the Chinese experience and that of the countries of Central and Eastern Europe regarding NIS reform is even sharper if the literature on the two paths of R&D system development are compared. Sources from and on the new member countries of the EU generally speak of at best modest performances in transforming old NISs of planned economies into new, competitiveness-oriented ones (Török, 1994; OECD 1999; OMFB, 1999b; Biegelbauer, 2000; Lankhuizen, 2000; Tamási, 2001; Kukliński, 2001; Müller, 2001; Zajac, 2001; Gorzelak et al., 2001; Aide à la Décision Économique, 2001).

At the same time at least one in-depth analysis of the NIS of China (Liu and White, 2001) described a successful transformation of the system. This analysis created the impression that China stands out among the transition economies regarding NIS reform, but Liu and White also stressed that huge regional imbalances in R&D capacities have not been much touched in China yet.

Furthermore these authors did not explicitly address a problem of key importance for the NISs of the transition economies of Europe, namely the strength and the degree of complexity of linkages between domestic business and domestic R&D, which is also a key point in assessing the evolutionary potential of these NISs. These linkages are weak in most if not all European transition economies, and it has not been proven that the Chinese case would be markedly different in this respect.

After these very brief remarks on China, it now seems practical to consider all those countries which are neither members of the OECD nor transition countries of Europe. Could they be regarded as elements of a more or less consistent third group?

4.6   R&D IN DEVELOPING COUNTRIES

Our main argument in this section is that the term 'developing country' is a very vague one if we try to apply it to that extremely heterogeneous group of countries which are neither members of the OECD nor transition economies, but may still have NISs of respectable quality and good competitiveness potential. This group of countries offers a string of intermediate cases where various parameters of economic development and R&D show degrees of consistency much below those observable either within the OECD or the transition group (although these latter two groups of countries overlap in the cases of Poland, Hungary, the Czech Republic, Slovakia and Slovenia, all admitted to the OECD in 1990s and to the EU in 2004).

The first surprising intermediate case from the Third World is that of Cyprus which is neither an OECD country nor a transition economy, and certainly not an industrial country either (Hadjimanolis and Dickson, 2001, 807). Still, it is considered a high-income country by the World Bank, and has been admitted to the European Union. This small country with only a 0.7 million population has a very low level of GERD/GDP ratio (0.2 per cent according to the latest available data which puts it in a position comparable to that of Thailand or Indonesia in this respect).

Cyprus has just one university, established as recently as in 1992, and only one or two research centres (Hadjimanolis and Dickson, 2001). Nevertheless the share of high-tech goods in Cypriot exports is larger than in New Zealand or Iceland (Hadjimanolis and Dickson, 2001, 809), both OECD countries with markedly higher levels of both per capita GDP and GERD/GDP than Cyprus.

So is Cyprus a developing country with respect to R&D? The impossibility of giving a fully acceptable answer to this question demonstrates another impossibility: finding an exact counterpart in NIS analysis of the term 'developing country' so often used in international economics. In their case study of

Thailand, Intarakumnerd et al. (2002) also argue that there seem to be three paths of NIS development (they do not consider transition economies a separate case): developed countries, 'learning-intensive' developing countries and developing countries (Intarakumnerd et al., 2002, 1445).

In spite of the lack of clarity in the usage of international economics terms for NIS analysis, we try to refer to developing countries when we mean non-OECD and non-transition countries. It was widely believed for decades that developing countries should not invest too much into R&D and innovation due to the low efficiency of their NISs. It was expected instead that foreign direct investment would transfer the necessary intellectual and physical capital to such countries in order to help them become major exporters of high-tech goods.

The World Development Report of 1998 largely contributed to changing this conviction. It demonstrated that developing countries might gain much from creating knowledge at home, and that 'some types of knowledge must be built from the ground up' (Mani, 2002, 27). Besides this, it seems evident that high-quality university education is needed in developing countries as well, but such capacities cannot be created without a country's own R&D of corresponding size and quality.

The NISs of the developing countries (LDCs = less-developed countries) can be divided into three main groups which correspond roughly to the GERD/GDP levels of these countries. The lack of data does not make it possible to set up an R&D scoreboard for the developing countries, but the comparison of their GERD/GDP levels shows, as a starting point, the relative sizes of their R&D capacities. Our focus is, for the time being, not the comparative analysis of R&D competitiveness in the Third World, but a structured assessment of their NISs based on the data available for the widest possible range of countries.[90] We can speak of the good performers, the underperformers and the non-performers within the group of Third World (or, more accurately, non-OECD and non-transition) countries.

The 'Good Performer' LDCs

The first group could be called that of the 'good performers' (only in the context of the Third World, of course) with more or less efficiently functioning NISs and relatively high levels of GERD (0.5 to 1 per cent of GDP, with some exceptions of still higher values in Israel, Singapore or Taiwan and lower ones in places like Argentina or Malaysia).

There seems to be a historical upper limit to GERD/GDP in Latin America: Katz observes that, as a rule, Latin American countries have never had GERD levels above 0.5 per cent of GDP out of which about 80 per cent has usually come from their governments (Katz, 2001, 4). He also points to the historical gap in GERD/GDP between industrial countries and South-East Asian economies on the one hand and Latin America on the other which cannot be explained merely by differences in economic development.

The efficiency of the NISs of the good performers would be, in most cases (that is with the exception of Israel, Singapore and Taiwan), not directly comparable to the input performance relationships in industrial countries. Their R&D outputs (publications and patents in the first place) compete rather with those of transition or Mediterranean OECD-countries.

Mani lists 16 developing countries (not necessarily good performers in R&D in our sense of the term) with their data for R&D intensity[91] given as the average for the years 1987 to 1997 (Mani, 2002, 41). Only three countries on the list, Korea (already a member of the OECD from 1996, therefore not a developing country in the strict sense of the term), Singapore and Taiwan have levels of R&D intensity above 1 per cent. Six others (Brazil, South Africa, Venezuela, India, Pakistan and China) are in the range of 0.49 to 1 per cent. Of the rest, five countries showed an R&D intensity higher than 0.2 per cent (Argentina, Tunisia, Syria, Malaysia and the Philippines). Finally, Thailand and Indonesia spent on an annual average less than 0.2 of their GNP on R&D between 1987 and 1997. This short list may convincingly indicate the extent to which the NISs of admittedly developing countries differ from each other.

Developing countries considered good performers in R&D have respectable economic potentials (measured by absolute GDP size) more often than not, and their NISs may benefit from some leveraging factors not present in transition economies of similar levels of R&D competitiveness.

For example the NISs of Brazil, Israel, South Africa, India or Pakistan are likely to be helped greatly by their regional power status, which creates a significant domestic market for defence-oriented R&D. Further, the fact that language of education is at least partly English in the latter four means a special competitive advantage in R&D as well.

Beside the countries mentioned above, in our opinion the good performers of the Third World also include Singapore, Malaysia, Taiwan, Chile and Argentina (not considering OECD members Korea and Mexico as developing countries). The good performers have a number of internationally quoted universities and research centres, their exports have a not-too-low content of high-tech goods (although Argentina with its 3.5 per cent[92] is a marked exception), and they are obviously visible in international patent and publication statistics.

What makes a real difference between these countries and the members of the OECD is that these economies are not so strongly integrated with the developed world as regards their factors of production and R&D as well as their policies. The economic, competition and technology policies of the developing countries are not directly influenced by OECD or EU standards. This gives their governments more ground for action in industrial policy and makes the preferential treatment of domestic firms less difficult as compared to their OECD competitors in industry or R&D.

The level of development of an economy (usually measured in per capita GDP) and its NIS are usually not too strongly correlated in the developing world, since the NISs of developing countries are usually islands of a highly educated, cosmopolitan and more or less adequately financed professional elite amidst seas of serious infrastructural, social and health problems. This can be demonstrated by the examples of the NISs of Brazil and India, and their subsequent comparison with Singapore – all three countries widely regarded as belonging to the (generally so-called) developing countries best performing in R&D.

According to World Bank data giving the average of the years 1987–97 quoted by Mani (2002, 41), India and Brazil had almost equal data of density of scientists and engineers per 1 million labour force (RSE indicator: 149 for India and 168 for Brazil) and also similar R&D intensity (GERD/GNP) indicators (0.73 for India and 0.81 for Brazil), while their per capita GDP (measured at PPP) shows an almost threefold difference (US$2,830 for India and US$7,710 for Brazil in 2002.[93])

On the other hand, Singapore stands out among the three countries for each of the three indicators, but her advantages are quite varied vis-à-vis her two competitors. Singapore's RSE value was 2,318 also on the average of the years 1987–97, and her R&D intensity 1.13 (Mani, 2002, 41). The Singaporean economy's advance over the two countries in R&D according to the measures used here may still appear modest if her per capita GDP on a PPP basis, US$27 030 is considered. In fact Singapore is about fifteen- to twenty-fold ahead Brazil and India both on per capita GDP and in the RSE indicator, and has an almost twofold advantage in relative R&D spending.

The NISs of the more advanced developing countries may suffer from several systemic or functional deficiencies. These are usually not often encountered in the advanced industrial countries, but are not exceptional at all in the transition countries, and bear some features of the 'random' model of innovation. The international opening of most Latin American economies has improved the efficiency of their NISs, albeit without appropriate increases in GERD levels for the time being (Katz, 2001).

The case of Brazil will be taken as an example for systemic deficiencies in 'good-performer NISs'. The analysis of Brazilian patent data has shown that even a more industrialized developing country's innovation system can suffer from an array of problems which deteriorates its competitiveness in international R&D (Da Motta, 2000, 1057–8):

- The large share of individuals in patents granted: a number of innovations realized with public (and perhaps also private) corporate financing are patented by participants of such projects on a private basis. Such innovations are therefore stolen (or 'privatized') as intellectual property. This has also repeatedly occurred in transition economies (see OMFB, 1999b), owing mainly to the legal loopholes of IP (intellectual property) regulation. Furthermore the diffusion systems of innovations are usually weak in LDCs which might explain why individual inventors (or micro-entrepreneurs) prefer to submit their patent applications themselves instead of channelling them through specialized firms of innovation management.[94]

- Little firm involvement in innovation: this problem is the flip side of the one explained above. There seems to exist a certain firm-level reluctance towards innovation, at least in the Brazilian case. Patents created within firms may leak from them because the protection of intellectual property is insufficient on the country and also on the firm level. In addition to this, a number of successful individual inventors are not interested in sharing their expected profits from innovations with firms, possibly because they do not work within firms, but as university or government employees. This structural bias (that is the relatively low number of R&D staff working in the corporate sector) is closely linked to the experience that the percentage share of BERD within GDP tends to increase with the level of economic development (see NSB, 2004, 4–50). The low interest of business in R&D and innovation has also been observed in most transition economies (Török, 1994; Biegelbauer, 2000; OMFB, 1999b; Lankhuizen, 2000; Tamási, 2001; Kukliński, 2001; Müller, 2001; Zajac, 2001; Gorzelak et al., 2001; Aide à la Décision Économique, 2001; Török, 2002).
- Lack of continuity in patenting: during the period of investigation (1980 to 1995), more than 60 per cent of the Brazilian inventor firms submitted only one patent application. This fact speaks of a low number of firms that could be considered innovative in a strategic approach. For most of the patent owners surveyed, innovation is not a continuous activity but it has rather a sporadic character: patent applications are submitted mainly when something is found, but looking for innovations seems to be a sporadic activity in most Brazilian firms surveyed.
- Low degree of sophistication in inter-firm technological division: innovation activities of Brazilian firms seem to be isolated not only in time, but also in space. This is again a problem related to the backwardness of the innovation diffusion system, observed also in European transition economies (see OMFB, 1999b; Gorzelak et al., 2001).
- Decline of patenting in the engineering industry: this happened in Brazil due to a fall in productive investment which shows the great degree of exposure of the NIS to business cycles. This high exposure is a sign of

the sensitivity of firms to changes in the financial climate and also of a certain lack of their financial strength, again a phenomenon not unknown in transition economies.

The above data were based on the number of patents granted by the Brazilian National Patent Office (INPI). Statistics from the United States Patent and Trademark Office (USPTO) show that Brazilian performance in patenting in the United States is good if other Latin American countries are used as a benchmark, but it does not compare well with the patenting performances of other developing countries with similar R&D capacities such as for example India (Mani, 2002, 283).

The intensity of innovation activities in developing countries is also influenced by differences between their patent systems and those in industrial countries, especially in the United States. The extension of patent protection in the United States in the 1990s was largely motivated by requests from high R&D intensity sectors, mainly the pharmaceutical industry. These claims were based on the fact that part of the benefits from American R&D had been transferred to Third World countries capitalizing on some loopholes in the American patent legislation, and also on its limited international scope (Jaffe, 2000, 548).

The 'good performers' may have a number of functional problems with regard to their NISs, but they are still active and, in some technological fields, quite competitive players in the international high-tech world. Their presence in the international R&D competition cannot be ignored even though their NISs do not have the coherence and the stability of those of most OECD countries, and they have only few innovative firms by international standards. These are, in any event, developing countries with R&D and innovation capacities not really typical in most parts of the Third World.

Such LDCs can be considered good performers which have demonstrated better performances in R&D and innovation than it could be expected judging from the level of their economic development. As the examples of Korea and Mexico have shown, LDCs with NISs comparable to those of advanced industrial countries may have the best chance of being accepted to the OECD, which can substantially boost both their imports of FDI and their access to R&D resources abroad.

The 'Underperforming' LDCs

The 'underperformers' are developing countries which have been able to reach a certain level of industralization and per capita GDP levels. Their R&D sector exists at least as far as the export performance of this sector is concerned, but its institutional profile is not too visible in many country cases. Their relatively high levels of development could bring them within range of visibility with the less-developed OECD countries. In marked contrast to the good performers however, the NISs of the underperformers are in no better shape than could be expected from their level of economic development.

These countries have PPP corrected per capita GDP data varying on a wide scale, roughly between the levels of Brazil and India. The GERD is below 0.5 per cent of the GDP, very often around 0.2 per cent only. Typical examples from this group are the Philippines, Indonesia, Thailand, Venezuela and Uruguay. These countries do not excel at all in international R&D output if publications or patents are considered.

In spite of that, some of them have surprising ratios of high-tech exports to total manufacturing exports. Based on data from 2001 (NSB, 2004, Appendix Table 6-1), the Philippines have a ratio of high-tech exports to total manufacturing exports of 48.2 per cent, Thailand 27.5 per cent and Indonesia 8.3 per cent. For comparison: the corresponding ratio reached 26.9 per cent in Mexico, 13.3 per cent in Brazil, 24.0 per cent in China, 48.4 per cent in Malaysia, 58.7 per cent in Singapore and 4.9 per cent in India.

This brief international comparison shows that more or less high levels of development of the economy or of the NIS are not necessary conditions for a good export performance in high-tech products.[95] The strategic question is however whether either of the two options 'strong domestic R&D *cum* weak high-tech export performance' or 'weak domestic R&D *cum* strong high-tech export performance' could be given a clear preference over the other.

This is of course a provocative or a pseudo-question, since the evidently best choice would be both strong domestic R&D and strong high-tech export performance. This however is not a feasible option for most developing countries except for such industrialized economies as Singapore, Malaysia or Mexico. Some of the rest, including Brazil and India, seem to prefer to invest in domestic R&D first and try to expand high-tech exports thereafter, whereas the underperformers (not in exports, but in domestic R&D) seem to have opted for the inverse sequencing. Some of them have become considerable exporters of high-tech goods but still lack an adequate domestic R&D potential.

We consider countries with poor indicators of R&D input and output to be underperformers regarding R&D in cases where they have assets for creating high-tech export capacities (even though the bulk of those assets is likely to come from multinational corporations), but these assets are apparently not used in domestic R&D. Thailand is a country with a medium indicator of high-tech export intensity, and an NIS in a condition which would make it difficult for Thailand to become a serious competitor in R&D with for example Turkey or Romania, both of which had similar levels of PPP corrected GDP per capita in 2002 (see www.economist.com/countries).

A case study on the NIS of Thailand (Intarakumnerd et al., 2002) calls this country an example of less-successful R&D and technological development. The authors are right in stating that international literature has focused on developing countries that were successful in building their technological capabilities and NISs (Intarakumnerd et al., 2002, 1445). Those less performing and visible in the catching-up process were neglected in the literature. The case study on Thailand is in a sense unique in trying to look into the factors of late and slow NIS development in the developing world.[96]

The country has 74 universities with more than 1 million students, but the quality of training is far from high and social sciences dominate the pattern of higher education (Intarakumnerd et al., 2002, 1451). The study analyses all those institutional players who might play a role in the NIS of an advanced country but most of them are clearly unprepared for playing such a role in the Thai economy. The government has some kind of industrial policy but this mutation of industrial policy is limited to the building of infrastructure and some export promotion, the only selective tool being the local content requirement for the car industry (Intarakumnerd et al., 2002, 1450). The vast majority of domestic firms come into contact with the world of modern technology only if they buy know-how or equipment 'off the shelf'. Multinational corporations use Thailand as an assembly base. As opposed to the transition economies where multinational firms have not yet taken much interest in domestic R&D (but could at least consider such an option), this option does not even exist in Thailand.

The article by Intarakumnerd et al. (2002) seems to have more importance for NIS research than just being an illustrative case study. It demonstrates that the NIS concept can work only for those countries where at least some of its building blocks have been in place before, and a critical mass of involvement by the government, by the learned and the business sector could be reached. If these factors are not available in an otherwise not very underdeveloped and performing economy, then it necessarily remains an underperformer in NIS terms and does not have a strong potential for evolution towards such an NIS which could play a significant role in economic development. Thailand's R&D competitiveness will also remain low even though certain indicators (for example the relative share of high-tech goods in manufacturing exports)[97] may seem to speak of a not unimpressive level of R&D competitiveness.

Thailand has a non-zero GERD/GDP indicator (0.13 per cent on average for 1987–97 as quoted by Mani, 2002, 41), although the country study by Intarakumnerd et al. (2002) does, quite unusually in the literature, not give any GERD figure for the country. The authors do not deserve any blame for that, since their article is just a strong argument in favour of proceeding to quantitative NIS analysis only if the institutional conditions for competitive R&D exist in a country. In any event this extremely low but non-zero GERD level offers Thailand a chance of starting a policy effort towards building its NIS. The study by Intarakumnerd et al. (2002) is concluded with a description of the first steps constituting such an effort.

The 'Non-performers'

Quite understandably, international R&D and innovation literature does not devote much space to the NISs of those developing countries which have neither any noticeable level of GERD, nor any other sign of the presence of high-tech or innovation-related activities such as a corresponding structure of exports. A considerable number of African economies including Senegal, Gambia, Ivory Coast, Kenya and Nigeria, some countries from Asia (Jordan, Syria, Cambodia, Myanmar) or a handful of Latin American countries such as Peru, Colombia and Ecuador can be included in this group.

The non-performers are not simply economies without any relationship to the world of advanced research and high technology or, to put it more bluntly, 'outsiders' to the high-tech world. These are countries with levels of economic development offering them some elbow room for spending on R&D, but having no apparent political interest in developing R&D as a sector. They may have scattered R&D capacities, even producing some internationally acclaimed results ('local peaks'),[98] but the NISs as such cannot be observed statistically in such countries. The lack of any systemic background for R&D is characteristic of the non-performers, which mostly have domestic universities and a respectable number of educated intellectuals but no R&D capacities worth mentioning in the country itself.

The sporadically good R&D output statistics of the non-performers might simply be symptoms of the same phenomenon as when countries not quoted in international sports (for example tiny Caribbean islands) win medals at the Olympics in individual branches of sport such as swimming or athletics. The sportsmen representing newcomer countries at the Olympics are probably citizens of such countries, but they study at North American or European universities, do their training work also there and have no strong organic relationships with their home countries. The same goes for R&D output statistics: the country of the author of a much-cited article might not at all be the place where he or she does research. This factor distorts the statistical picture of international R&D to a significant extent only in the case of developing countries, mainly non-performers where there is no domestic R&D background to explain sometimes surprisingly good indicators of R&D output.

The case of non-performers shows a marked difference with such underdeveloped (in the true sense of the term probably not even developing) countries where no sign of the presence of modern R&D or high-tech activities can be found at all. We could possibly call these countries non-tech economies.

Such countries include several Sub-Saharan republics of Africa, a few countries in Latin America (for example Bolivia, Honduras or Nicaragua) and Asia (Nepal, Bhutan or Laos) where a great part of the population lives in a subsistence economy and neither infrastructural, nor human capital-related conditions are given for even the lowest-level assembly of modern products – not to mention high-tech goods as we have seen in for example the exports of the Philippines or Thailand.

A Possible Typology of LDCs with Respect to R&D

We have tried to show the great degree of heterogeneity of the so-called Third World or developing countries as far as their participation in international R&D competition is concerned. We have left aside such exceptional cases as the small oil exporters (for example Kuwait, Qatar or Brunei), where high levels of per capita GDP have no relation whatsoever to the quality of domestic factors of production such as human and physical capital or technology. Intermediate cases between developing and transition economies were also disregarded such as former Soviet republics of Europe or Central Asia (for example Armenia and Georgia from Europe, or Turkmenistan, Uzbekistan or Kyrgizstan from Central Asia) from which no reliable information on the condition of the NIS was available.

In addition to the above, we did not consider the few remaining Communist countries with undeniable R&D capacities but a very low level of exposure to international R&D and rare or completely missing relationships with the international R&D community. There seem to be two such countries left in the world: Cuba and North Korea.

Four groups of countries were established in decreasing order of importance regarding the weight and quality of their R&D sectors and NISs. We now summarize the findings of this effort of classification of LDCs.

The theoretical concept of NIS offers a good analytical tool for assessing country-level structures and performances in international R&D competition. The problem is that it was originally invented for countries where institutional structures and policy frameworks are transparent, with the condition of the NIS reflecting the overall welfare level and competitive positions of the economy quite well.

Moving toward the bottom of the list where countries are ranged according to their GDP per capita makes the picture less and less transparent. The

Table 4.2 A classification scheme of non-OECD countries according to the condition and performance of their National Innovation Systems*

Group	GERD/GDP	Level of economic development (per capita GDP, PPP)	Elements of NIS	R&D and high-tech output	Examples
'Good performers'	> 0.5%	Middle or low-middle	Existing, very well or relatively well organized	Comparable to several new members of EU or better	Israel, Brazil, Chile, India, China, Taiwan, Singapore, Pakistan, Republic of South Africa
'Underperformers'	> 0.2%	Middle or low-middle	Existing but either in initial stage or disorganized	Good only in some elements, high-tech exports may be strong	Malaysia, Philippines, Thailand, Venezuela, Uruguay, Argentina, Egypt, Tunisia, Morocco
'Non-performers'	0–0.2%	Low-middle or low	Only a few exist, scattered	'Local peaks' may exist, usually very weak	Colombia, Ecuador, Nigeria, Kenya, Senegal, Gambia, Jordan, Vietnam, Myanmar
'Non-tech' countries	≈ 0	Among lowest in the world	None	None	Sub-Saharan Africa, Nepal, Bhutan, Bolivia, Honduras, Nicaragua

Note: *OECD members Korea, Mexico and several transition countries not included; a few country cases may not completely fit into group.

organic link between a country's level of economic development and the condition and performance of its NIS gets increasingly weaker and the pattern of R&D or innovation policy more and more vague. A country's competitive positions in international R&D can be measured with a number of techniques surveyed in the previous chapters, but creating an institutional model of innovation with a good explanatory power for Third World countries too is still a daunting task.

5. The big picture

The ranking lists have shown that international R&D competition is basically dominated by the countries of the 'Triad', North America (mainly the United States), the Far East (particularly Japan) and the European Union. The leaders however do not constitute a homogeneous group and shifts in their relative positions are of major importance for the development of this competitive scene. Nevertheless the R&D competitiveness position of the leaders and followers can perhaps best be understood in the context of the Triad.

5.1 CAPACITIES AND PERFORMANCES IN INTERNATIONAL R&D: LEADERS AND FOLLOWERS

The gap in R&D capacities and performances between the United States (and to a lesser extent Japan) and the European Union is evident, and it exists in a number of respects (Rodrigues, 2003, 52–4). Spending on R&D expressed by the GERD/GDP ratio, the relative share of R&D financed by business, the number of patents per million of population, the relative share of researchers within the population, and the recently introduced indicator of 'knowledge investment'[99] are all lower in the European Union than in the United States. The existence of these gaps speaks of a clear advantage of the United States over Europe in R&D, but the size and the trend of this advantage cannot be measured exactly by simply listing such indicators which describe various dimensions of the R&D gap between the United States and the EU.

The Lisbon Strategy of the European Union has formulated a number of ambitious goals for European integration, including the building of a knowledge-based society in Europe (Rodrigues, 2003, 52). The programme considers a more ambitious policy for R&D to be a key tool of achieving this strategic objective, and it has also set a benchmark for the EU against which its effort towards improving its R&D performance can be measured. The benchmark is the United States, and the Lisbon Strategy has set the date of 2010 for catching up with the United States in a number of fields, including R&D.

A similar problem exists if the potential contribution of the new member states of the European Union to the R&D capacities and performances of the

EU-25 is to be identified. Most new EU members (except for Cyprus, Malta and Slovenia) have levels of economic development significantly behind even the laggards the EU-15, Greece and Portugal. The R&D indicators of some of the new Central European member countries are however directly comparable with if not better than those of a couple of EU-15 countries (again primarily Portugal and Greece, but also Ireland in some comparisons).

This apparent contradiction shows that comparisons of national R&D or innovation systems can produce different international ranking lists to those produced by comparisons of the levels of economic development. Could there be any acceptable method for ranking countries with respect to their roles in international R&D and innovation?

Tentative answers to this question have been given by a number of previous publications, but mainly with respect to innovation, and simply by putting together a number of diverse ranking lists based on a variety of indicators of R&D and innovation. In doing so, most of the authors apparently circumvented the problem of theoretical background. It remained unclear:

- How are such comparisons related to the theories of R&D and innovation?
- What kinds of units of R&D and innovation (individual researchers, R&D organizations, firms or countries) could be subject to such comparisons?
- What could be an appropriate theoretical frame of reference for comparing different characteristics or elements of R&D input and output in an international approach?

The analytical framework of comparative international R&D and innovation analysis has been provided by the model of national innovation systems (NIS, also referred to as NSI, national systems of innovation, in the literature) and, in a broader scope, a number of findings of evolutionary economics (see Nelson, 1995). A number of publications, mainly those by Laursen (2000) and Godin (2003), made it clear that the only statistically but also theoretically feasible way of making international comparisons of R&D capacities and performances is by using countries as the units of comparison. This approach can be accepted despite the fact that many individual R&D and innovation efforts can be linked to countries only in a controversial way.

Still, a number of indicators used in international economic comparisons such as GDP, exports, FDI (foreign direct investment) or government expenditure are country specific. The same applies for practically all the widely used indicators of R&D and innovation (GERD, R&D employment, patents, publications or the TBP – technology balance of payments). In the current stage of development of international economics, the intellectual influence of Smith,

Ricardo and the Heckscher-Ohlin theory can still be felt rather strongly. This is probably one of the main reasons why most international comparisons are carried out only among countries even if an increasing number of decisions substantially affecting the development of the world economy are taken not in cabinet rooms but at corporate headquarters.

The changes in relative international economic positions of countries can be partly attributed to their competitive efforts, and one possible approach to grasping the reasons and describing the impacts of these relative changes is competitiveness analysis. Its acceptance in the theory of international economics is far from general. It is used mainly in business analysis and strategy work, but also in global comparisons of the economic performances of national economies. Even if it still lacks a really solid theoretical background, its relationship with neoclassical and post-neoclassical (for example neo-technological) theories of international trade is undeniable.

The analyses of economic competitiveness usually go in two directions. One approach is the competitiveness of exports, where the main question asked is how the competitive positions of the exporting country have changed vis-à-vis its main competitors. This kind of competitiveness analysis can yield good results mainly if comparability is taken into account, that is only those countries are compared whose products really compete with each other on a large scale.

The second possible approach is comprehensive competitiveness analysis, when the overall condition of various national economies is compared based on the assumption that a well-functioning economy should be competitive. This is a somewhat controversial approach since good macroeconomic performance does not necessarily mean that the economy in question has competitors abroad. For example let us imagine a closed national economy that imports a negligible share of its inputs and is not export oriented either. Competitiveness analysis for such a country could be only of limited validity, if any at all.

Furthermore, a striking characteristics of competitiveness related research consists in its methodological diversity. A wide range of methods is combined in most well-known comprehensive analyses of competitiveness, while models of export competitiveness are, in many cases, rather one-sided. A co-existence of analyses of export competitiveness based on inputs (for example unit labour costs) and outputs (for example trade performance) can be observed, but very few if any analyses of competitiveness have tried explicitly to combine the input- and the output-oriented approaches. No surprise if, even for the same national economy, input- and output-based evaluations of competitiveness may yield quite different results.

In spite of this methodological pluralism (not to say confusion), competitiveness analysis is usually a challenging task promising interesting insights into the patterns of economic development and the factors of success or failure of various national economies. National economies seem to compete with each other in fields much wider than just exports, including sectors where economic analysis faces a number of previously unknown methodological difficulties. Such a sector is R&D and innovation, where the concept of competitiveness analysis has not been applied before to a wide sample covering most of the world economy.

There seem to be several good reasons for extending the scope of competitiveness analysis to R&D and innovation. The inputs and the outputs of these activities are relatively easy to identify and to measure, even if a wide range of inputs and outputs may not be completely visible.

For example visible inputs of R&D include GERD and human resources, whereas the high quality of a country's education system or the good condition of its R&D infrastructure are invisible inputs not measurable directly. There are also a number of invisible inputs to it, such as for example a consistent effort of institution development and building or the development of the national education system.

Similarly, visible outputs of R&D (or of the NIS of a country) are publications and patents, while invisible outputs can be the increase of the tacit knowledge base of the economy on the one hand, and innovations and other products of R&D used entirely within a company (that is not made public at all) or sold without any patent protection on the other. Besides the fact that some invisible outputs of R&D are difficult to measure and compare across countries, patent registrations do not reflect innovations in an exact manner, and can be understood only as a more or less reliable proxy of just one kind of output of innovation activities.

In spite of all these methodological uncertainties, we believe competitiveness analysis in R&D and innovation can bring considerable results if both their most important and visible inputs and outputs are appropriately taken into account. In fact the logic of competitiveness analysis would require that each country's R&D and innovation outputs reflect its R&D inputs to a considerable extent, and this is the case for the majority of OECD countries.

Still, the examples of transition economies have shown that there can be important exceptions to this observation (for example decreasing GERD/GDP ratios do not necessarily entail worse performances in publications). On the other hand, the NISs of a number of developing countries also seem to behave in such ways that the supposedly causal links between inputs and outputs of R&D and innovation are far from obvious.

Reviewing a number of different international comparisons of capacities and performances of the NISs of a wide range of countries has produced important insights. These go significantly beyond assessing the value of various measurement techniques of inputs and outputs in this sector.

In the most advanced industrial economies for example, generous R&D financing from governments and business (with a high percentage share of the latter) coupled with relatively high levels of R&D employment yield corresponding results in terms of patents and publications. These are two kinds of output of the NIS which can be measured in a quite reliable way for a significant number of countries.

This result of our research cannot be regarded at all as a direct confirmation of the 'linear' model of innovation, since this model is less about the conversion of R&D inputs into outputs of R&D and innovation, than about the sequencing of the different stages of the innovation process. It may be telling however that some input and output parts of the 'black box' (as the innovation process is sometimes described, with reference to the apparently missing link between R&D inputs and outputs of R&D and innovation) are quite transparent in several advanced industrial economies. In this respect transparency means that innovation is 'mass-produced', R&D is more or less helping this mass production and, for a given amount of R&D inputs, relatively reliable estimates can be made on what kind and amount of outputs would be yielded by those inputs.

Transparency is also related to efficiency of R&D and innovation. If the 'black box' is not 'black' any more, then relatively few R&D inputs will be wasted before appropriate measures of correction are taken.

A string of advanced industrial economies are world leaders according to most of the measures of R&D input and output. These countries are heading, without any doubt, the world ranking list of competitiveness in R&D, practically independently from the technique with which R&D competitiveness is measured or approximated.

This result has been corroborated by our quantitative analysis using several indicators of R&D input and output regardless of whether the indicator of high-tech exports was used or not. The real world leaders in R&D both stand out whether absolute or per capita measurement techniques are used. The combination of different ranking lists has produced a clear picture in both cases. Four countries – the United States, Germany, Japan and South Korea – belong in the first ten countries on our world ranking list reflecting R&D competitiveness or, in a slightly different approach, efficiency.

This group of world leaders in R&D comes as a slight surprise only if South Korea is considered. South Korea is an economy with one of the highest GERD/GDP ratios in the world, and with a long-time policy record of coordinated efforts towards improving competitiveness through building an innovative-based and (to borrow one of the key terms of the Lisbon strategy) knowledge-based economy.[100] In addition to that, the size of the country's population makes it comparable with France or the United Kingdom, former great powers but still important players in international R&D.

No doubt the British or the French NISs still belong to the best performing in the world, but they have lost some ground in international R&D competition due to various reasons. Their spending on R&D is either lower than in the four world leader countries or, as the French example shows, the proportion of their R&D financing provided by business is surprisingly low. It may be interesting to note at this point that these two countries are the only nuclear powers within the European Union.[101]

Belonging to the top ranks of international R&D is also a matter of country size. The reason is a number of countries that are very efficient and competitive in R&D cannot be placed high in the synthetic ranking list of R&D competitiveness due to their limited market power, that is their relatively small country size. Such countries with relatively small sizes of population can obtain high positions only on the relative or per capita lists of R&D competitiveness, but they fall somewhat behind on the absolute lists.

These countries include, mainly, those members of the European Union which can be considered outliers in terms of the Lisbon Strategy. Their GERD/GDP ratios belong to the highest in the world, and their per capita indicators of R&D and innovation output are also among the best. They have already fulfilled the Lisbon objectives regarding both spending on R&D and the qualitative aspects of their NISs, but their low statistical weight within the European Union implies that their excellent indicators cannot entail a substantial improvement of the EU average. These countries include Sweden and Finland and, along with them, Switzerland, the Netherlands, Norway and Denmark.

Non-European countries that also belong to the top category of international R&D competitiveness include Israel and Canada. Israel is the only such outstanding performer in international R&D which is not an OECD member. Israel has benefited from the substantial inflow of qualified manpower from the former Soviet Union – a positive externality for the NIS of the country. Although R&D statistics on Israel usually do not include military research-related information, civilian research in Israel probably enjoys some of the positive side-effects of military R&D.

The group of the countries performing best in international R&D poses relatively little problems of international comparison since the quantitative aspect of their R&D input and performance shows a quite homogenous picture. These are basically the only countries in the world where high-quality inputs lead to corresponding output. There is a quite strong linkage between the input and the output side of their R&D competitiveness, and all the relevant information speaks of the fact that the best competitors in international R&D are those countries where R&D is a top policy priority for the government.

In these countries, spending on R&D is regarded as an investment, the risks and yields of which can be more or less calculated in advance. In other words, the factor of uncertainty of spending on R&D is relatively insignificant in such countries since policies, infrastructures, and human and financial resources are effectively combined in order to achieve the best possible R&D performance.

It may be telling from a Lisbon Strategy point of view that less than half of the EU-15 could be considered to be part of the top group (Ireland, Belgium, Luxembourg, Austria, Italy, Portugal, Spain and Greece do not belong here by any measure) and none of the ten new EU members is even close to it.

The next field of R&D competitiveness is much more varied and coloured. The example of Spain demonstrated that different aspects of the R&D competitiveness of industrial countries which are strong but not top-level in international R&D show a multifaceted picture. Spain is also a typical case for this group of countries because its positions on the different ranking lists vary to a great extent, but the country is placed between tenth and twentieth on most of them. New Zealand, Austria and Italy have similar characteristics. The remaining EU-15 countries are also participants of international R&D competition which are well ranked in most comparisons, but cannot be considered such influential players in international R&D competition as their North American or North European counterparts are.

R&D is still close to being a strategic priority in these countries, but innovation is not sufficiently focused upon in policy implementation. These countries have quite well-developed R&D infrastructures, adequate but not generous financing for competitive R&D, and high-quality R&D manpower as well. Their NISs are well organized but, as the examples of Austria, Spain or Italy show, not too close to the business world.

This is also reflected by trade statistics: in spite of the fact that the high-tech content of manufacturing exports is considered a rather unreliable indicator for assuming an adequate domestic R&D background, the export structures of the three countries referred to above speak of relatively low levels of high-tech exports. This is not necessarily a sign of the weak competitive potential of their R&D, but it certainly shows that domestic R&D is not much used by the country's exporters. It does not seem at all surprising in these countries that their BERD/GERD ratios are rather small as compared to the top competitors in R&D.

This second group of countries competing in international R&D concludes that section of the composite ranking list of R&D competitiveness in which long-term government support for R&D and well-organized NISs can be considered as evidence, reflecting the strategic priorities described in evolutionary economics literature. In these economies R&D is a sector which obtains and delivers along well-established rules, and support for R&D is not regarded as a waste of taxpayers' or business money. R&D output and performance may not be strong in these countries, but it is solid and sufficient for maintaining a more or less extensive infrastructure for R&D and innovation.

The next group of countries is 'transitional' in several senses of the term (although it includes some member countries of the EU-15 such as Greece and Portugal, sometimes considered as advanced industrial economies in broader international comparisons), not only because it includes a string of transition countries, but also because it represents a field of competitiveness between that of the strong players in international R&D with well-organized NISs on the one hand, and the field of countries with poor R&D competitiveness and not quite transparent NISs on the other.

The NISs of most transition countries also combine certain characteristics of the NISs of advanced industrial and developing economies. They are interesting examples of the coexistence of traditional, centralized and modern, open and flexible institutional systems of R&D with a number of characteristics shared by this group of countries. Their R&D inputs show a strange combination of poor financing and sometimes quite good endowment with highly qualified manpower, but the usually very low exposure of their NISs to business makes these systems extremely sensitive to the fluctuations of government financing.

R&D is not a strategic sector in these countries, at least not in reality in spite of the fact that their governments' rhetorics regularly come back to evoking the strategic importance of R&D in improving competitiveness. If however governments cut their spending in order to reduce budget deficits, the NISs of transition economies usually fall among the first victims. One of the reasons for this seems to be the weak political weight of R&D in the transition countries.

This political underrepresentation of the R&D sector in the transition economies (eight among them new members of the EU) can be explained by two main factors. First, the number of researchers per head of population is lower in most transition countries than the EU average. Second, the weak links of these NISs to business mean that taking the innovation challenge and implementing appropriate measures is not a priority for the governments of the transition countries.

The NISs of the transition economies perform surprisingly well in spite of all the organizational, structural and political difficulties they regularly have to face. Regarding R&D competitiveness, this means a rather efficient production (low unit cost) of publications and patents, as for example in Poland and Hungary but also in less-developed transition economies such as Romania or Bulgaria.

One of the reasons for this apparent efficiency is low labour cost, which helps in attracting foreign direct investment in manufacturing, but the counterpart of FDI does not exist in R&D (except for some recent examples in the Czech and Hungarian car, electronics or software industries). What happens instead is that inexpensive labour produces an amount of refereed publications and patents comparable to outputs of much better-paid researchers in more advanced countries. Qualitative differences between these outputs are difficult to measure. If this measurement were possible, it could also happen that the production of low-cost human resources of R&D would be given a less favourable assessment.

The underfinancing of R&D is an issue quite often mentioned with regard to transition or developing countries, which has two distinct aspects. First, comparatively low GERD/GDP ratios in these countries lead to such situations in which these countries spend proportionally even less on R&D than their more advanced counterparts in North America and Western Europe from their higher domestic disposable income. This is the purely statistical aspect of the underfinancing problem. On the other hand however, there is a technical aspect as well: the more or less dramatic lack of financial resources available for labour, equipment, journal subscriptions, software, building maintenance or travel costs.

In the long run these problems surely cause the competitiveness of R&D in the less advanced countries to deteriorate, and contribute to the very uneven performances of their NISs. It is common in transition or Third World countries that some selected or well-placed universities and research centres work in conditions comparable to those of their partner institutions in the developed world, while the rest have to survive with more or less pariah-like infrastructures and financing. This is why the homogeneity of the NISs of such countries is usually not assured, and the data on their inputs and outputs reflect only national averages but not the extremely different situations of the R&D organizations coexisting in such countries.[102] At least however such countries can still come up with quite respectable performances in R&D and, as it has been mentioned before, fairly good indicators of R&D efficiency if publications are taken into account.

Our composite ranking lists include only a few countries from those below the group of transition and developing countries with regard to R&D competitiveness. Quite logically, they are at the bottom of the ranking lists which is no surprise. They are however also players in international R&D competition, and their presence is felt in most fields of international science in spite of the modest resources they can use for R&D purposes.

There are about 40 Third World countries performing some R&D activities but not covered regularly by international R&D statistics. These countries have been included in our analysis of different NISs in the world, but they have been omitted from the composite ranking lists owing to their inadequate statistical coverage. Some researchers representing such countries have published frequently quoted articles in refereed journals or registered patents at American or European patent offices, but these personal achievements were usually reached outside of their respective home countries. These are the country cases (for example Moldova, Senegal or Vietnam) where individual performances in R&D or innovation are not sufficient for the country to reach statistically relevant levels of R&D competitiveness.

5.2 A PICTURE OF INTERNATIONAL R&D COMPETITIVENESS: THE 'WORLD MAP'

The 'world map' of international R&D competitiveness includes hardly more than 100 countries, out of which less than 50 are real players. Their patterns of R&D performance and competitiveness show an amazing diversity, and it seems to be a challenging task for comparative R&D research to explore the specifics of the NISs of the participants of international competition in R&D.

Our starting point is the result of a cluster analysis which was carried out for more countries and less indicators than covered by our analysis producing the composite lists of R&D competitiveness.[103] The cluster analysis helped us somewhat to create more or less homogenous country groups, the 'world map' of international R&D.

The country groups constituting this map consist of countries with largely similar indicators of R&D competitiveness either in an absolute or a per capita approach. An overview of this map is given below with the remark that a certain number of countries important in international R&D has been omitted from our world map.

The reason is either inconsistency between the various indicators of R&D competitiveness of a given country which made it impossible to include it in one group or another in an appropriate way (such cases are Russia and Turkey), or the lack of certain data important for identifying an appropriate cluster for each country. On top of this, we did not want to create too-long country lists for each cluster. This is why only a couple of country names are given for each of the groups.

The top of the hierarchy in international R&D competitiveness is the group of the G-7+1 countries (United States, Japan, Germany, France, the United Kingdom, Canada and Italy as the G-7, and South Korea in the light of our composite lists of R&D competitiveness) which produce, depending on the indicators used, 80 to 90 per cent of the world's R&D output. These countries are in the centre of the world map of R&D competitiveness due to their outstanding performance in both the absolute and the per capita approach.

There are also other countries with considerably less impressive indicators of R&D competitiveness whose ranking positions are similar on the absolute and the per capita ranking lists. This group of countries form the 'centre court' of the world map along with the cluster of the G-7+1.

One group of the 'centre court' has European countries ranking in the international midfield for both the absolute and the per capita indicators, partly because they have neither too small nor too large economies measured by the size of their GDP or population. For such countries such as Hungary, the Czech Republic and Spain, neither the absolute nor the per capita ranking method is significantly more favourable, but they are generally placed in the first 30 of the international ranking lists for most of the indicators used.

Another group still within the 'centre court' also has countries whose positions are similar in absolute and per capita comparisons of R&D competitiveness, but they rank significantly lower than the 'midfielders'. This group includes for example Malaysia, Kuwait and Venezuela.

A third group in the 'centre court' has one important characteristic: the countries belonging here cannot boast of good indicators of R&D competitiveness either in an absolute or in a per capita approach. These are in fact the 'non-performers' mentioned in the comparative analysis of the NISs of LDCs: their group has been put in the 'centre court' due to the fact that their R&D performance is entitled to the same judgement both on an absolute and a per capita basis.

In addition to the 'centre court', the world map has two additional 'courts': the one of countries which are important competitive players on the basis of their absolute indicators of R&D competitiveness, and the other of countries important in a per capita approach. Size is the decisive factor in the competitive performance of the countries shown as parts of the first 'court', and efficiency is the important criterion for the countries of the second.

Close to the group of the G-7+1 countries is, in the 'court' based on the per capita approach, the group of small and successful countries. They stand out by the high level of efficiency of their R&D, and some of them can boast of the highest GERD/GDP and per capita publication or patent counts in the world. Due to their relatively small size however, they cannot exert a strong general influence on R&D competition in the world, but there are important niches in which they are dominant players.

Members of this group include Switzerland, Israel, Sweden, Finland and Denmark, and a couple of other small countries with low population numbers and efficient NISs such as Norway, Austria or Singapore could be added to it. The Netherlands and Ireland are not clear cases because the Netherlands has a population size three times that of Finland or Switzerland, whereas Ireland is a country with relatively low indicators of R&D output in the light of its remarkable record of economic growth from the early 1980s on.

The 'absolute court' consists of three groups of economies which are rather large in size and have more or less remarkable indicators of R&D only if the absolute ranking lists are considered. Several countries in this 'court' have sizeable NISs (marked by for example huge researcher populations), with considerable differences in quality between domestic universities and research centres. The measured level of R&D competitiveness is, in most cases, strongly related to the levels of economic development. Countries from the European continent can be found only in the first group.

The first group contains fairly industrialized countries with R&D outputs of a respectable size yet with poor efficiency in R&D. Such countries, including Brazil, Poland and to a lesser extent Ukraine, are more or less significant players in international R&D competition based on their large NISs. Their levels of economic development also make them increasingly important locations for foreign direct investment, but their exports have low contents of high-tech products. They are still mainly used by multinational firms as bases for their assembly lines rather than places where their R&D activities could be outsourced.

The 'absolute court' has a very special group not really fitting any of the others, and showing a special behaviour as compared to other countries on this 'court' as well. Countries of the world's largest populations, China and India, belong here. These countries also share improving indicators of R&D competitiveness. Such improvements are due to several factors such as former efforts of establishing important domestic R&D capacities when self-sufficiency (economic isolation from the rest of the world) was the governing ideology, or the abundant and high-quality R&D manpower available in both countries.

Students from both countries, especially from China, go abroad in large numbers to earn PhD degrees (see NSB, 2004) and these countries are fast becoming priority investment targets for multinational firms (see UNCTAD, 2003). Due to the very large population sizes of these countries however, most of their per capita indicators of R&D competitiveness are still among the lowest in the world and can be expected to remain at low levels for several years to come. Nonetheless China and India are already important players in global R&D competition.

The third group in the 'absolute court' contains developing countries with some signs of activity in R&D, but present on the world map mainly due to R&D output coming from the research centres or universities a large country can be expected to maintain. These countries, such as Iran, Indonesia and Pakistan, also have a certain political and strategic weight in their respective regions which obliges them to a certain extent to maintain strong domestic R&D facilities.

The world map presented in Figure 5.1 is an attempt to show international competition in R&D according to the relative positions of some of its main actors. It can also be regarded as a summary of our analysis of the various patterns of R&D competitiveness in the world which has shown that the number of key players is limited, and the strategically most important part of this competition takes place between North America (or the United States) and

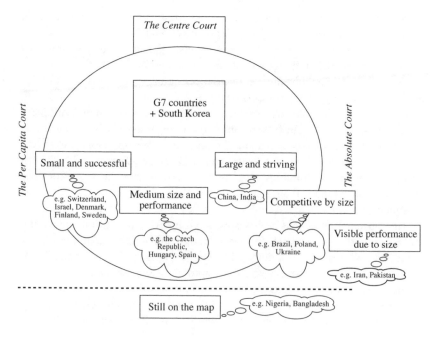

Figure 5.1   The 'world map' of R&D competitiveness

the European Union. There are about 35 countries in the world (most of them OECD members) which can more or less adequately spend on R&D and also reap corresponding benefits from such investment. Far-reaching institutional changes and great improvement in policy backgrounds and financing conditions would be needed in the other countries for them to become noteworthy players in international R&D competition. But have we come any nearer to the meaning of the concept of R&D competitiveness for economic analysis?

5.3   POLICIES TOWARDS IMPROVING COMPETITIVENESS IN R&D

After all our deliberations on inputs and outputs, resources and performances in international R&D and innovation the ultimate question remains the following. Could it be asserted or not that competitiveness is a conceptual framework appropriate for giving a good comparative picture of the development of this strategic sector of the world economy?

We believe yes, if in the first place a quite general approach to competitiveness is applied. Such a general approach would allow it to amalgamate the input and the output side of competitiveness analysis and to consider both above-average inputs and outputs as key factors of R&D competitiveness. Countries investing proportionately more into R&D in a narrow sense, and innovation-related activities, education and IT infrastructure in a broader approach, can expect better comparative and competitive performances in three respects.

First, their direct R&D outputs such as publications and patents will likely increase.[104] This will, mainly in the long run, improve the international standing of their universities and research centres and make these countries more attractive places for talented and productive researchers. This kind of locational advantage will likely give a further leverage to the improvement of R&D competitiveness of these countries.

Second, if applied with appropriate framework conditions, the indirect outputs of increased national R&D efforts are likely to improve the innovation performance of a number of firms in these countries even if this does not necessarily appear in formal indicators of R&D output (publications and patents). The improvement of the innovative capacity of domestic business might make it a more attractive target for foreign direct investment and increase its competitiveness in sales. An additional advantage resulting from better innovation performances in business is that the R&D related spending of firms will also likely increase. As has been demonstrated in our text, there seems to be a strong relationship between the increase of the BERD/GERD ratio and the improvement of national R&D competitiveness.

A third conclusion is that in some cases higher R&D competitiveness measured on the input side can contribute to better trade performance. The examples of countries with well-performing domestic R&D sectors and high relative shares of high-tech goods in manufacturing exports (for example Finland or Switzerland) show that the structures of exports may benefit from the improvement of R&D competitiveness which can also increase the capacity of domestic business to contribute more to the national R&D effort.

It is important however to take account of the institutional factors of R&D competitiveness as well. Only the best performers in international R&D seem to have NISs that allow the measurement of a more or less transparent and efficient conversion of R&D inputs into R&D outputs. These are almost exclusively OECD countries. The best supply of internationally comparable and homogenous R&D data is also offered by the OECD, but only on its member countries.

A certain number of new members of the OECD however, mainly from Central and Eastern Europe, have NISs which still bear the mark of economic and political transition. These countries can boast of high-quality human resources for R&D and sometimes good indicators of efficiency in producing R&D outputs. Their NISs suffer, at the same time, from weak links between

R&D and business, sometimes incomplete legal frameworks for innovation (mainly IP protection) and poor government and business financing of R&D. The lack of clear government policies and strategic commitments regarding the future of domestic R&D in these countries is also a handicap for them.

The cases of these countries may be considered as laboratories for exploring the institutional and policy changes necessary for middle-income countries to catch up with the most competitive players in international R&D. The fields of competitiveness in international R&D can change mainly as a result of such catching-up processes as the examples of South Korea and Israel have shown in the recent past. A string of other industrializing economies of the Third World (such as Singapore, Taiwan, Hong Kong) are increasingly present in global R&D, but Brazil, China and India are also good candidates for belonging to the club of leaders in international R&D within the next 15 to 25 years. It is worth noting also for strategy analysts that none of these countries is from Europe.

The analysis of R&D competitiveness confirms that Europe (and the European Union) is slowly losing ground in international R&D competition. The tendency has been recognized by the authors of the Lisbon Strategy and appropriate strategic action was recommended to reverse the trend. The 2004 report of the European Commission on the first three-year balance sheet of the Lisbon Strategy has noted only moderate progress towards the R&D related objectives of the strategy (European Commission, 2004).

The new member countries of the EU could also contribute to the success of the Lisbon effort, but their NISs are not prepared in an institutional sense. This is why it would be important to solve the apparent contradictions between their as yet relatively satisfactory levels of R&D competitiveness, the poor financial, institutional and policy backgrounds and innovation performance below average. Finding appropriate institutional and political solutions could help these countries give additional leverage to the EU's strategic effort of catching up with the United States in general, but especially in terms of R&D competitiveness by the years around or not too long after 2010.

Appendix A

Table A.1   *Ranking list of the countries of the world according to their total numbers of publications, 1990–98*

Position	Country	No. of publications
1	USA	1 763 421
2	United Kingdom	468 660
3	Japan	454 302
4	Germany	394 409
5	France	307 733
6	Canada	234 620
7	Russia	211 662
8	Italy	188 313
9	Australia	125 666
10	The Netherlands	124 478
11	Spain	117 001
12	Sweden	98 928
13	India	95 885
14	Switzerland	87 901
15	China	80 486
16	Israel	59 930
17	Belgium	59 269
18	Poland	50 572
19	Denmark	49 907
20	Taiwan	42 790
21	Finland	41 896
22	Brazil	39 064
23	Austria	38 988
24	South Korea	36 014
25	Ukraine	32 085
26	Norway	29 874
27	New Zealand	25 779
28	South Africa	25 004
29	Czech Republic	24 029
30	Hungary	23 022

Table A.1   continued

Position	Country	No. of publications
31	Greece	22 580
32	Argentina	21 053
33	Mexico	19 164
34	Turkey	17 456
35	Hong Kong	15 065
36	Egypt	14 079
37	Rep. of Ireland	12 954
38	Bulgaria	12 362
39	Portugal	11 477
40	Chile	10 548
41	Singapore	10 327
42	Slovakia	9 593
43	Yugoslavia	8 567
44	Belarus	8 319
45	Romania	7 645
46	Saudi Arabia	7 381
47	Nigeria	5 361
48	Venezuela	4 894
49	Croatia	4 833
50	Thailand	4 831
51	Slovenia	4 491
52	Malaysia	3 701
53	Kenya	3 688
54	Morocco	3 485
55	Pakistan	3 352
56	Uzbekistan	3 169
57	Estonia	3 033
58	Iran	2 798
59	Lithuania	2 592
60	Armenia	2 348
61	Colombia	2 278
62	Latvia	2 276
63	Kuwait	2 201
64	Kazakhstan	2 132
65	Philippines	2 028
66	Tunisia	2 026
67	Algeria	1 942
68	Georgia	1 899
69	Indonesia	1 896

Table A.1   continued

Position	Country	No. of publications
70	Cuba	1 895
71	Azerbaijan	1 828
72	Moldova	1 778
73	Jordan	1 733
74	Iceland	1 693
75	Bangladesh	1 661
76	Senegambia	1 447
77	Zimbabwe	1 394
78	Tanzania	1 320
79	Uruguay	1 276
80	Vietnam	1 252
81	United Arab Emirates	1 238
82	Eritrea	1 163
83	Peru	1 075
84	Costa Rica	1 015
85	Sri Lanka	1 012
86	Cameroon	1 007
	World total	**5 031 587**

(*Source*:   Schubert, 2003)

Table A.2   Ranking list of the countries of the world according to the average number of citation per publication, 1990–98

Position	Country	Citation/publication
1	Switzerland	6.178
2	USA	5.526
3	The Netherlands	4.834
4	Iceland	4.815
5	Denmark	4.575
6	Sweden	4.519
7	Belgium	4.400
8	United Kingdom	4.361
9	Germany	4.360
10	Finland	4.343
11	Canada	4.174
12	Senegambia	4.114
13	France	4.049

Table A.2   continued

Position	Country	Citation/publication
14	Austria	3.951
15	Israel	3.812
16	Italy	3.752
17	Australia	3.563
18	Norway	3.550
19	Rep. of Ireland	3.463
20	Japan	3.418
21	Uruguay	3.308
22	Spain	3.157
23	New Zealand	3.028
24	Costa Rica	3.003
25	Colombia	2.968
26	Hungary	2.830
27	Portugal	2.788
28	Tanzania	2.627
29	Thailand	2.598
30	Estonia	2.583
31	Slovenia	2.562
32	Chile	2.517
33	Hong Kong	2.482
34	Singapore	2.466
35	Greece	2.465
36	Kenya	2.458
37	Philippines	2.387
38	Indonesia	2.366
39	Mexico	2.330
40	Poland	2.300
41	Peru	2.288
42	Brazil	2.279
43	Czech Republic	2.263
44	Argentina	2.248
45	Venezuela	2.244
46	South Korea	2.215
47	Lithuania	2.171
48	Croatia	2.120
49	South Africa	2.112
50	Cameroon	2.103
51	Taiwan	2.057

Table A.2   continued

Position	Country	Citation/publication
52	Slovakia	1.950
53	Vitenam	1.932
54	Bangladesh	1.803
55	Cuba	1.734
56	Latvia	1.723
57	Zimbabwe	1.717
58	China	1.642
59	Eritrea	1.604
60	Romania	1.574
61	Sri Lanka	1.545
62	Tunisia	1.533
63	Bulgaria	1.518
64	Yugoslavia	1.511
65	Malaysia	1.473
66	Iran	1.472
67	Algeria	1.472
68	India	1.469
69	Morocco	1.466
70	Turkey	1.361
71	Russia	1.274
72	Saudi-Arabia	1.252
73	United Arab Emirates	1.180
74	Georgia	1.135
75	Kuwait	1.129
76	Pakistan	1.124
77	Armenia	1.107
78	Egypt	1.021
79	Jordan	0.943
80	Belarus	0.914
81	Ukraine	0.893
82	Moldova	0.855
83	Nigeria	0.798
84	Uzbekistan	0.663
85	Kazakhstan	0.486
86	Azerbaijan	0.379
	World average	**3.745**

(*Source*:   Schubert, 2003)

Competitiveness in research and development

Table A.3   Ranking list of the countries of the world based on the relative number of citations, 1990–98

Position	Country	Relative number of citations
1	Switzerland	1.239
2	Iceland	1.237
3	Senegambia	1.227
4	Finland	1.181
5	Denmark	1.181
6	The Netherlands	1.157
7	Sweden	1.146
8	Belgium	1.136
9	Tanzania	1.130
10	Germany	1.123
11	United Kingdom	1.106
12	USA	1.085
13	Austria	1.074
14	Rep. of Ireland	1.072
15	Norway	1.057
16	Canada	1.050
17	France	1.047
18	New Zealand	1.035
19	Australia	1.024
20	Italy	0.994
21	Japan	0.981
22	Costa Rica	0.966
23	Uruguay	0.960
24	Colombia	0.960
25	Singapore	0.952
26	Kenya	0.940
27	Slovakia	0.935
28	Estonia	0.933
29	Israel	0.929
30	Czech Republic	0.920
31	Lithuania	0.919
32	Thailand	0.918
33	Indonesia	0.913
34	Russia	0.909
35	Spain	0.905
36	Philippines	0.904

Table A.3   continued

Position	Country	Relative number of citations
37	Hong Kong	0.898
38	Vietnam	0.890
39	Poland	0.885
40	Portugal	0.882
41	Hungary	0.880
42	Chile	0.874
43	Slovenia	0.870
44	Greece	0.865
45	Cameroon	0.861
46	South Africa	0.861
47	Latvia	0.844
48	South Korea	0.832
49	Belarus	0.804
50	Croatia	0.782
51	Venezuela	0.780
52	Zimbabwe	0.772
53	Taiwan	0.771
54	Romania	0.767
55	Bangladesh	0.766
56	Mexico	0.765
57	Brazil	0.762
58	Argentina	0.752
59	Peru	0.749
60	Uzbekistan	0.742
61	Moldova	0.737
62	Ukraine	0.737
63	Iran	0.732
64	Eritrea	0.729
65	Malaysia	0.721
66	China	0.718
67	Cuba	0.717
68	Bulgaria	0.715
69	Tunisia	0.702
70	Turkey	0.698
71	Algeria	0.694
72	Sri Lanka	0.686
73	Yugoslavia	0.677
74	Morocco	0.671

Table A.3   continued

Position	Country	Relative number of citations
75	Saudi-Arabia	0.660
76	India	0.646
77	Kuwait	0.634
78	Egypt	0.624
79	United Arab Emirates	0.621
80	Georgia	0.611
81	Armenia	0.598
82	Kazakhstan	0.579
83	Pakistan	0.552
84	Jordan	0.551
85	Nigeria	0.531
86	Azerbaijan	0.457
	World average	**1.000**

(*Source*:   Schubert, 2003)

Appendix B

Table B.1 R&D indicators (2000)

Country	Number of researchers	GERD (1000 US$)	Import of measurement equipment (1000 US$)	Domestic patents granted	Number of scientific publications (1999)	High-tech export (1000 US$)	GERD as a % of GDP[g]	Researchers per million population[h]	Publications per million population[h]	Patents per million population[h]
Argentina	26420	1247699	263331	145	2361	849695	0.4378	760	68	4.2
Australia	65805	5936646	1012185	1301	12525	4340161	1.5282	3641	693	72.0
Austria	18715[b]	3503360	796812	1122	3580	7861895	1.4897	2326	445	139.4
Belgium	30219[c]	4919152[c]	1098002	750	4896	21467226	2.1501	2981	483	74.0
Brazil	55103	6259672	945674	400	5144	6958558	1.0513	346	32	2.5
Bulgaria	9479	66477	38228	144	801	224336	0.5542	1128	95	17.1
Canada	90810	13217988	4346120	1117	19685	35467747	1.8867	3094	671	38.1
Chile	5629	394910	112078	32	879	123615	0.5598	396	62	2.3
China	695062	10819562	3002327	6475	11675	56006711	1.0018	580	10	5.4
Colombia	4240	146596	124368	21	207	337645	0.1803	110	5	0.5
Cyprus	303	22628	15892	0	46	52675	0.2601	407	62	0.0
Czech Rep.	13852	685570	393603	272	2005	3737315	1.3502	1341	194	26.3
Denmark	18438[c]	3784073[c]	414339	313	4131	9196935	2.3251	3527	790	59.9
Finland	34847	4071251	400264	25	4025	13737644	3.3559	6822	788	4.9
France	160424[c]	28494523	3421968	10303	27374	71602930	2.2017	2759	471	177.2
Germany	257774	46597625	5679813	16901	37308	103000000	2.497	3157	457	207.0
Greece	14828[c]	809970	234152	3	2241	864265	0.719	1418	214	0.3
Hong Kong	4423	798019[b]	1490173	41	1817	6027014	0.573	712	293	6.6
Hungary	14406	373450	374913	176	1958	7914250	0.8184	1410	192	17.2
Iceland	1719[e]	231377	39475	2	114	29326	2.703	6438	427	7.5
India	95428[b]	2303000[b]	497729	600	9217	2102291	0.54	103	10	0.6
Indonesia	92900	72071	246232	0	142	7405065	0.047	470	1	0.0
Ireland	8217	1089294	475100	34	1237	32294676	1.1427	2277	343	9.4
Israel	9161[a]	5391713	520474	455	5025	10229554	4.8849	1713	939	85.1
Italy	64886[c]	11470496	2630595	618	17149	27723113	1.068	1132	299	10.8
Japan	647572	141929977	4756835	112269	47826	152000000	2.9784	5161	381	894.8
Korea (South)	108370	12245828	3180852	22943	6675	61822698	2.6784	2411	148	510.4
Malaysia	3415[b]	287877[b]	1642629	52	416	51685646	0.3211	171	21	2.6
Mexico	21879[c]	2065881	2782714	113	2291	46928104	0.3596	240	25	1.2
Netherlands	40623[c]	7192120	1945014	2820	10441	51200614	1.9463	2628	675	182.4

Table B.1 continued

Country	Number of researchers	GERD (1000 US$)	Import of measurement equipment (1000 US$)	Domestic patents granted	Number of scientific publications (1999)	High-tech export (1000 US$)	GERD as a % of GDP[g]	Researchers per million population[h]	Publications per million population[h]	Patents per million population[h]
New Zealand	8264[a]	577583	118895	547	2375	397684	1.1374	2293	659	151.8
Norway	19024[e]	2661805[c]	278523	395	2598	2166714	1.8157	4364	596	90.6
Panama	286	44647	22017	0	37	16458	0.45	109	14	0.0
Poland	55174	1104990	457787	939	4523	2562169	0.7005	1430	117	24.3
Portugal	16667	842033	361305	49	1508	2105108	0.7929	1681	152	4.9
Romania	20476	138265	134346	865	785	772916	0.3767	903	35	38.1
Russia	506420	2742012	518554	14444	15654	2436499	1.0919	3418	106	97.5
Singapore	16633	1744941	2695652	40	1653	81124903	1.8916	4785	476	11.5
Slovakia	9955	131684	138149	83	871	794403	0.6886	1856	162	15.5
South Africa	26000[d]	956834[d]	377241	0	2013	1133099	0.76	649	50	0.0
Spain	76670	5264660	1354069	1730	12289	11562212	0.9386	1929	309	43.5
Sweden	42958[e]	9266500[e]	1073815	2082	8326	21205527	3.858	4867	943	235.9
Switzerland	25755	6316568	1021269	1345	6993	19989671	2.6381	3618	982	189.0
Thailand	4409[a]	155548[a]	648782	153	470	21279950	0.1273	75	8	2.6
Turkey	20065[c]	1277555	480063	26	2761	2149526	0.6389	326	45	0.4
Ukraine	104970	292730	88629	4921	2194	581013	0.921	2037	43	95.5
UK	157662[b]	26537286	5040259	4170	39711	86281529	1.8591	2690	678	71.2
US	1114100	265179600	13295848	85071	163526	226000000	2.7031	4146	608	316.6
Venezuela	4688	404830	196973	14	448	100329	0.3359	215	21	0.6
Sources	UNESCO	UNESCOf	UNCTAD	WIPO	NSF	UNCTAD				

Notes:
a.) 1997.
b.) 1998.
c.) 1999.
d.) 2001.
e.) linear interpolation from 1999 and 2001 data.
f.) national currencies converted into US$ using the Pacific Exchange Rate Service of the University of British Columbia.
g.) computed from GDP data (UNCTAD) and GERD (UNESCO and supplementary sources).
h.) population data: UNCTAD.

Supplementary sources and information:
GERD for Hong Kong: http://www.info.gov.hk/censtatd/eng/hkstat/fas/st/rd_index.html.
GERD for India: http://www.science.org.hk/Newsevents-ReportTable.htm. The researcher number for India was taken from the OECD Science, Technology and Industry Scoreboard 2003.
GERD and researcher data for the Philippines and Indonesia: ASEAN – Building competitiveness through S&T. Public information series 2003.
GERD for South Africa: Department of Science and Technology: National survey of research and experimental development. High-level key results. 2004.
The GERD for Ukraine was calculated at 5.59 hryvna/dollar exchange rate.

Table B.2 R&D indicators (1995)

Country	Number of researchers	GERD (1000 US$)	Import of measurement equipment (1000 US$)	Domestic patents granted	Number of scientific publications	High-tech export (1000 US$)	GERD as a % of GDP[k]	Researchers per million population[l]	Publications per million population[l]	Patents per million population[l]
Argentina	22927[d]	1136427[d]	270720	209	1742	397854	0.4405	659	50	6.0
Australia	58781[h]	5969847	978245	1074	11742	2573882	1.6016	3253	650	59.4
Austria	9356[g]	3576403[d]	778614	1470	3148	5778558	1.5208	1163	391	182.7
Belgium	22918	5784193[d]	874046	880	4531	13477207	2.0892	2261	447	86.8
Brazil	26754	5762119[d]	693194	525	3134	1631090	0.8184	168	20	3.3
Bulgaria	13990	23389[d]	0	168	882	3905	0.1785	1664	105	20.0
Canada	80510	10213421[d]	2712636	743	21653	18774940	1.7514	2743	738	25.3
Chile	5158[d]	414290	128058	19	768	56322	0.6353	363	54	1.3
China	422700	4863818[d]	1893965	1530	6995	19391095	0.6951	353	6	1.3
Colombia	3277[d]	282433[d]	156964	87	152	147955	0.3053	85	4	2.3
Cyprus	237[f]	18621	14712	0[e]	38	41589	0.21	319	51	0.0
Czech Rep.	11935	605530[d]	437508	577	1825	1796681	1.1636	1155	177	55.9
Denmark	15954	3390541[d]	364583	367	3946	6467171	1.8811	3052	755	70.2
Finland	16863	2958017	365607	860	3655	7264179	2.2878	3301	716	168.4
France	151249	33259027	3076094	15299	26265	52962182	2.1414	2602	452	263.1
Germany	231128	51806989[d]	4309811	19727	34442	81517813	2.1075	2830	422	241.6
Greece	10972[e]	556382[e]	170195	222	1874	304767	0.4733	1050	179	21.2
Hong Kong	574	354456	818181	25	1372	7632504	0.2546	92	221	4.0
Hungary	10499	324826	161823	534	1657	1406915	0.7272	1028	162	52.3
Iceland	1076	106948	19872	0	138	40724	1.5350	4030	517	0.0
India	136503[c]	2391319[c]	406474	415	8727	1429070	0.6770	147	9	0.4
Indonesia	26666	106641	376940	11[h]	115	1795569	0.0527	135	1	0.1
Ireland	8368	1013191[d]	285720	503	1054	14963098	1.5227	2319	292	139.4
Israel	7620[d]	1890431	330439	328	5269	3601378	2.1426	1425	985	61.3
Italy	75536	11591801	2327390	687	15660	22618087	1.0565	1318	273	12.0
Japan	673421	130111921[d]	3391024	94804	42338	138940649	2.4588	5367	337	755.6
Korea (South)	100456	11657934	3558933	6575	3234	38416024	2.3828	2235	72	146.3
Malaysia	2090[h]	218333	1041625	29	343	30258587	0.2458	104	17	1.4
Mexico	19434	876040[d]	1007897	148	1616	16444942	0.3061	213	18	1.6
Netherlands	34038	7405429	1675823	1144	10899	31769074	1.7853	2202	705	74.0
New Zeeland	6104	732232	159118	198	2181	322586	1.2041	1694	605	54.9
Norway	15931	2510748	355868	321	2576	1911908	1.7127	3655	591	73.6
Panama	313[d]	30608[d]	14029	15	32	15855	0.3871	119	12	5.7
Poland	49787	845437	333257	1619	4186	1153716	0.6654	1290	108	41.9

Table B.2 continued

Country	Number of researchers	GERD (1000 US$)	Import of measurement equipment (1000 US$)	Domestic patents granted	Number of scientific publications	High-tech export (1000 US$)	GERD as a % of GDP[k]	Researchers per million population[l]	Publications per million population[l]	Patents per million population[l]
Portugal	11648	614424	233903	22	867	1438715	0.5731	1175	87	2.2
Romania	30988	145448	127580	1791	596	197673	0.4100	1366	26	79.0
Russia	591930[i]	3781886[d]	481659	20861	18512	2027670	1.1197	3996	125	140.8
Singapore	7695	964547	1550169	0	1064	63171304	1.1567	2214	306	0.0
Slovakia	9711	188571	108202	149	1059	412374	1.0261	1810	197	27.8
South Africa	37192[b]	1088097	435936	0	2120	438683	0.72	0	53	0.0
Spain	47342	4459904	1248989	547	9870	8167116	0.7635	1191	248	13.8
Sweden	33665	7430945	1057503	1604	8117	15041279	3.0938	3814	920	181.7
Switzerland	21635[d]	8081870[d]	983231	2226	6603	16226906	2.6304	3039	928	312.7
Thailand	6899	207632	703043	40[h]	303	13836835	0.1234	117	5	0.7
Turkey	15854	643419	341280	54	1560	507353	0.3784	258	25	0.9
Ukraine	163299	442579	82075	1139	2643	416673	1.1962	3169	51	22.1
UK	144735[d]	22372035[d]	3874975	5242	39980	62341792	1.9712	2470	682	89.4
United States	1040900[d]	171000000	7345269	55739	179051	144217538	2.3302	3873	666	207.4
Venezuela	4258[a]	204795[j]	142006	220[h]	386	62637	0.2646	0	18	10.1
Sources	UNESCO	UNESCOj	UNCTAD	WIPO	NSF	UNCTAD				

Notes:
a.) 1992.
b.) 1993.
c.) 1994.
d.) 1996.
e.) 1997.
f.) 1998.

g.) linear interpolation from 1993 and 1998 data.
h.) linear interpolation from 1994 and 1996 data.
i.) linear interpolation from 1994 and 1997 data.
j.) national currencies converted into US$ using the Pacific Exchange Rate Service of the University of British Columbia.
k.) computed from GDP data (UNCTAD) and GERD (UNESCO and supplementary sources).
l.) population data: UNCTAD.

Supplementary sources and information:
For Romania the 1996 November exchange rate used.
The GERD for Ukraine was calculated at 1.4731 hryvna/dollar exchange rate.
GERD for Philippines and researchers for Indonesia: ASEAN – Building competitiveness through S&T. Public information series 2003.
GERD for South Africa: Department of Science and Technology: National survey of research and experimental development. High-level key results. 2004. The high-tech export and import of measurement equipment were given for South Africa customs union.
The GERD for Colombia was calculated with an exchange rate from http://www.jeico.com/cnc57col.html.
For Cyprus the GERD/GDP rate (0.21) was estimated from the GDP/GNP and the 1992 GERD/GNP ratio (0.19).

Table B.3 Correlation coefficients between the R&D indicators (2000)

	1.	2.	3.	4.	5.	6.	7.	8.	9.	10
1. Number of researchers	1	0.84	0.78	0.79	0.83	0.77	0.24	0.25	0.06	0.51
2. GERD (thousand US$)		1	0.87	0.89	0.96	0.87	0.34	0.32	0.21	0.60
3. Import of measurement equipment (th. US$)			1	0.70	0.92	0.94	0.35	0.29	0.27	0.48
4. Domestic patents granted				1	0.75	0.80	0.34	0.35	0.11	0.84
5. Number of scientific publications					1	0.86	0.33	0.31	0.26	0.46
6. High-tech export (thousand US$)						1	0.40	0.36	0.26	0.63
7. GERD as a % of GDP							1	0.76	0.82	0.52
8. Researchers per million population								1	0.73	0.44
9. Publications per million population									1	0.30
10. Domestic patents granted per million pop.										1

Notes

1. Research and experimental development (OECD, 2002, 30).
2. We consider this an equally good argument against price-based measurements of competitiveness, see later.
3. Really modern and technically demanding analyses of competitiveness have to cover aspects of product quality besides the development of market shares (Pitti, 2002, 15). A good technique for measuring this is offered by the method of hedonic price indexes which helps in correcting price changes with the impacts of technological development and other changes in consumer utility or demand. This method is quite useful in giving a realistic picture of the price trends of the output of the 'New Economy'.
4. Such products were only seldom discussed in earlier literature, but modern microeconomics treats explicitly such luxury goods whose demand increases or decreases faster than income (Varian, 1999). Literature on the car industry mentions several brands (for example Rolls-Royce, Bentley, Ferrari or larger models of Mercedes and BMW) whose demand could potentially go down if prices were cut. See American examples on this in Scherer (1996, 303).
5. The OECD has made other methodological manuals for S&T analysis available. One of these, the Oslo Manual (*Proposed Guidelines for Collecting and Interpreting Technological Innovation Data*) will be referred to in this text. The others are listed in the Frascati Manual (OECD, 2002, 16).
6. Some authors consider it only as a by-product of other activities including education, industrial consulting, government-sponsored applied research or technological development. This opinion was markedly represented by one of the pioneers of scientometrics in the foreword of his bestseller written for his Hungarian readers, whom he warned against a too-strong orientation towards basic academic research (De Solla Price, 1979, 13).
7. 'Basic' is put in quotation marks by us, and not the authors cited.
8. The terms 'backward linkage' and 'forward linkage' were introduced by Albert O. Hirschman (1958). 'Backward linkage' means that the development of a sector or a firm is influenced by its clients or 'downstream' partners. The opposite of this is a 'forward linkage' when the supplier's behaviour or structure influences the development of its clients from an 'upstream' direction.
9. This relationship is explained in detail by a number of institutional models of R&D as, for example, the 'technology push' or the 'linear' models to be discussed later.
10. The exact meaning of this term will be explained later.
11. Exceptions to this observation are constituted by the cases of international outsourcing of R&D.
12. Natural, administrative and strategic barriers to entry.
13. On the theory of networks of innovation see Kreis-Hoyer and Grünberg (2002), Pyka and Küppers (2002), and especially Küppers (2002) and Ahrweiler et al. 2002). On measurement issues see Balconi et al. (2004).
14. As a case study of the development of the systemic and institutional factors of competitiveness in R&D, the specifics of the NISs of transition countries will be also surveyed in our text.
15. For instance successful R&D organizations – or national innovation systems in a broader context – manage to harmonize the personal goals of the researchers and research teams, the handling of the 'scientific challenge' and innovation (or we may even say local or domestic value added), yet the level of harmonization is high in the developed countries

and low – or the R&D is not visible enough – in less-developed economies. The transition economies are in essence between the two worlds and we hypothesize that in the long run their R&D and innovation systems will either catch up or slide down.

16. Unlike in the United States, psychology is considered as part of the social sciences in European countries.

17. Trade structure is understood here, both on the export and the import side, as the percentage distribution of commodity groups within exports and imports.

18. It is also true however that he does not speak of what this theoretical background should be.

19. Some derivates of it are also used for comparisons of competitiveness, but these comparisons are based on special quantitative techniques of establishing ranking lists of the different key parameters. We shall see them later.

20. A similar assessment was given by Cosh et al. (1993) of the British economic development of the 1980s.

21. In fact the trade performance of high-tech sectors can be considered as an indicator of both competitiveness in manufacturing and, albeit in a less direct way, competitiveness in R&D. Owing to the primarily international trade theory background of this topic, it is discussed in this chapter.

22. This is true in spite of the fact that Audi is doing substantial engine development work in Győr and GE has one of its R&D centres for lighting products in Budapest.

23. Korea's relative share of global high-tech exports went up from 2 per cent in 1980 to 7.3 per cent in 2001 (NSB, 2004, O-17). Its GERD level was 2.65 per cent in 2000, almost equal to the indicator of the United States and immediately above the Swiss, German and French GERD levels (NSB, 2004, 4–51).

24. This section was written using background material and calculations prepared by András Bakács and Gábor Túry in October 2003.

25. It seems worth noting at this point that Michael Porter entirely rejects the idea of the 'New Economy' (Porter, 2001). His argument rests on two points. First, the 'New Economy' is nothing else in his view than the traditional economic model made much more effective with a technological improvement. Second, he recognizes that this technological improvement, the Internet, does not make the usual management techniques and factors of competitiveness obsolete, but it helps their even better application.

26. Such cases include some industrial countries with good endowments with natural resources (for example Norway or Canada). The contribution of their primary sectors to GDP and exports is quite high, and this is why their R&D output finds industrial application partly abroad.

27. Our source lists these indicators as tools for measuring US-performance in R&D in an international comparison, and this is why some indicators are expressed in US-related terms. This is due to the fact that the list was originally produced by the National Science Foundation.

28. The applicability of the scientometrics approach for analysing R&D competitiveness will be discussed in a separate subchapter later.

29. For a description of this case along with two others when Nobel Prizes were given for scientific merits not standing the judgment of posteriority see Hargittai (2001, 75).

30. Török (2002) (still before Godin's recapitulation and evaluation of the NSF list was published).

31. A similar distortion occurs when international comparisons of productivity are made on the basis of per capita GDP data since these express the relative share of individuals in GDP rather than their relative contribution to it (the inactive have their share in GDP but they do not contribute to it). Therefore international comparisons of productivity using per capita GDP should be done only including such countries which have identical ratios of active population.

32. Source: UNCTAD Secretariat (2002). Parts of the assessment from Deli (2004) were also used in this section.

33. The analytical value of this third indicator will be discussed later in this chapter.

34. Karsai's study on venture capital (VC) financing (Karsai, 2002) also shows the consider-

able statistical problems of obtaining internationally comparable VC data. In fact both the NVCA and the EVCA sources were needed to compile an international database of VC/GDP ratios.

35. For American examples see Scherer (1996), especially p. 229. Important European sources on the block exemption system include: 'Decision of 23 December 1971 (Case No. 72/41 – Henkel /Colgate)', OJ L 14/14, 18 January 1972; 'Regulation No. 418/85 of 19 December 1984 on the Application of Article 85(3) of the Treaty of Categories of Research and Development Agreements', OJ L 53, 22 February 1985. For the legal background of this regulation see Korah (1997, 216–17).

36. Three criteria have to be fulfilled for a new firm to be considered as part of this group: (1) the founder of the new firm (the respondent to the questionnaire) took real steps during the last 12 months in order to launch the process; (2) the respondent will be at least a partial owner of the new firm; (3) the firm did not pay full wages at all during the last three months before the survey was closed.

37. Since our main research objective consists in producing a synthetic ranking list of countries based on their R&D competitiveness.

38. It might be interesting to note at this point that, out of the two main indicators of macro-economic performance, GNP is more national in character than GDP because it is calculated from the contributions of domestically owned (but not necessarily domestically operated) factors of production to the national product. GNP is however quite rarely used due to data collection problems: its exact measurement would require the reliable identification of all domestically owned assets operated abroad, and also a reliable evaluation of revenues realized from them.

39. On the transition of its R&D system see in detail Müller (2001).

40. On the transition of their R&D systems see in detail Biegelbauer (2000), Tamási (2001), Kukliński (2001), Zajac (2001).

41. Our OECD source contains GERD data for the Czech Republic, Poland and Hungary from 1990 onwards and BERD data for the same countries from 1995 onwards.

42. The author cited makes a reference to methodological problems with the Czech data. These problems are reflected in the wide gap between the Czech and the Slovak figures of decrease of R&D employment. The dismantling of the pre-1993 federal R&D system with a heavy weight of Czech R&D meant a loss of R&D jobs primarily in the Czech regions after the splitting of the country into two republics.

43. The author's personal experience tells that there was a considerable exodus from social sciences research in Hungary and Poland after 1988, and pre-1993 Czechoslovakia after 1989. This occurred due to the explosion of demand from business for skilled economists and lawyers with advanced language skills which created very promising career opportunities for underpaid researchers. I know of dozens of examples in Hungary when not necessarily very highly rated researchers in economics or other social sciences became prominent business leaders just months after they left the academic world between 1989 and 1992. Some of them however later proved unable to resist competitive pressure from younger MBAs who graduated either abroad or in the off-shore business schools of the region, and they lost their coveted jobs in business.

44. The author thanks András Schubert for his valuable intellectual support to the writing of this section. His survey paper (Schubert, 2003) has also been gratefully used. All the errors regarding misinterpretations of terms or results of scientometrics are however entirely the author's responsibility.

45. The mean observed citation rate is defined as the ratio of citation count to publication count. It reflects the factual citation impact of a country, region, institution, research group and so on.

46. The mean expected citation rate of a single paper is defined as the average citation rate of all papers published in the same journal in the same year. Instead of the one-year citation window to publications of the two preceding years as used in the Journal Citation Report (JCR), a three-year citation window to one source year is used, as explained above. For a set of papers assigned to a given country, region or institution in a given field or subfield, the indicator is the average of the individual expected citation rates over the whole set.

47. A rather provocative but very abstract question can be asked at this point: What could be the percentage of publications which have been written with the purpose of generating a high number of citations only?
48. For a very recent comparison see King (2004).
49. It has to be noted at this point that patent counts may suffer from an analogous bias as literature-based innovation measures. Small firms tend to submit proportionately less of their own inventions for patent protection than larger ones (Kingston, 2001, 417).
50. These can also be called 'procedures' or 'scenarios' for carrying out R&D projects.
51. On 'Alternative protection from imitation' see (Scherer and Ross, 1990, 626–30).
52. We have seen examples of both cases in our interviews carried out with innovative Hungarian firms in the 1990s (for an English-language summary of that research, see OMFB, 1996). In the first example, a medium-sized Hungarian firm patented an apparently important invention (high-voltage transmission technology). The firm was financially too weak to continue the innovation process on its own. Furthermore it had good technicians but lacked qualified marketing and legal staff. It started negotiations with a German partner on the sale of the patent, but the price quoted by the patent owner was considered too high by the potential buyer. In order to obtain a justification of this high price, it requested more and more details on the invention. After obtaining the critical amount of information, it left the negotiating table. It turned out subsequently that the German firm put together the pieces of the puzzle and succeeded in reproducing the invention. The original owner of the patent was unable to bear the costs of the legal procedure abroad, and had to give up the game due to its lack of business experience. In fact it was probably this lack of experience which became plain to the negotiating partner during the bargaining process and made this unfair solution feasible for it.

    In the second case, a Hungarian pharmaceutical firm (still before its privatization) successfully finished the pre-clinical tests of a new drug. The drug was developed for elderly patients, therefore it was likely to find sizeable markets mainly in industrial countries. The company was financially not strong enough to undertake the clinical tests in the European Union, Japan and the United States (the main target markets), so it concluded a strategic alliance with a Japanese pharmaceutical firm. The Japanese company obliged itself to carry out all the clinical tests and the processes of licensing in the industrial countries. It obtained exclusive marketing rights in the industrial world while the Hungarian firm's future sales were limited by the agreement to Central and Eastern Europe, Africa and parts of Asia.
53. This usual formula seems to be an exaggeration here due to the following discomforting reason. Gender bias is very strong regarding the distribution of most scientific awards. For example only 0.2 per cent of the Nobel Prize winners until 2001 were women (Palló, 2001).
54. Pairwise comparison is hardly enough to arrange the objects into a linear ranking due to the circular dominances. The mathematical background of partially ordered sets and their projection to linear rankings are not discussed here. We focus on the statistical problem.
55. The main sources were UNESCO (number of researchers, GERD), UNCTAD (population, GDP, high-tech export, import of measurement equipment), the World Intellectual Property Organisation (patents), the National Science Foundation (publications), and the Pacific Exchange Rate Service (http://fx.sauder.ubc.ca/data.html) of the University of British Columbia. Exchange rates were needed to calculate GERD from national currencies to US dollars. For some countries individual sources were used (these will be mentioned in later sections). Altogether, data for 49 countries was collected. For basic indicators see the Appendix.
56. Hereinafter we will sometimes call the indicators 'variables'.
57. Let us consider a linear combination of the studied indicators so that the aggregate indicator depends on the chosen weights. The multidimensional representatives of the countries are projected onto the single straight line determined by the weights and their ranking is the natural order of them along this straight line. The method is simple, the result is very clear and can be easily visualized and interpreted. Yet it can be justified only if the weights are generally accepted. If not, difficulties emerge: each choice of the weights might have its rationale and advantage in the interpretation, while one can develop easily a counter-

example which demonstrates that the particular choice of the weights results in a misleading ranking and false interpretation.

58. Certainly, we had hoped for this situation in advance, because the correlation coefficients are high among the relative and absolute indicators (see the Appendix). Niwa and Tomizawa (1995) also used principal components to determine R&D positions for a few countries.
59. See Goldberg (1989) for a detailed discussion on genetic algorithms.
60. For some unknown reason, Indonesia reported three times more researchers in 2001 than in the mid-1990s.
61. One principal component is extracted explaining 71 per cent of total variance.
62. The rank correlation coefficient is 0.99.
63. For the sake of simplicity, we do not include the 'trade' indicators in the DEA analysis. The inclusion of high-tech exports and the imports of measurement equipment in the analysis would have had far-reaching consequences beyond our topic of discussion.
64. There are evaluation methods efforts to measure even the profitability or value added generation capability of R&D activities. but we are not in the position to present such output figures on country level. For a summary of R&D evaluation methodologies see EPUB (2002).
65. The input-oriented model assumes that the outputs are given and the goal is to minimize the input.
66. The peer countries themselves are not necessarily on the same level of efficiency. Their comparison can be given using the 'super-efficiency' scale. This tool is not used in our current analysis.
67. Given computing capacity, the problem can be extended and solved for n dimensions. This is the four-dimensional case.
68. Nevertheless, we shall also see later that constructing one single ranking list is possible with DEA. To do so, we need to separate the outputs and compute separately publication efficiency and patent efficiency.
69. Further, in DEA it would be ideal if the reference countries, or their general characteristics at least, did not change – a condition that is not self-evident.
70. We remind the reader that previously the efficiency-based ranking lists computed by the DEA were used only with respect to the same reference countries. One single ranking list would be insufficient for helping R&D policymaking in the reference countries.
71. It is clear that GERD and the number of researchers are not independent variables since a large portion of GERD is spent on personnel (researcher) costs. This effect is handled by the first two methods in an appropriate way, while in DEA we could only assume that certain combinations of these two inputs delineate enough to describe efficiency. This is a statistical problem and does not make the robustness of DEA questionable.
72. This is confirmed by conventional statistics as well. Their R&D spending is more than 72 per cent of all the 49 countries in our database. The same figures are 80 per cent and 50 per cent for domestic patents granted and scientific publications respectively. They import 38 per cent of the measurement equipment and export 42 per cent of the high-technology products sold in world trade.
73. This was the case even in the Soviet Union where the politically motivated exclusion of the famous Nobel Prize winner dissident Andrei Sakharov from the Academy was, in the early 1980s, blocked by the fact that the ballot on this issue had to be secret and the members of the Academy voted against his exclusion.
74. Reform of the Hungarian small business sector in 1982 had interesting organizational implications for some more practice-oriented institutes of the Academy of Sciences. The 1982 regulation made it possible for employees of state enterprises (or other organizations) to found simple partnerships between themselves which were allowed to work for the mother firm if it lacked extra capacity. Such partnerships called VGMK (literally translated 'Intra-Enterprise Business Groups') were also created within some academic research centres, usually with leading researchers as their members. These small firms could carry out on a contractual basis part of the projects of their mother institutes commissioned from outside, and were paid by the mother institute as any subcontractor. The possibility of

participating in the activities of these small firms (and thus earning extra income) was offered as an incentive for junior research staff to perform better in their routine research work.

75. Data based on the author's own experience.

76. It is interesting to note at this point that in 1999, 20 per cent of S&E (science and engineering) doctoral students in the United States were from China, and 2 per cent each from the former Soviet Union and Poland (Science and Engineering Indicators, OM, 2002, vol 1, Figure 3-21). All these figures had been probably close to zero ten years before. If Vietnam with its almost 2 per cent figure is added it means more than one-quarter of PhD students in S&E studies at American universities are already from former socialist countries. Two other countries' data also include an unspecifiable amount of former East European students: Germany (4 per cent) and Israel (close to 1 per cent, but not figuring in the graph cited).

77. Business expenditure on research and development, see later in detail.

78. Gross expenditure on research and development, also presented later.

79. The Hungarian Academy of Sciences was gradually nationalized between 1945 and late 1949 as were all the Academies of the countries under Soviet occupation. On the details of the process see Péteri (1989).

80. The Prussian Academy of Sciences was founded by Alexander von Humboldt. The Hungarian Academy of Sciences was created by Count István Széchenyi who offered his year's income in 1825 for a 'Scientific Society for the cultivation of national language and science' to be established.

81. Biegelbauer quotes an assessment by the US National Academy of Sciences (1994) saying that the Hungarian Academy of Sciences was, during the first 120 years of its existence, an Academy of Sciences in the classical sense: 'a private, non-profit, self-perpetuating society of distinguished scholars engaged in scientific . . . research, dedicated to the furtherance of science and technology and their use for general welfare' (Biegelbauer, 2000, 42).

82. National Academies may be very different in character, although they exist in some form in most European countries. Their current roles and structures all reflect their origins and former roles in politics and in science. This is why the debate on the futures of the Academies going on in most Central and East European countries in the early 1990s was quite Beckettian in some cases: one argument cited the Finnish example as one to be followed (the Finnish Academy of Sciences is a purely honorary body with a maximum number of 12 members) while another pointed at the Académie Française with its meritocratic structure recognizing achievements both in science and in art. Central and East European Academies of Science usually limit their membership to scientists, but most of them match the sizes of smaller parliaments with respect to membership numbers.

83. Source: OM (2002, 5).

84. The necessity of having a well-performing R&D diffusion system was understood only about five years later, but the outcome of this effort was of a rather questionable value (Török, 1996a).

85. On the NIS of Cyprus see Hadjimanolis and Dickson (2001). Malta is not mentioned at all in NSB (2004), and no references whatsoever to its NIS have been found in the literature, but some NIS-related data of the country figure in European Innovation Scoreboard (2003).

86. Our survey of the 2003 Trendchart uses the data calculated and published in Balogh (2004). For the Trendchart itself see European Innovation Scoreboard (2003).

87. See Biegelbauer (2000, 181) for a comparison of the influences of different institutions on the R&D sector in Austria, Slovenia and Hungary. Very interestingly, this comparison shows that the degree of influence of business on the domestic R&D sector is not significantly higher in Austria than in Slovenia or Hungary. Such Central European, that is 'non-systemic' characteristics of the NISs in the region have remained largely unexplored by literature so far.

88. Literature on R&D and innovation in the transition countries has dealt extensively with this problem. For such sources see Török (1994), Török (1996a), Török (1997a), Glatz (1998), OMFB (1999a), Biegelbauer (2000), Balogh (2001), Berényi (2001), Balogh (2002), Dőry (2002), Inzelt (2002), Román (2002), Mogyorósi et al. (2003), Nikodémus (2003), Siegler (2003).

89.   For detailed data see Eurostat online (Statistics in Focus: www.europa.eu.int/comm/euro-stat).

90.   Our quantitative comparison of R&D competitiveness (Chapter 4) will only include less than 20 Third World countries on which all the necessary R&D data were available.

91.   The GNP-based counterpart of GERD, R&D spending per GNP in a year in a country.

92.   Own calculation from NSB (2004, Appendix Table 6-1).

93.   PPP corrected GDP per capita data for Brazil, India and Singapore were downloaded on 5 July 2004 from www.economist.com/countries.

94.   The weakness of the R&D diffusion system has also been demonstrated for Hungary (see Török, 1996a; OMFB, 1999). The lack of an appropriate 'institutional fabric' directed at supporting innovation at all institutional levels of the Latin American economies is noted by Sutz (2000, 288).

95.   In the case of Brazilian manufacturing for example, Costa and de Queiroz (2002) have shown that domestic firms only have capabilities of building their own technological potential.

96.   The study by James (2000) deals with labour-intensive development in Sub-Saharan Africa. This is however not a NIS analysis, and Sub-Saharan countries could not be even called 'underperformers' due to their close to complete lack of R&D resources and capacities.

97.   The useability of this indicator in R&D competitiveness analysis was discussed in Chapter 3.

98.   A few 'non-performers' such as Gambia can boast of excellent scientometric indicators as compared to their GERD or publication efforts.

99.   It contains spending on research, education, training and software. The relative share of 'knowledge investment' within GDP reached 7.7 per cent in the EU, but 9.0 per cent in the United States in 1999 (Rodrigues, 2003, 54).

100. On various aspects of Korea's catching-up efforts see Inoue et al. (1993), Lee and Lim (2001), Kim and Lee (2002), Sakakibara and Cho (2002).

101. This fact that could possibly serve as a partial explanation of why one part of their R&D budget seems to be spent without providing appropriate leverage to their visible performance in R&D and innovation. Any attempt to prove this very raw hypothesis would however require appropriate data which are not available.

102. For an analysis of well-performing R&D institutions in the Czech Republic, Hungary, Poland, Slovakia and Slovenia see Borsi, Dévai, Papanek and Rush (2004).

103. In our cross-sectional analysis the following data from 59 countries were used: the number of researchers, GERD as a percentage of GNP, number of researchers per million population, the number of scientific publications, the number of scientific publications per million population.

104. These two indicators reflect R&D competitiveness only in an indirect way, but they do it in a reliable manner according to our measurement results.

References

Abbott, Roderick, Claus-Dieter Ehlermann, Ulrich Immenga, Alexis Jacquemin, Frédéric Jenny, François Lamoureux, Jean-François Marchipont, Ernst-Ulrich Petersmann and Jean-François Pons (1995), 'Competition policy in the new trade order: strengthening international competition and rules', report by the group of experts, manuscript, Brussels.

Academy of Finland (2000), *The State and the Quality of Scientific Research in Finland, A Review of Scientific Research and Its Environment in the Late 1990s*, publications of the Academy of Finland, 7/00.

Acs, Zoltan J., Luc Anselin and Attila Varga (2002), 'Patents and innovation counts as measures of regional production of new knowledge', *Research Policy*, **31**, pp. 1069–85.

Acs, Zoltan J., László Szerb, József Ulbert and Attila Varga (2002), *GEM 2001 Magyarország (Global Entrepreneurship Monitoring 2001 Hungary)*, University of Baltimore/University of Pécs.

Agenda 2000 (1997), *Agenda 2000: The Opinion of the European Commission on Hungary's Application to the European Union*, Budapest: Ministry of Foreign Affairs.

Ahrweiler, Petra, Simone De Jong and Paul Windrum (2002), 'Evaluating innovation networks', in Pyka-Küppers (eds) *Innovation Networks. Theory and Practice*, Cheltenham UK and Northampton US: Edward Elgar, pp. 197–214.

Aide à la Décision Économique SA, in association with the University College London School of Slavonics and European Studies and the Maastricht Economic Research Institute on Innovation and Technology (2001), *Innovation Policy Issues in Six Candidate Countries: The Challenges*, European Commission Directorate-General for Enterprise EUR 17036, 189 pages.

Amable, Bruno and Robert Boyer (2001), 'Europe's system(s) of innovation', in Pascal Petit and Luc Soete (eds), *Technology and the Future of European Employment*, Cheltenham, UK and Northampton, US: Edward Elgar, pp. 425–50.

Balassa, Bela (1965), 'Trade liberalization and "revealed" comparative advantage', *Manchester School of Economic and Social Studies*, **32** (2), pp. 99–123.

Balassa, Bela (1977), 'A Stages Approach to Comparative Advantage', World Bank staff working paper 256, May.

Balázs, Péter (1996), *Az Európai Unió külkapcsolatai és Magyarország [The EU's International Relations and Hungary]*, Budapest: KJK.

Balconi, M., S. Breschi and F. Lissoni (2004), 'Networks of inventors and the role of academia: an exploration of Italian patent data', *Research Policy*, **33**, pp. 127–45.

Balogh, Thomas (1955), 'Factor intensities of American foreign trade and technical progress', *Review of Economics and Statistics*, **37** (4), pp. 425–27.

Balogh, Tamás (2001), 'A szakértői bírálattól a portfólió-elemzésig. Az alkalmazott kutatás-fejlesztés értékelése' [From expert evaluation to portfolio analysis. An assessment of applied research and development], *Magyar Tudomány*. **3**, pp. 328–39.

Balogh, Tamás (2002), 'Hol állunk Európában? A magyarországi kutatás-fejlesztés helyzete' [Where do we stand in Europe? The situation of R&D in Hungary], *Magyar Tudomány*, **3**, pp. 361–70.

Balogh, Tamás (2004), 'A magyarországi innováció helyzete az új Európában' [The situation of innovation in Hungary in the new Europe], *Európai Tükör*, **2**, May, pp. 45–60.

Barabási, Albert-László (2003), *Behálózva. A hálózatok új tudománya [Linked. The New Science of Networks]*, Budapest: Magyar Könyvklub Publishers.

Baumol, William, Joseph Panzar and Robert Willig (1982), *Contestable Markets and the Theory of Industry Structure*, New York: Harcourt Brace Jovanovich.

Berényi, Dénes (2001), 'A magyar tudomány a világversenyben' [Hungarian science in world competition], *Magyar Tudomány*, **2**, 217.

Biegelbauer, Peter S. (2000), *130 Years of Catching Up with the West: A Comparative Perspective on Hungarian Industry, Science and Technology Policy-making since Industrialization*, Contemporary Trends in European Social Sciences, Aldershot: Ashgate Publishing.

Bork, Robert H. (1993), *The Antitrust Paradox: A Policy at War with Itself*, New York: Free Press (1st edition 1978).

Borsi, Balázs, Katalin Dévai, Gábor Papanek and Howard Rush (eds) (2004) *The RECORD Manual: Benchmarking Innovative Research Organisations in European Accession Countries*, Budapest University of Technology and Economics and European Commission, Brussels, O EUR 21238, 75 pages.

Borsi, Balázs and András Telcs (2004), 'A K+F tevékenység nemzetközi összehasonlítása országstatisztikák alapján' [An international comparison of R&D based on national statistics], *Közgazdasági Szemle*, **51**, February, pp. 153–72.

Bowden, Roger J. (1983), 'The conceptual basis of empirical studies of trade in manufactured commodities: a constructive critique', *Manchester School of Economic and Social Studies*, **3**, pp. 209–34.

Brander, James A. and Barbara Spencer (1983), 'International R&D rivalry and industrial strategy', *Review of Economic Studies*, **50**, pp. 707–22.

Brandsma, Andries, Nikolaus Thumm and Thübke, Alexander (2002), *Economic Transformation. European Commission Directorate General JRC*, Joint Research Centre Institute for Prospective Technological Studies (IPTS), Enlargement Futures Series, 01/2. final report, June.

Braun, Ernest and Wolfgang Polt (1988), 'High technology and competitiveness: an Austrian perspective', in Christopher Freeman and Bengt-Åke Lundvall (eds), *Small Countries Facing the Technological Revolution*, London and New York: Pinter Publishers, pp. 203–25.

Braun, Tibor, Wolfgang Glänzel, Éva Kovács-Németh and Zsuzsa Szabadi-Peresztegi (2002), 'Magyarország helyzete a természettudományi alapkutatás világában: tudománymetriai tájkép a második évezred végén' [Hungary's Situation in the World of Basic Scientific Research: A Scientometric Landscape at the End of the Second Millennium], *Magyar Tudomány*, **7**, pp. 935–45.

Braun, Tibor, Zsuzsa Szabadi-Peresztegi and Éva Kovács-Németh (2003), 'About Abels and similar international awards for ranked lists of awardees as science indicators of national merit in mathematics', *Scientometrics*, **56** (2), pp. 161–8.

Bruton, Henry J. (1998), 'A reconsideration of import substitution', *Journal of Economic Literature*, **36**, June, pp. 903–36.

Buzás, Norbert (2003), 'Organizational elements of knowledge transfer in Hungary: towards a functional system of innovation', in Imre Lengyel (ed.) *Knowledge Transfer, Small and Medium-sized Enterprises, and Regional Development*, Szeg ed: JATEPress, pp. 32–46.

Caminal, Ramon and Xavier Vives (1996), 'Why market-shares matter: an information-based theory', *RAND Journal of Economics* **27** (2), Summer, pp. 221–39.

Cantner, Uwe and Andreas Pyka (2001), 'Classifying technology policy from an evolutionary perspective', *Research Policy*, **30**, pp. 759–75.

Carlsson, Bo et al. (2002), 'Innovation systems: analytical and methodological issues', *Research Policy*, **31**, pp. 233–45.

Carlton, Dennis W. and Jeffrey M. Perloff (2000), *Modern Industrial Organization*, 3rd edition, Reading, MA: Addison-Wesley.

Caves, Richard E. (1964), *American Industry: Structure, Conduct, Performance*, Englewood Cliffs, NJ: Prentice Hall.

Caves, Richard E. (1982), 'Multinational enterprise and economic analysis', *Cambridge Surveys of Economic Literature*, Cambridge University Press.

Caves, Richard E. and Ronald W. Jones (1985), *World Trade and Payments: An Introduction*, Boston, MA and Toronto: Little, Brown & Company.

Charnes, A., W.W. Cooper and E. Rhodes (1978), 'Measuring the efficiency of decision making units', *European Journal of Operational Research*, **2** (6), pp. 429–44.

Chikán, Attila (1998), *Vállalatgazdaságtan* [*Economics of the Firm*], Budapest: Aula Publishers.

Clark, Woodrow W., Jr. (2002), 'Intrapreneurship: commercialization of research and development by firms: the United States case', in A. Varga and L. Szerb (eds), *Innovation, Entrepreneurship, Regions and Economic Development: International Experiences and Hungarian Challenges*, Pécs: University of Pécs. pp. 107–21.

Coase, Ronald W. (1937), 'The nature of the firm', *Economica*, **4**, pp. 386–405.

Cohen, Stephen S. (1994), 'Speaking freely: foreign affairs', July–August. www.foreignaffairs.org/19940701faresponse5134/none/the-fight-over-competitiveness.html

Commissione (V) Bilancio, Tesoro e Programmazione del Parlamento Italiano (2000), *Documento conclusivo dell'indagine conoscitiva sulla competitività del sistema-paese di fronte alle sfide della moneta unica e della globalizzazione dei mercati*, June 20, Rome.

Coriat, Benjamin and Fabienne Orsi (2002), 'Establishing a new intellectual property rights regime in the United States: origins, content and problems', *Research Policy*, **31**, pp. 1491–507.

Cosh, Andy, Kirsty Hughes and Bob Rowthorn (1993), 'The competitive role of UK manufacturing industry 1979–2003', in Kirsty Hughes (ed.), *The Future of UK Competitiveness and the Role of Industrial Policy*, London: Policy Studies Institute, pp. 7–27.

Costa, Ionara and Sérgio Robles Reis de Queiroz (2002), 'Foreign direct investment and technological capabilities in Brazilian industry', *Research Policy*, **31**, pp. 1431–43.

Coupé, Tom (2003), 'Revealed performances: worldwide rankings of economists and economics departments', *Journal of the European Economic Association*, **1**, pp. 1309–45.

Coupé, Tom (2004), 'What do we know about ourselves? On the economics of economics', *Kyklos*, vol. 57 – Fasc. 2, pp. 197–216.

Cournot, Augustin (1838), *Recherches sur les principes mathématiques de la théorie des richesses*, reprinted in English (1897) *Research into the Mathematical Principles of the Theory of Wealth*, London: Macmillan.

Csörgő, Sándor, Lajos Rónyai and Imre Ruzsa (2003), 'Mi mennyi?' [What is how much?] *Magyar Tudomány*, **48** (9), pp. 1174–79.

Czakó, Erzsébet (2004), Miért versenyképes a versenyképesség? – a versenyképességi listák újdonságai [Why is competitiveness competitive? Innovations in the competitiveness lists], in Erzsébet Czakó, Imre Dobos and Anita Kőhegyi (eds), *Vállalati versenyképesség – logisztika – készletek* [*Company-level Competitiveness – Logistics – Inventories*], essays in honour of the 60th birthday of Attila Chikán, Budapest University of Economics, Department of Business Economics, pp. 119–27.

Da Motta e Albuquerque, Eduardo (2000), 'Domestic patents and developing countries: arguments for their study and data from Brasil (1980–1995)', *Research Policy*, **29**, pp. 1047–60.

Dasgupta, P. and J. Stiglitz (1980), 'Uncertainty, industrial structure and the speed of R&D', *Bell Journal of Economics*, **11**, pp. 1–28.

David, Paul A. et al. (2000), 'Is public R&D a complement of substitute for private R&D? A review of the econometric evidence', *Research Policy*, **29**, pp. 497–529.

De Castro Eduardo Anselmo et al. (2000), 'The triple helix model as the motor for creative use of telematics', *Research Policy*, **29**, pp. 193–203.

De Solla Price, Derek J. (1961), *Science since Babylon*, New Haven, CT: Yale University Press.

De Solla Price, Derek J. (1963), *Little Science, Big Science*, New York: Columbia University Press.

De Solla Price, Derek J. (1979), *Kis tudomány – nagy tudomány* (*Little Science, Big Science*), Budapest: Akadémiai Kiadó.

Deli, Zsuzsa (2004), 'The scoreboards of R&D activities in an international context', *Development and Finance*, **2**, pp. 32–41.

Devlin, Keith (1990), *Mathematics: the New Golden Age*, Harmondsworth: Penguin Books.

Dőry, Tibor (2002), 'Towards a regional innovation system: regional policy issues and problems in the Central Transdanubian region', in A. Varga and L. Szerb (eds) *Innovation, Entrepreneurship Regions and Economic Development: International Experiences and Hungarian Challenges*, Pécs: University of Pécs, pp. 247–64.

EPUB (2002), *RTD Evaluation Toolbox. Socio-economic Evaluation of Public RTD Policies*, IPTS-Joanneum Research.

Erdei, Tamás (2002), 'A magyar bankok versenyképessége' [The competitiveness of Hungarian banks], lecture at the conference, 'Hungary at the Gate of the European Union' organized by GKI Economic Research, Budapest, 13 November.

European Commission (1995), *Green Paper on Innovation*, Luxembourg: Office for Official Publications of the European Communities.

European Commission (2002), 'Competitiveness and benchmarking', *European Competitiveness Report 2002*, commission staff working document (SEC(2002) 528), Luxembourg: Office for Official Publications of the European Communities.

European Commission (2003), *A European Initiative for Growth. Investing in Networks and Knowledge for Growth and Jobs*, final report to the European Council, Brussels, COM (2003) 690, 26.

European Commission (2004), *Delivering Lisbon, Reforms for the Enlarged Union*, final report from the Commission to the Spring European Council, Brussels, 21 January, COM(2004) 29.

European Commission (2001), *European Competitiveness Report*, Brussels: EC.

European Innovation Scoreboard (2003), 'Indicators', assessed 5 June, 2004 at http://trendchart.cordis.lu/scoreboard2003 /html/indicators/indicators.html.

EVCA (1999–2001), *Yearbook*, Zaventem: European Venture Capital Association.

Faber, Jan and Anneloes Barbara Hesen (2004), 'Innovation capabilities of European nations: cross-national analyses of patents and sales of product innovations', *Research Policy*, **33**, pp. 193–207.

Färe, R., S. Grosskopf and C.A. Lowell (1994a), *Production Frontiers*, Cambridge: Cambridge University Press.

Färe, R., S. Grosskopf, M. Norris and Z. Zhang (1994b), 'Productivity growth, technical progress and efficiency changes in industrialised countries', *American Economic Review*, **84**, pp. 66–83.

Fertő, Imre and Lionel J. Hubbard (2002), 'Megnyilvánuló komparatív előnyök és versenyképesség a magyar élelmiszer-gazdaságban' [Revealed comparative advantages and competitiveness in the Hungarian food sector], *Külgazdaság*, **46**, September, pp. 46–58.

Fisher, Irving (1925), 'Our unstable dollar and the so-called business cycle', *Journal of the American Statistical Association*, **20**, pp. 179–202.

Fleischer, Holger (1997), 'Mißbräuchliche Produktvorankündigungen im Monopolrecht – Lehren aus United States vs. Microsoft', *Wirtschaft und Wettbewerb*, **47**, (3) (March), pp. 203–10.

Flor, M.L. and M.J. Oltra (2004), 'Identification of innovating firms through technological innovation indicators: an application to the Spanish ceramic tile industry', *Research Policy*, **33**, pp. 323–36.

Freeman, Christopher (1988), 'Technology gaps, international trade and the problems of smaller and less-developed countries', in Christopher Freeman and Bengt-Åke Lundvall (eds), *Small Countries Facing the Technological Revolution*, London and New York: Pinter Publishers, pp. 67–84.

Freeman, Chris (2002), 'Continental, national and sub-national innovation systems – complementarity and economic growth', *Research Policy*, 31, pp. 191–211.

Freeman, Christopher and Bengt-Åke Lundvall (eds) (1988), *Small Countries*

Facing the Technological Revolution, London and New York: Pinter Publishers.

Fudenberg, Drew and Jean Tirole (1991), *Game Theory*, Cambridge, MA and London: MIT Press.

Fujita, Masahisa, Paul Krugman and Anthony J. Venables (1999), *The Spatial Economy. Cities, Regions and International Trade*, Cambridge, MA and London: MIT Press.

Furman, Jeffrey L., Michael E. Porter and Scott Stern (2002), 'The determinants of national innovative capacity', *Research Policy*, **31**, pp. 899–933.

Gavigan, James P., Mathias Ottitsch, Sami Mahroum (1999), *Knowledge and Learning. Towards a Learning Europe*, European Commission Directorate General JRC, Joint Research Centre Institute for Prospective Technological Studies (IPTS), Futures Programme no. 14, 81.

Giesecke, Susanne (2000), 'The contrasting roles of government in the development of biotechnology industry in the US and Germany', *Research Policy*, **29**, 205–23.

Glänzel, Wolfgang, András Schubert and Tibor Braun (2002), 'A relational chart approach to the world of basic research in twelve science fields at the end of the second millennium', *Scientometrics*, **55** (3), pp. 335–48.

Glänzel, Wolfgang, András Schubert and Tibor Braun (2003), 'Eggyel kevesebb' [One less], *Magyar Tudomány*, **48** (9), pp. 1180–83.

Glänzel, W., M. Meyer, B. Schlemmer, M. du Plessis, B. Thijs, T. Magerman, K. Debackere and R. Veugelers, (2003), 'Biotechnology – an analysis based on publications and patents', Steunpunt O&O Statistieken K.U. Leuven, accessed November at http://www.steunpuntoos.be/biotech_b.html.

Glatz, Ferenc (1998), *Tudománypolitika az ezredforduló Magyarországán* [*Science Policy in Hungary at the Turn of the Century*], Budapest: Hungarian Academy of Sciences.

Godin, Benoît (2003), 'The emergence of S&T indicators: why did governments supplement statistics with indicators?' *Research Policy*, **32**, pp. 679–91.

Goldberg, D.E. (1989), *Genetic Algorithms in Search, Optimization, and Machine Learning*, Menlo Park, NY: Addison-Wesley.

Gorzelak, Grzegorz, Éva Ehrlich, Lubomir Faltan and Michal Illgner (eds) (2001), *Central Europe in Transition: Towards EU Membership*, Regional Studies Association Polish Section, Warsaw: Wydawnictwo Naukowe.

Gregersen, Brigitte (1988), 'Public sector participation in innovation systems', in Christopher Freeman and Bengt-Åke Lundvall (eds) (1988), *Small Countries Facing the Technological Revolution*, London and New York: Pinter Publishers, pp. 262–77.

Griliches, Zvi (1990), 'Patent statistics as economic indicators: a survey', *Journal of Economic Literature*, **28**, December, pp. 1661–707.

Group of Lisbon (1995), *Limits to Competition*, Cambridge, MA and London: MIT Press.

Grubel, H.G. and P.J. Lloyd (1995), *Intra-Industry Trade*, London: Macmillan Press.

Guellec, Dominique and Bruno van Pottelsberghe de la Potterie (2001), 'The internationalisation of technology analysed with patent data', *Research Policy*, **30**, pp. 1253–66.

Hadjimanolis, Athanasios and Keith Dickson (2001), 'Development of national innovation policy in small developing countries: the case of Cyprus', *Research Policy*, **30**, pp. 805–17.

Hagedoorn, John and Myriam Cloodt (2003), 'Measuring innovative performance: is there an advantage in using multiple indicators?', *Research Policy*, **32**, pp. 1365–79.

Hara, Takuji (2003), *Innovation in the Pharmaceutical Industry. The Process of Drug Discovery and Development*. Cheltenham, UK and Northampton, MA, USA: Edward Elgar.

Hargittai, István (2001), *The Road to Stockholm, Nobel Prizes, Science and Scientists*, Oxford: Oxford University Press.

Hayashi, Takayuki (2003), 'Effect of R&D programmes on the formation of university–industry–government networks: comparative analysis of Japanese R&D programmes', *Research Policy*, **32**, pp. 1421–42.

HEBC (Hungarian EU Enlargement Business Council) (2003), *Célegyenesben. Magyarország sikeres integrációja. A Magyar EU Bővítési Üzleti Tanács ajánlásai.* [*Approaching the Target. Hungary's Successful Integration to Europe, Recommendations of the Hungarian EU Enlargement Business Council*], Budapest: HEBC.

Heller, Farkas (1947), Közgazdaságtan I. kötet, *Elméleti közgazdaságtan.* [*Economics I. Theoretical Economics*], Budapest: Institute for Higher Engineer Training.

Hicks, Diana et al. (2001), 'The changing composition of innovative activity in the US: a portrait based on patent analysis', *Research Policy*, **30**, pp. 681–703.

Hirsch, Seev (1974), 'Hypothesen über den Handel zwischen Entwicklungs- und Industrieländern', in H. Giersch and D. Haas (eds), *Probleme der weltwirtschaftlichen Arbeitsteilung*, Kiel: Institut für Weltwirtschaft, pp. 69–88.

Hirsch, Seev (1975), 'The product cycle model of international trade', *Oxford Bulletin of Economics and Statistics* (**1**).

Hirschman, Albert O. (1958), *The Strategy of Economic Development*, New Haven, CT: Yale University Press.

Hoffmeyer, E. (1958), 'The Leontief Paradox critically examined', *Manchester School Review*, May, pp. 160–75.

Horváth, Gyula (2001), 'A magyar régiók és települések versenyképessége az európai gazdasági térben' [The competitiveness of Hungarian regions in the European economic space], *Tér és Társadalom*, **2**, pp. 203–31.

Hotelling, H. (1933), 'Analysis of a complex of statistical variables into principal components', *Journal of Educational Psychology*, **24**, pp. 417–41, 498–520.

Hughes, Kirsty (1986), *Exports and Technology*, Cambridge: Cambridge University Press.

IMD (2003), *The World Competitiveness Yearbook*, Lausanne: IMD School of Management.

IMF (2000), *World Economic Outlook October 2000, Focus on Transition Economies*, IMF.

Information Society (1997), *Information Society. The Green Paper on the Information Society in Portugal*, Missâo para a Sociedade da Informaçâo no 87, Lisbon, May.

Inotai, András (1997), *Útközben. Magyarország és az Európai Unió* [*On the Road. Hungary and the European Union*] Budapest: Belvárosi Publishers.

Inotai, András (1999), *Magyarország és a többi közép- és kelet-európai ország szerkezeti átalakulása a Németországba irányuló export tükrében* [*Structural Change in Hungary and in the Other Countries of Central and Eastern Europe as Reflected by Exports to Germany*], Budapest: Institute for World Economics and OMFB.

Inoue, Ryuichiro, Hirohisa Kohama, Shujiro Urata (eds) (1993), *Industrial Policy in East Asia*, Tokyo: JETRO.

Intarakumnerd, Patarapong et al. (2002), 'National innovational system in less successful developing countries: the case of Thailand', *Research Policy*, **31**, 1445–57.

Inzelt, Annamária (2002), 'Restructuring and Financing R+D: New Partnerships', in A. Varga and L. Szerb (eds), *Innovation, Entrepreneurship, Regions and Economic Development: International Experiences and Hungarian Challenges*, Pécs: University of Pécs. pp. 27–50.

IPTS (2001), *Impact of Technological and Structural Change on Employment, Prospective Analysis 2020*, Synthesis Report. European Commission Directorate General JRC, Joint Research Centre Institute for Prospective Technological Studies (IPTS), Report EUR 20131 EN, 47.

Jaffe, Adam B. (2000), 'The US patent system in transition: policy innovation and the innovation process', *Research Policy*, **29**, pp. 531–57.

James, Jeffrey (2000), 'Trait-making for labour intensive technology in Sub-Saharan Africa', *Research Policy*, **29**, pp. 757–66.

Jiménez-Contreras, Evaristo, Félix de Moya Anegón and Emilio Delgado López-Cózar (2003), 'The evolution of research activity in Spain. The impact of the National Commission for the Evaluation of Research Activity (CNEAI)', *Research Policy*, **32**, pp. 123–42.

Johnson, Björn (1988), 'An institutional approach to the small-country problem', in Christopher Freeman and Bengt-Åke Lundvall (eds), *Small Countries Facing the Technological Revolution*, London and New York: Pinter Publishers, pp. 279–97.

Kaiser, Robert and Heiko Prange (2004), 'The reconfiguration of national innovation systems: the example of German biotechnology', *Research Policy*, **33**, pp. 395–408.

Kaldor, Nicholas (1978), *The Effect of Devaluations on Trade in Manufactures*, London: Duckworth.

Karsai Judit (2002), 'A kockázati tőke részvétele az innováció finanszírozásában' [The participation of venture capital in financing innovations], unpublished manuscript, University of Veszprém.

Katrak, Homi (2002), 'Does economic liberalisation endanger indigenous technological developments? An anlysis of the Indian experience', *Research Policy*, **31**, pp. 19–30.

Katz, Jorge (2001), 'Structural reforms and technological behaviour: the sources and nature of technological change in Latin America in the 1990s', *Research Policy*, **30**, pp. 1–19.

Keller, Wolfgang (2004), 'International technology diffusion', *Journal of Economic Literature*, **12**, September, pp. 752–82.

Kim, Youngbae and Byungheon Lee (2002), 'Patterns of technological learning among the strategic groups in the Korean electronic parts industry', *Research Policy*, **31**, pp. 543–67.

Kindleberger, Charles P. (1962), *Foreign Trade and the National Economy*, New Haven, CT: Yale University Press.

King, David A. (2004), 'The scientific impact of nations', *Nature*, **430**, 15 July, pp. 311–16.

Kingston, William (2001), 'Innovation needs patents reform', *Research Policy*, **30**, pp. 403–23.

Kiss, Ferenc, Iván Major and Pál Valentiny (2000), *Információgazdaság és piacszabályozás* [*Information Economy and Market Regulation*], Budapest: Akadémiai Kiadó.

Koestler, Arthur (1959), *The Sleepwalkers*, London: Hutchinson.

Korah, Valentine (1997), *An Introductory Guide to EC Competition Law and Practice*, 6th edn, Oxford: Hart Publishing.

Kreis-Hoyer, Petra and Jutta Grünberg (2002), 'Inter-Organizational Knowledge Networks: A Theoretical Foundation', European Business School IMC working paper no 3, December.

Krugman, Paul (1994), 'Competitiveness: a dangerous obsession', *Foreign Affairs*, (2), pp. 28–44.

Krugman, Paul (1996), *The Age of Diminished Expectations*, Cambridge, MA: MIT Press (1st edn 1994) revised and updated.

Krugman, Paul and Maurice Obstfeld (1991), *International Economics: Theory and Policy*, 2nd edition, New York: HarperCollins Publishers.

Krugman, Paul and Maurice Obstfeld (2000), *International Economics: Theory and Practice,* 5th edn, Addison-Wesley Publishing Company.

Kukliński, Antoni (2001), 'Science and technology in Poland at the turn of the centuries', G. Gorzelak et al. (eds), *Central Europe in Transition: Towards EU Membership*, Warsaw: Regional Studies Association Polish Section, Wydawnictwo Naukowe, pp. 224–34.

Kulikov, Ivan (2004), 'The comparative assessment of telecommunications restructuring in Russia', MA thesis, CEU Economics Department, Budapest.

Kühn, Kai-Uwe, Paul Seabright and Alasdair Smith (1992), *Competition Policy Research: Where Do We Stand?* CEPR occasional paper 8, London.

Küppers, Günter (2002*), Complexity, Self-Organization and Innovation Networks: A New Theoretical Approach*, in A. Pyka and G. Küppers (eds), *Innovation Networks. Theory and Practice*, Cheltenham UK and Northampton, MA: Edward Elgar, pp. 22–54.

Laband, David and Robert Tollison (2000), Scientific Collaboration, *Journal of Political Economy*, **108**, pp. 632–62.

Laffont, Jean-Jacques and Jean Tirole (1993), *A Theory of Incentives in Procurement and Regulation*, Cambridge, MA: MIT Press.

Lall, Sanjaya (2003), 'Indicators of the relative importance of IPRs in developing countries', *Research Policy*, **32**, pp. 1657–80.

Landry, Réjean et al. (2001), 'Utilization of social science research knowledge in Canada', *Research Policy*, **30**, pp. 333–49.

Lankhuizen, Maureen (2000), 'Shifts in foreign trade, competitiveness and growth potential: from Baltics to "Bal-techs"?' *Research Policy*, **29**, pp. 9–29.

Lányi, Beatrix (2002), 'A K+F nemzetközi versenykepéssége. Közép-európai OECD országok kutatási és fejlesztési tevékenységének értékelése [International competitiveness in R&D. The assessment of R&D in Central European OECD countries], working paper 22, University of Veszprém.

Lary, Hal B. (1968), *Imports of Labor-Intensive Manufactures from Less Developed Countries*, New York: National Bureau for Economic Research.

Laursen, Keld (2000), *Trade Specialization, Technology and Economic Growth. Theory and Evidence from Advanced Countries*, Cheltenham, UK and Northampton, MA, USA: Edward Elgar.

Lee, Keun and Chaisung Lim (2001), 'Technological regimes, catching-up and leapfrogging: findings from the Korean industries', *Research Policy*, **30**, pp. 459–83.

Lembke, Johan (2002), *Competition for Technological Leadership. EU Policy for High Technology*, Cheltenham, UK and Northampton, MA, USA: Edward Elgar.

Lemola, Tarmo (2002), 'Convergence of national science and technology policies: the case of Finland', *Research Policy*, **31**, pp. 1481–90.

Lengyel, Imre (2000), 'A regionális versenyképességről' [On regional competitiveness], *Közgazdasági Szemle*, **12**, pp. 962–87.

Lengyel, Imre (ed.) (2003), *Knowledge Transfer, Small and Medium-Sized Enterprises, and Regional Development*, Szeged: JATEPress, University of Szeged.

Leoncini, Ricardo and Sandro Montresor (2001), 'The automobile technological systems: an empirical analysis of four European countries', *Research Policy*, **30**, pp. 1321–40.

Leontief, Wassily (1954), 'Domestic production and foreign trade: the American capital position re-examined', *Economia Internazionale*, **2**.

Leontief, Wassily (1956), 'Factor proportions and the structure of American trade: further theoretical and empirical analysis', *Review of Economics and Statistics*, **38** (4) (November) pp. 386–407.

Lesourne, Jacques (ed.) (1979), *Facing the Probable and Managing the Unpredictable. The Interfutures Report*, Paris: OECD.

Leydesdorff, Loet (2000), 'The triple helix: an evolutionary model of innovations', *Research Policy*, **29**, pp. 243–55.

Linder, Staffan Burenstam (1961), *An Essay on Trade and Transformation*, Stockholm: Handelshögskolan.

Lipczynski, John and John Wilson (2001), *Industrial Organisation. A Theory of Competitive Markets*, Harlow, UK: Pearson Education.

Liu, Xiaohui and Chenggang Wang (2003), 'Does foreign direct investment facilitate technological progress? Evidence from Chinese industries', *Research Policy*, **32**, pp. 945–53.

Liu, Xielin and Steven White (2001), 'Comparing innovative systems: a framework and application to China's transitional context', *Research Policy*, **30**, pp. 1091–114.

Lloyd, P.J. (1998), 'Globalisation and competition policies', *Weltwirtschaftliches Archiv*, **134** (2), pp. 161–85.

Lotka, A.J. (1926), 'The frequency distribution of scientific productivity', *Journal of the Washington Academy of Science*, **16**, pp. 317–23.

Lundvall, Bengt-Åke and Peter Nielsen (1999), 'Competition and transformation in the learning economy – illustrated by the Danish case', *Revue d'Économie Industrielle*, (**88**) (2e trimestre) (numéro spécial: L'économie de la connaissance), pp. 67–90.

Lundvall, Bengt-Åke (ed.) (1992), *National Systems of Innovation: Towards a Theory of Innovation and Interactive Learning*, London: Pinter.

Major, Iván (2003), 'What makes Hungarian SMEs perform poorly?' *Acta Oeconomica*, **53**, 2, pp. 109–44.

Mani, Sunil (2002), *Government, Innovation and Technology Policy. An International Comparative Analysis*, Cheltenham, UK and Northampton, MA, USA: Edward Elgar.

Marcy, Gérard (1976), *Économie internationale*, Paris: Presses Universitaires de France.

Maskin, Eric and Jean Tirole (1988), 'A theory of dynamic oligopoly I. Overview and quantity competition with large fixed costs', *Econometrica*, **56** (3), pp. 549–69, quoted in Tirole (1988) pp. 340–46.

Mathews, John A. (2002), 'The origins and dynamics of Taiwan's R&D consortia', *Research Policy*, **31**, pp. 633–51.

Matsumoto, Koji (1991), *The Rise of the Japanese Corporate System*, London and New York: Kegan Paul International.

Milgrom, Peter and John Roberts (1992), *Economics, Organization and Management*, Englewood Cliffs, NJ: Prentice Hall.

Mogyorósi, Péter, Márton Vilmányi and Balázs Révész (2003), 'Experiences in the Fields of Innovation Services in Hungary at the Age of Millennium', in I. Lengyel (ed.) *Knowledge Transfer, Small and Medium-sized Enterprises, and Regional Development*, Szeged: JATEPress. pp. 47–59.

Moore, J. I. (2001), *Writers on Strategy and Strategic Management. Theory and Practice at Enterprise, Corporate Business and Functional Levels*, 2nd edn, London: Penguin Business.

Mucchielli, Jean-Louis and Michel Sollogoub (1980), *L'échange international. Fondements théoriques et analyses empiriques*, Paris: Economica, p. 220.

Mulligan, Casey B. and Xavier Sala-i-Martin (1995), 'Measuring aggregate human capital', National Bureau of Economic Research working paper, no 5016, Cambridge, MA.

Mustar, Philippe and Philippe Larédo (2002), 'Innovation and research policy in France (1980–2000) or the disappearance of the Colbertist state', *Research Policy*, **31**, pp. 55–72.

Müller, Karel (2001), 'The Czech Republic: Science, Technology and Education', in G. Gorzelak et al. *Central Europe in Transition: Towards EU Membership*, Warsaw: Regional Studies Association Polish Section, Wydawnictwo Naukowe. pp. 186–206.

Nalymov, Vassily Vassiliyevitch, and Zinaida Maximovna Mulchenko (1980), *Tudománymetria [Scientometrics]*, Budapest: Academy Publishers, (original: V.V. Nalymov and Z.M. Mulchenko: *Naukometria – izuchenie razvitiya nauki kak informatsionnogo processa* (1969), Moscow: Nauka).

Narula, Rajneesh (2002), 'Innovation systems and "inertia" in R&D location: Norwegian firms and the role of systemic lock-in', *Research Policy*, **31**, pp. 795–816.

National Academy of Sciences (1994), see Biegelbauer, 2000, p. 42, National Academy Press, Spring.

National Science Board (1998), *Science and Engineering Indicators 1998*, Arlington, VA: National Science Board.

Neary, J. Peter (2003), 'Competitive versus comparative advantage', *World Economy*, **26**, (4), April, pp. 457–70.

Negassi, S. (2004), 'R&D co-operation and innovation a microeconomic study on French firms', *Research Policy*, **33**, 365–84.

Nelson, Richard R. (1993), *National Innovation Systems: A Comparative Analysis*, Oxford and New York: Oxford University Press.

Nelson, Richard R. (1995), 'Recent evolutionary theorizing about economic change', *Journal of Economic Literature*, **33**, March, pp. 48–90.

Nelson, Richard R. (2004), 'The market economy, and the scientific commons', *Research Policy*, **33**, pp. 455–71.

Nelson, Richard R. and Sidney Winter (1982), *An Evolutionary Theory of Economic Change*, Cambridge, MA: Harvard University Press.

Nikodémus, Antal (2003), 'A hazai innováció perspektívái EU-csatlakozásunk előestéjén' [Perspectives of Hungarian innovation on the eve of EU-accession], *Külgazdaság*, **47** (12), pp. 37–52.

Niwa, F. and H. Tomizawa (1995), *Composite Indicators: International Comparison of Overall Strengths in Science and Technology*, National Institute of Science and Technology Policy report 37.

NSB (2002), *Science and Engineering Indicators 2002*, vol I, Arlington, VA: National Science Board, National Science Foundation.

NSB (2004), *Science and Engineering Indicators 2004*, vol I, Arlington, VA: National Science Board, National Science Foundation.

Nyitrai, Ferencné (2003), 'A K+F finanszírozása a fejlett világban és Magyarországon' [The financing of R&D in the advanced world and Hungary], *Development and Finance*, **3**, pp. 3–11.

Oblath, Gábor and Petra Pénzes (2003), 'A hazai gazdaság nemzetközi versenyképessége: értelmezések, mutatók és néhány tanulság' [International competitiveness of the domestic economy. Concepts, indicators and some conclusions], *Competitio*, **2** (2), November, pp. 20–41.

OECD (1968), *Gaps in Technology: General Report*, Paris: OECD,

OECD (1971), *Conditions for Success in Technological Innovation*, Paris: OECD.

OECD (1978), *Report of the Second Ad Hoc Review Group on R&D Statistics*, Paris: OECD.

OECD (1992), 'Proposed guidelines for collecting and interpreting technological innovation data', in *Oslo Manual, 1992*, Paris: OECD.

OECD (1990), 'Proposed standard method of compiling and interpreting technology balance of payments data', in *TBP Manual*, 1990, Paris: OECD.

OECD (1994), *Using Patent Data as Science and Technology Indicators*, Paris: OECD.

OECD (1999), *OECD Country Studies. Hungary*, Paris and Budapest: OECD.

OECD (2001), *Science, Technology and Industry Scoreboard 2001, Towards a knowledge-based economy*, Paris: OECD.

OECD (2002), www1.oecd.org/publications/e-book/9201131E.PDF.

OECD (2002). *Proposed Standard Practice for Surveys on Research and Experimental Development* [Frascati Manual], Paris. OECD.

OECD (2002), *The Measurement of Scientific and Technological Activities. Proposed Guidelines for Collecting and Interpreting Technological Innovation Data* [Oslo Manual], Paris: OECD.

OM (2002), *Kutatás-fejlesztés Magyarországon* [*Research and Development in Hungary*], Budapest: Oktatási Minisztérium [Ministry of Education].

OMFB (1996), *Evaluation of the Applied R&D Programme* 1991–1995, OMFB (National Committee for Technological Development), Budapest, 1996, 34.

OMFB (1999a), *Research and Development in Hungary*, KSH-OMFB.

OMFB (1999b), *National Innovation System in Hungary*, Budapest: OMFB (National Committee for Technological Development).

Özcelik, Emre and Erol Taymaz (2004), 'Does innovativeness matter for international competitiveness in developing countries? The case of Turkish manufacturing industries', *Research Policy*, **33**, pp. 409–24.

Pajarinen, Mika, Pentti Rouvinen and Pekka Ylä-Anttila (1998), *Small Country Strategies in Global Competition: Benchmarking the Finnish Case*, Helsinki: ETLA – SITRA.

Palkovits, István (2002), '*Autonóm szereplők, piaci erők és regionális gazdaságfejlődés*' [*Autonomous players, market powers and regional economic development*], PhD thesis, University of Pécs, Faculty of Economics.

Palló, Gábor (2001), 'Nobel preferenciák' [Nobel preferences], *Magyar Tudomány*, **46** (12), pp. 1426–36.

Papanek, Gábor (ed) (1999), *A magyar innovációs rendszer főbb összefüggései* [*Main Patterns of the Hungarian Innovation System*], Budapest: OMFB.

Papanek, Gábor (2003), 'The "European Paradox" in the Hungarian R&D sector', *Development and Finance*, **4**, pp. 40–7.

Papp, Zoltán (2004), 'A tudományos teljesítmény mérésének problémáiról' [On the problems of measuring scientific performance], *Magyar Tudomány*, **110** (2), pp. 232–40.

Patel, Pari and Keith Pavitt (1995), 'Patterns of technological activity: their measurement and interpretation', in P. Stoneman (ed.), *Handbook of the Economics of Technical Change*, Oxford: Basil Blackwell, pp. 14–51.

Pavitt, Keith (1984), 'Sectoral patterns of technical change: towards a taxonomy and a theory', *Research Policy*, **13**, pp. 343–73, reprinted in Pavitt (1999). pp. 15–45.

Pavitt, Keith (1987), 'The objectives of technology policy', *Science and Public Policy*, **14** (4), August, pp. 182–8, reprinted in Pavitt (1999), pp. 3–14.

Pavitt, Keith (1991), 'What makes basic research economically useful?' *Research Policy*, **20**, pp. 109–19, reprinted in Pavitt (1999), pp. 222–32.

Pavitt, Keith (1996), 'National policies for technical change: where are the increasing returns to economic research?', proceedings of the National Academy of Sciences, 93, November, 12693–12700, reprinted in Pavitt (1999), pp. 233–47.

Pavitt, Keith (1999), *Technology, Management and Systems of Innovation*, Cheltenham, UK and Northampton, USA: Edward Elgar.

Pavitt, Keith and Pari Patel (1991), 'Large firms in the production of the world's technology: an important case of "non-globalisation",' *Journal of International Business Studies*, **22** (1), pp. 1–21, reprinted in Pavitt (1999), pp. 125–48.

Pearson, K. (1901), On lines and planes of closest fit to system of points in space, *Philosophical Magazine*, **2** (6th series), pp. 559–72.

Penyigey, Krisztina (1996), 'Structure of the Hungarian consumer goods market: an analysis with the help of product tests', *Ipargazdasági Szemle/Review of Industrial Economics*, special issue, pp. 61–74.

Perez, Carlota (1988), *New Technologies and Development*, in Christopher Freeman and Bengt-Åke Lundvall (eds) *Small Countries Facing the Technological Revolution*, London and New York: Pinter Publishers, pp. 85–97.

Péteri, György (1989), 'Születésnapi ajándék Sztálinnak. Vázlat a Magyar Tudományos Akadémia államosításának történetéhez 1945–49' (A birthday present to Stalin. An outline of the nationalisation of the Hungarian Academy of Sciences, *1945–1949*], *Századvég*, **1–2**, pp. 18–35.

Petit, Pascal (1999), '*Les aléas de la croissance dans une économie fondée sur le savoir*', *Revue d'Économie Industrielle*, (88) (2e trimestre) (numéro spécial: L'économie de la connaissance), pp. 41–66.

Petit, Pascal and Luc Soete (eds) (2001), *Technology and the Future of European Employment*, Cheltenham, UK and Northampton, MA, USA: Edward Elgar.

Petrenko, Galyna (2003), *New Economy and ICT Development: The Case of EU Accession Countries*, MA thesis, CEU Economics Department, Budapest.

Peyrefitte, Alain (1976), *Le mal français*, Paris: Librairie Plon.

Pitti, Zoltán (2002), 'A versenyképesség, mint napjaink legújabb kihívása'

[Competitiveness as the most recent challenge of our times], *Vezetéstudomány*, **33** special issue, pp. 14–22.

Plasschaert, Sylvain (1995), 'Recent books on transfer pricing: a review article', *Transnational Corporations*, **4** (1) April, pp. 97–112.

Porter, Michael E. (1990), *The Competitive Advantage of Nations*, New York: Free Press.

Porter, Michael E. (2001), 'Strategy and the Internet', *Harvard Business Review*, March, HBR OnPoint, pp. 62–78.

Porter, Michael E. (2003), 'Building the microeconomic foundations of prosperity: findings from the microeconomic competitiveness index', in *The Global Competitiveness Report*, World Economic Forum, pp. 23–45.

Porter, Michael E. and Scott Stern (1999), *The New Challenge to America's Prosperity: Findings from the Innovation Index*, Washington, DC: Council on Competitiveness.

Posner, M.V. (1961), 'International trade and technical change', Oxford Economic Papers.

Pritchard, A. (1969), 'Statistical bibliography or bibliometrics?' *Journal of Documentation*, **24**, pp. 348–49.

Pyka, Andreas and Günther Küppers (2002), *Innovation Networks. Theory and Practice*, Cheltenham, UK and Northampton, USA: Edward Elgar.

Rodrigues, Maria João (2003), *European Policies for a Knowledge Economy*, Cheltenham, UK and Northampton, MA, USA: Edward Elgar.

Román, Zoltán (2000), 'Az Európai Unió innovációpolitikája' [Innovation Policy in the European Union], *Európai Tükör*, (3) 33–47.

Román, Zoltán (2002), 'A kutatás-fejlesztés teljesítményértékelése' [Performance Evaluation in R&D], *Közgazdasági Szemle*, **49**, April.

Romer, Paul (1990), 'Endogenous technical change', *Journal of Political Economy*, **98** (5), pp. 71–102.

Sachs, Jeffrey (2000), 'A new map of the world. Today's world is divided not by ideology but by technology', This demands, Jeffrey Sachs argues here, bold new thinking on development. *The Economist*, 24 June, pp. 99–101.

Sakakibara, Mariko and Dong-Sung Cho (2002), 'Cooperative R&D in Japan and Korea: a comparison of industrial policy', *Research Policy*, **31**, pp. 673–92.

Salgó, István and Ádám Török (1980), 'Importverseny a gépipari fogyasztási cikkek piacán' (Import Competition on the Market of Engineering Products for Consumption). *Külgazdaság*, **12**, pp. 47–56.

Salter, Ammon and Ben R. Martin (2001), 'The economic benefits of publicly funded basic research: a critical review', *Research Policy*, **30**, 509–32.

Salvatore, Dominick (2002), 'International Competitiveness, Multifactor Productivity and Growth in the United States, Europe, Japan and Asia', in Roger Grawe and András Inotai (eds), *Trade, Integration and Transition:*

International Conference in Memoriam Bela Balassa, Budapest: World Bank and Institute for World Economics, Hungarian Academy of Sciences, pp. 25–37.

Scherer, F.M. (1994), *Competition Policies for an Integrated World Economy*, Washington, DC: The Brookings Institution.

Scherer, F.M. (1996), *Industry Structure, Strategy and Public Policy*, New York: Harper Collins College Publishers.

Scherer, F.M. and David Ross (1990), *Industrial Market Structure and Economic Performance*, 3rd edition, Boston: Houghton Mifflin.

Schubert, András (2003), 'Magyarország helyzete a világ országai között a tudománymetriai mutatószámok alapján készített rangsorokban és térképeken' [Hungary's position in the world in ranking lists and maps prepared on the basis of scientometric indicators], unpublished manuscript, Budapest, June.

Schumpeter, Joseph A. (1912), *Theorie der wirtschaftlichen Entwicklung*, Berlin and München: Duncker und Humblot.

Schumpeter, Joseph A. (1954/1986), *History of Economic Analysis*, New York: Oxford University Press.

Servan-Schreiber, Jean-Jacques (1967), *Le défi américain*, Paris: Flammarion.

Slovenian Ministry of Education, Science and Sport (2002), *Science in Slovenia*, Ljubljana: Republic of Slovenia Ministry of Education, Science and Sport.

Sherry, Edward F. and David J. Teece (2004), 'Royalties, evolving patent rights, and the value of innovation', *Research Policy*, **33**, pp. 179–91.

Shy, Oz (1995), *Industrial Organization*, Cambridge, MA: MIT Press.

Siegler, András (2003), 'Az európai kutatási térség és Magyarország' [The European Research Area and Hungary], *Európai Tükör*, **2**, pp. 33–53.

Simon, Herbert A. (1999), 'The many shapes of knowledge', *Revue d'Économie Industrielle*, **88**, (2e trimestre) (numéro spécial: L'économie de la connaissance), pp. 23–40.

Simonovits, András (2004), 'Publikációs szelekció a közgazdaságtanban' [Publicational selection in economics], *BUKSZ*, **16**, p. 158.

Simonyi, Károly (2001), 'A magyarországi fizika kultúrtörténete' [The cultural history of physics in Hungary], *A Természet Világa*, special issue 1, p. 14.

Spearman, C.E. (1904), 'Proof and measurement of association between two things', *American Journal of Psychology*, **15**, pp. 72–101.

Steinbock, Dan (1998), *The Competitive Advantage of Finland. From Cartels to Competition*, Helsinki: Taloustieto Oy.

Stout, David and Peter Swann (1993), 'The non-price competitiveness of British firms', in Kirsty Hughes (ed.), *The Future of UK Competitiveness and the Role of Industrial Policy*, London: Policy Studies Institute, pp. 28–39.

Sutton, John (1991), *Sunk Costs and Market Structure. Price Competition, Advertising and the Evolution of Concentration*, Cambridge, MA: MIT Press.

Sutz, Judith (2000), 'The university – industry – government relations in Latin America', *Research Policy*, **29**, pp. 279–90.

Swerling, C.B. (1954), 'Capital shortage and labor surplus in the United States', *Review of Economics and Statistics*, **36** (3), pp. 286–9.

Szentes, Tamás (2002a), *Globalizáció, regionális integrációk és nemzeti fejlődés korunk világgazdaságában* [*Globalisation, Regional Integrations and National Development in the Modern World Economy*], Szombathely: Savaria University Press.

Szentes, Tamás (2002b), 'Néhány gondolat a "humán tőkére" és a tudományos kutatásokra fordított költségek kérdéséhez' [Some thoughts on the costs of 'human capital' and scientific research], *Magyar Tudomány*, **5**, pp. 636–47.

Tamási, Péter (2001), *Education, Science and Technology in Hungary*, in G. Gorzelak et al. (eds), *Central Europe in Transition: Towards EU Membership*, Warsaw: Regional Studies Association Polish Section, Wydawnictwo Naukowe. pp. 207–23.

Tchalakov, I. (2001), 'Innovating in Bulgaria: two cases in the life of laboratory before and after 1989', *Research Policy*, **30**, pp. 391–402.

Temple, Paul and Giovanni Urga (1997), 'The competitiveness of UK manufacturing: evidence from imports', *Oxford Economic Papers*, **49**, pp. 207–27.

Tirole, Jean (1988), *The Theory of Industrial Organization*, Cambridge, MA: MIT Press.

Török, Ádám (1986a), *Komparatív előnyök. Nemzetközi példák, hazai tapasztalatok* [*Comparative Advantages. International Patterns, Domestic Experience*], Budapest: KJK.

Török, Ádám (1986b) 'Belső szabadkereskedelem és világgazdasági integrálódás. Gondolatok a Cockfield-jelentés nyomán' [Internal free trade and integration in the world economy. Thoughts provoked by the Cockfield Report], *Külgazdaság*, **30** (6), pp. 3–12.

Török, Ádám (1989), 'Komparatív előnyök, versenyképesség, piacműködés' [Comparative advantages, competitiveness and the functioning of markets], *Ipargazdasági Szemle*, (3), pp. 23–34.

Török, Ádám (1994), 'Human resources and technology change in Eastern Europe', *International Journal of Technology Management*, (1), pp. 3–4.

Török, Ádám (1996a), 'A K+F diffúziós rendszere Magyarországon' [The system of R&D diffusion in Hungary], *Külgazdaság*, **5**, pp. 63–72.

Török, Ádám (1996b), *Piacműködés és iparvédelem* [*Market Performance and the Protection of Domestic Industry*], Pécs: Janus Pannonius University Publishers.

Török, Ádám (1997a), 'Az első átfogó projektértékelési kísérlet Magyarországon' [The first comprehensive effort of project evaluation in Hungary], *Közgazdasági Szemle*, **44**, pp. 69–82.

Török, Ádám (1997b), 'A versenyképesség-elemzés egyes módszertani kérdései' [Some methodological issues of competitiveness analysis], *Gazdaság – Vállalkozás – Vezetés*, **3**, pp. 2–13.

Török, Ádám (1999a), *Verseny a versenyképességért? Mikroszféra-kezelési politikák az Európai Unióban és Magyarországon* [*Competing for Competitiveness? Policies Affecting Business in the EU and Hungary*], Budapest: Prime Minister's Office.

Török, Ádám (1999b), 'A verseny- és a K+F-politika keresztútján. Bevezetés a csoportmentességi szabályozás elméletébe' [At the crossroads of competition and R&D policy. Introduction in the theory of block exemptions] *Közgazdasági Szemle*, **41**, June, pp. 491–506.

Török, Ádám (2000), 'Reális-e a magyar tudomány 20. helyezése a (képzeletbeli) világranglistán?' [Is the 20th position of Hungarian science realistic on an [imaginary] world ranking list?], *Magyar Tudomány*, **11**, pp. 1307–28.

Török, Ádám (2001), 'Piacgazdasági érettség többféleképpen? Néhány alapfogalom értelmezése és alkalmazása a világgazdaság három nagy régiójában' [Mature in several ways for market economy? The application and interpretation of some basic terms in three large regions of the world economy], *Közgazdasági Szemle*, **48** (September), pp. 707–25.

Török, Ádám (2002), *Hungarian Science and Technology in the Top Twenty?* in A. Varga-L. Szerb (eds), *Innovation, Entrepreneurship, Regions and Economic Development: International Experiences and Hungarian Challenges*, Pécs: University of Pécs. pp. 11–26.

Trajtenberg, Manuel (2001), 'Innovation in Israel 1968–1997: a comparative analysis using patent data', *Research Policy*, **30**, pp. 363–89.

Trebilcock, Michael J. and Robert Howse (1995), *The Regulation of International Trade*, London and New York: Routledge.

Turkkan, N. (1999), 'GENETIK. Floating point genetic algorithm for minimization problems', Excel file, V2, June, Université de Moncton: School of Engineering, Canada.

UNCTAD (1995), *World Investment Report 1995, Transnational Corporations and Competitiveness*, New York and Geneva: United Nations.

UNCTAD (2002), *World Investment Report 2002: Transnational Corporations and Export Competitiveness*, New York and Geneva: United Nations.

UNCTAD (2003), *World Investment Report 2003: FDI Policies for Development: National and International Perspectives*, New York and Geneva: United Nations.

UNCTAD Secretariat (2002), *Indicators of the Technology Development*, Geneva: United Nations.

UNESCO (1998), *World Science Report*, London: UNESCO Publishing – Elsevier.

Utterback, James and Fernando Suarez (1993), 'Innovation, competition and market structure', *Research Policy*, **22** (1), 1–21.

Varga, Attila and László Szerb (eds) (2002), *Innovation, Entrepreneurship, Regions and Economic Development: International Experiences and Hungarian Challenges*, Pécs: University of Pécs.

Varian, Hal R. (1999), *Intermediate Microeconomics*, New York and London: W.W. Norton & Company.

Varsakelis, Nikos C. (2001), 'The impact of patent protection, economy openness and national culture on R&D investment: a cross-country empirical investigation', *Research Policy*, **30**, pp. 1059–68.

Vernon, Raymond (1979), 'The product cycle hypothesis in a new international environment', *Oxford Bulletin of Economics and Statistics*, **41** (4) (November), pp. 255–67.

Vickers, John (1995), 'Concepts of Competition', *Oxford Economic Papers*, **47**, pp. 1–23.

Viotti, E.B. (1997), 'Passive and active national learning systems', PhD dissertation, New School for Social Research, New York, cited by Freeman (2002).

Walls, Vivien (1988), 'Technology and the competitiveness of small countries: a review', in Christopher Freeman and Bengt-Åke Lundvall (eds), *Small Countries Facing the Technological Revolution*, London and New York: Pinter Publishers, pp. 37–66.

Walsh, Vivien (1988), 'Technology and the competitiveness of small countries: a review', in Chris Freeman and Bengt-Åke Lundvall (eds), *Small Countries Facing the Technological Revolution*, London: Pinter Publishers, pp. 37–66.

Wells, L. (1969), 'Test of a product cycle model of international trade', *Quarterly Journal of Economics*, **83** (1) (February), pp. 152–62.

Williamson, Oliver E. (1985), *The Economic Institutions of Capitalism*, New York: Free Press.

Wilson, David and Vangelis Soutiaris (2002), 'Do Germany's federal and land governments (still) co-ordinate their innovation policies?', *Research Policy*, **31**, pp. 1123–40.

World Economic Forum (WEF) (1999), *The World Competitiveness Yearbook 1999*, Geneva-Davos: World Economic Forum.

Wyatt, Geoffrey (1986), *The Economics of Invention. A Study of the Determinants of Inventive Activity*, Brighton: Wheatsheaf Books, Harvester Press.

Zajac, Štefan (2001), 'Science, technology, education in Slovakia', in G. Gorzelak et al. *Central Europe in Transition: Towards EU Membership*, Warsaw: Regional Studies Association Polish Section, Wydawnictwo Naukowe, pp. 243–63.
Zellner, Christian (2003), 'The economic effects of basic research: evidence for embodied knowledge transfer via scientists' migration', *Research Policy*, **32**, pp. 1881–95.

Index